THE
EXECUTIVE
TRAP

HOW TO PLAY YOUR PERSONAL BEST
ON THE GOLF COURSE AND ON THE JOB

JAY HALL, Ph.D.

Simon & Schuster

New York   London   Toronto   Sydney   Tokyo   Singapore

SIMON & SCHUSTER
Simon & Schuster Building
Rockefeller Center
1230 Avenue of the Americas
New York, New York, 10020

DESIGNED BY BARBARA MARKS
Manufactured in the United States of America

1   3   5   7   9   10   8   6   4   2

Library of Congress Cataloging-in-Publication Data
Hall, Jay, date
The executive trap: how to play your personal best on
the golf course and on the job/Jay Hall.
p. cm.
1. Executive ability.   2. Leadership.
3. Performance.   4. Golf.   I. Title.
HD38.2.H345   1992
658.4'09—dc20   92-8071
CIP
ISBN: 0-671-74575-1

For the children . . .

yours and mine,

you and me.

Contents

*The game is played mainly on a
five-and-a-half-inch course . . .
the space between your ears.*

Bobby Jones, gentleman golfer
and only winner of the Grand Slam

Introduction:

THE FAILURE OF SUCCESS

Jim Flick, golf author and 1988 PGA Teacher of the Year, told me a story about the failure of success. He once worked with a top executive from a major corporation who, despite a good game overall, could not get out of greenside sand traps successfully. She started with a faulty concept of what to do and followed with even poorer execution. Like many among us, she tried to "pick" the ball off the sand with her golf club. Moreover, she shifted her weight left as she swung her club, which caused her to move on the ball just enough to catch it with the leading edge of her sand wedge. The resulting shot never got more than three feet off the ground. The ball either plugged into the bank, still in the trap, or soared a good thirty yards over the target. She was totally helpless when faced with a buried lie (a ball embedded in the sand). "Any time I hit a sand trap," she confided in Jim, "I know I've just added at least four strokes to my score!"

Flick explained she should hit sand first, not the ball. He told her that if she hit into the sand two or three inches behind the ball, the ball would literally ride a cushion of sand up and out of the trap. The executive was dubious, but she tried hitting the sand first. She was so tentative that she didn't follow through and complete her swing. She just banged her club into the sand behind the ball and stopped. The ball popped up and traveled about two feet, plopping once again into the sand. Flick suggested she think about the *shape* of her full swing. "Try to make a 'U-shaped' swing," he said. "Back and up, then down and through and up again."

The executive made four or five proper swings, then Flick showed her how to open the face of her club to take full advantage of the sand wedge design. She agreed she could feel the club slipping under the sand.

Then Flick lined up three balls in the sand, touching one another in a straight line toward the green. "Now," he said, "if you make a full swing and stay down at the bottom long enough, you should be able to lift all three balls at once."

The executive gave it a try. On her third attempt, all three balls lifted out of the trap and landed softly on the practice green. "Wow," she marveled, "I'll never be afraid of just one ball again."

Flick left her gleefully hitting recoveries from the sand. The next morning he spotted the executive practicing in the bunker. She was lifting her club about halfway up, shifting her weight forward, and catching the ball first— just exactly what she had been doing before. Flick watched her scull four balls over the green. As he approached her, the executive looked up to see him coming. "Your way just doesn't *feel* right!" she said with a smile.

Jim's story struck a nerve with me, for I have run into the same sort of enigma in my own work with executives —good people wanting to do a good job but mysteriously opting for more familiar practices guaranteed to make them fail.

As a psychologist and educator, I have worked since the early sixties with people who run organizations. I have tried to spread the good news about effective management, revealed by research in the behavioral sciences, and what can happen when executives manage for a full release of the human potential at their disposal. But my message does not always fall on receptive ears. Something ingrained and hard to penetrate seems more important to many executives than becoming effective agents of productive and healthy organizations. They are reluctant to act in their own best interests, much less in anyone else's. They seem ambivalent, desiring success and wanting to do a good job but unable to let go of something holding them back. Like the executive in the sand trap, some still conclude, "It just doesn't *feel* right." Apparently, *knowing* how to do a better job is no assurance that executives will *do* a better job.

I have seen executives who have committed themselves publicly to new and better ways later get downright creative at ducking the issue. I have seen some get angry so often about honestly reported information that people learn not to report it anymore! And I've known many who use euphemisms and half-truths to divert attention from real concerns and, thereby, obscure the problem and forestall unpleasant solutions. Many I've seen have their hands perennially tied by some anonymous authority, leaving them blameless for any lack of action. All the while I have witnessed human potential being discouraged, wasted, and obstructed by the people in charge of such a precious resource.

Now, some people might simply say, "So what? So some executives resist doing a good job. What's so earthshaking about that? Why should it be a reason for anyone to get upset?" That attitude, in fact, is another part of the problem. All of us are affected by executive acts, but a lot of us are reluctant to evaluate executive effectiveness—our own or anyone else's. For reasons known only to ourselves, we have simply accommodated ourselves to neglect, abuse, inaction, and dishonesty. We have looked the other way and lowered our expectations.

I have written this book because I believe we are facing

a crisis of leadership. Not just at the top, as some would like to believe. Faulting the CEOs and executive VPs in our lives is a favorite pastime for those of us trying to let *ourselves* off the hook. I'm talking about leadership at all levels —on the factory floor, in the mail room, at the corner grocery, at school, and at home—wherever the decisions and practices of one person affect the productivity and well-being of scores of others.

It concerns me when leaders all but refuse to act in the best interests of themselves or others, when doing so is easy and clearly consistent with their professed goals and aspirations. The symptoms are all around us. Poor quality of workmanship, loss of productive capacity, trade imbalances, spiraling medical costs, schools that do not teach, and families who live together without communication— these are the fruits of flawed leadership. This is a problem not only in large corporations, but in our communities and families as well.

It has been hard for me to understand why so many of us seem hell-bent on defeating not only ourselves but one another. I have pondered the problem for some time. And the missing appreciation of what has happened to executive leadership came to me one day on a plane while reading Timothy Gallwey's book, *The Inner Game of Golf*. It suddenly dawned on me why I couldn't always help people become more productive simply by offering them new principles and scientific data. Reading Gallwey, I realized that every executive, like every golfer, is playing *two* games, one outside and one inside, one public and apparent and one private and hidden. Game and player, management and manager, are different entities. The principles and skills for managing others' potential and releasing their competence concern the public game of being an executive. But how we apply these principles depends on how well we play the private game within ourselves. It dawned on me that I, and others like me, had been concentrating on the *wrong* game.

Gallwey set me straight. He helped me glimpse that "something else" going on with the executives I had known, and pointed me in a new direction of inquiry. I began looking at executive games. And it was then I began to realize that executives not only play games they don't know they are playing, but they play all their games the *same* way! We can't separate what goes on in the executive suites of our formal organizations from what goes on in our schoolrooms and family kitchens. Executives take their games with them. They play the same games wherever they happen to be—as bosses at work, as teachers in the classroom, as parents at home, and even as just folks at play. And some of the games are not very good.

In the process of playing their favorite games, executives teach the rest of us to play games too. We take these games to work with us, carry them home and even to the ballpark—and they are not very productive, either. These are the things Gallwey helped me see more clearly, and pieces of the executive puzzle began to fall into place.

Gallwey's basic premise is simple: *Performance = Potential − Interference.* The left side of the equation, *performance,* represents what Gallwey calls an "outer game." It concerns the behaviors and practices we use, a public game that all can see, based on principles and strategies derived from logic, information, and personal experience. It can be both scientific and objective. It can be taught. This is where most of us mistakenly focus our attention. The right side of the equation, *potential minus interference,* represents an "inner game." It concerns what we *think* and *feel,* a private game that is unseen and subjective. It is a game of constant interplay between our thoughts and feelings, our aspirations and our apprehensions, which, if known at all, is known only to ourselves. Many of us are totally unaware of this game. Yet we play it all the time. Few of us have mastered it because most of us have ignored it. But mastery of the private game is the key to masterly performance of all our games because, at its core, it is the game of *judgment*. It is the executive game of choice and consequence.

I think Gallwey's premise speaks to what I consider the crisis of leadership facing us today. Many of us are openly concerned with performance, our own and others'. Not so with the private interplay of potential and interference. The potential Gallwey refers to varies from person to person. It may be a potential for accomplishing a particular task well, or it could be a special aptitude for excellence. In any case, it is our potential for *personal productivity*. Unfortunately, it can be dulled and misdirected by interference of one kind or another.

The interference that concerns Gallwey most is self-interference. We get so tangled up in our own foibles, fears, and doubts that we inhibit our own potential. Gallwey focuses his attention on techniques for quieting that self-interference. I, on the other hand, am concerned in this book about *why* such interference can assume such a dominant role in our lives, *why* we allow our own executive potential to be negated by forces we ourselves set in motion, and *why* we then interfere with the potential of those we manage. I think answers to such questions will shed light on the dilemma and offer a way out of the Executive Trap.

The interplay between potential and interference is enormously important, personally and organizationally. Mental health experts tell us people's inability to realize their potential is a major cause of their unhappiness and unproductive behavior. These same experts believe that when people are unable to realize their potential, it is because "they have been mismanaged by other people." The executives in their lives—the parents, teachers, supervisors, and others in authority—have let them down somehow rather than preparing them for healthy, productive, and happy lives. That's why executives are the target of this book. If executives can first learn to realize their own potential, then perhaps they can do a better job of encouraging and enabling those in their charge to do the same.

If we look deeply enough, we will find that the real game is in our heads, and each of us can learn to master it if we really want out of the trap. As it turns out, the productivity most executives want may begin with each of us personally. To succeed, we must first become willing to work on our personal productivity. We must untrap ourselves and begin to realize our own potential. How to do this is what *The Executive Trap* is about.

FORE!

Learning to Manage the Game Within the Game

Every golfer scores better when he learns
his true capabilities.
Tommy Armour

"WELCOME TO THE ACADEMY!" the Pro says on opening day to the men and women who have come to improve their games. "I hope you're looking forward to our time together as much as the staff and I are. There are a couple of things, however, I need to mention before we get to work.

"This golf school may be a little different from others. We'll spend plenty of time *playing* the game, but our real emphasis is going to be on *management*. The great Ben Hogan believed that good play boils down to good management. In fact, he said, 'If you can't manage your own game, you can't play in the tournament.'

"So we'll be learning to manage our own games. That means becoming more aware of how we play the game and why we play it the way we do. And we hope that will lead you to a new level of personal awareness, because awareness is the real key to good management and to the solid performance you can enjoy for a lifetime."

•

We can discover much from playing and studying our games, for games have been a window to greater awareness since the beginning of recorded time.

The ancient Greeks were lovers of public games. They were fascinated by the thrill of victory and the agony of defeat. They admired winners and bestowed honor, wealth, and status on those who excelled. They even paid handsomely—more than they were willing to pay their physicians, scholars, and teachers—just to be entertained by those they admired.

The poets and philosophers of the time believed that people were captivated by what the performances revealed about the players themselves. The poet Pindar noted the dedication, discipline, and character that equipped some players to persevere. Others, like Plato and Pythagoras, were equally alert to displays of confusion, fear, and exhaustion that caused other players to falter, withdraw, or collapse altogether. Games, they deduced, are metaphors of life.

So why not use a game as a diagnostic tool for understanding executives? Maybe we can learn about the games executives play in an office environment or in their homes by watching them play on the golf course. "There's no question," Jim Flick observes, "that all of us are affected by similar things in our life-styles and in our golf." And, more to the executive point, Ford Motor's Harold (Red) Poling, chairman of the board and 8-handicapper, says he tries to imbue his management style with the same strong focus on strategy he uses in golf.

Golf is, after all, one of the better simulators of life. Nothing duplicates the subtle nuances, the exhilaration and bad breaks, the temptations and moral dilemmas, of life quite as well as golf. Michael Murphy, in his book *Golf in the Kingdom*, likens the symbolic parallels of golf with the human experience. "Why does golf bring out so much in a man, so many sides of his personality?" he asks. "Why is it such an X-ray of the soul?"

The answer: Because we play all our games the same. Maybe we can learn something about the game of life by watching how our executives play golf.

Let's return to the Academy.

•

TWO DAYS AFTER the opening session, Larry Freeman, CEO of a large franchise operation, shares a golf cart with the Pro. They are about to join Tim McBride and Frank Fortis on the 18th tee for some on-course instruction. Tim is the Dean of Student Affairs at a small midwestern university. Frank is the entrepreneurial owner of a financial management company.

They see Tim and Frank waiting impatiently on the 18th tee. "The agenda for today," the Pro begins, "is to explore the subtle elements of course management. How to read terrain, effects of the elements, lie of the ball, design of the hole, and then be able to come up with the correct shot."

Number 18 is a 439-yard par four that bends to the left. A lake guards the left of the green. The Pro takes the threesome to the center of the fairway, 220 yards from the tee. He drops three balls.

"Okay, gentlemen, here are your tee shots. What do you plan to do?"

"Well," Frank says, "this isn't as far as my drives usually go, but I'll bring it in over the lake and fade it back to the pin. That will set me up for a birdie."

"Larry?"

"I think I'll play for bogey. One over par might satisfy even Jack Nicklaus from here. I'm two hundred nineteen yards from the front of the green. There's disaster on the left and a twenty-mile-per-hour crosswind. Frankly, I don't believe I've got the talent to go for the green this time. So, I'll lay it up with my six-iron about fifty or sixty yards short of the green. Then I can pitch it up in three. I figure I can get down in two putts for a five. If I get lucky, I might get close enough for par."

"Tim?"

"I'm calling in sick!" Tim laughs. "No, seriously, I'll hit a nine-iron down to the front of the lake and then an eight-iron onto the green. A nine may be too much, but I'm real comfortable with my short irons. They're *magic*."

"All right, gentlemen—execute."

Frank takes out his two-iron, makes one practice swing, addresses the ball, and lets it fly. The ball heads straight for the pin.

Tim gasps. "That's beautiful, Frank."

Suddenly, caught by the crosswind, the ball bends left and falls in the water. Frank looks at the club as if he can't believe the results.

Then Larry takes out his six-iron. He makes three practice swings, then checks his target one more time. Then he puts the ball safely down the right side, fifty-five yards from the flag. Satisfied, he retrieves his divot and tamps it back in place.

Tim takes his nine-iron and walks to the ball. Before grounding the club, he plants a kiss on its face. "Come on, baby," he says, "do your stuff."

Tim makes his best swing of the day. But it's too much club, and the ball lands right in the middle of the lake.

"Okay, gentlemen, now we have some choices," says the Pro. "Larry, you've already got your sand wedge out, so I know what you're thinking. Frank and Tim, the rules allow you to hit again from here, drop two club lengths back from the lake or drop anywhere behind the lake as long as the point where you entered the lake is between you and the flag. You'll be hitting your fourth shot."

Frank throws a ball down. "I'll hit from here. The two-iron is the right shot." He hits the ball, and once again it is blown into the water. Frank slams his club into the turf, leaving an ugly scar.

"Tim?"

"Hey, this ain't the U.S. Open. One ball lost is enough," Tim says. "I'll take a pickup six and call it a day. If you can't trust a nine-iron, what can you trust?'' His chuckle is not convincing.

Back in the clubhouse, Frank tells the Pro, ''I want you to tell me—us—how to become good golfers. You've seen us play. What do I do next to realize my full potential?''

''I can't tell you how to realize your potential,'' the Pro replies. ''Nobody can.''

''Why not?'' sputters Frank. ''That's what I'm paying you for!''

''Because golf is *two* games,'' the Pro says. ''There is a Public Game and a Private Game. The Public Game is the one everyone can see. The goal is simply to use as few strokes as possible in 18 holes. We play it on the golf course. I can teach you that.

''The Private Game is more subtle. We play it in our minds. It can be more important to performance than all the skills of the Public Game. And unlike those of the Public Game, the goals of the Private Game differ from person to person.''

''Why can't you teach the Private Game, too?'' asks Larry.

''Just getting somebody to *acknowledge* there is a Private Game is hard enough,'' the Pro says. ''I see a lot of denial in my line of work. Many people work hard to hide their Private Games.

''But the hardest part is getting past the fear that paralyzes folks' desire for a good game. The Private Game is a game of *ambivalence*. It's a game of managing the tensions between our desire to do well and the fear of what we will have to give up to realize our desires. In a way, it's like trying to steal second base without risking leaving first.

''The Private Game is very personal,'' the Pro continues. ''I don't know why you play the game or why you *choose* to play it the way you do. I don't know how you make decisions or approach problems. I can't *teach* any of these things. I can, however, help you *discover* them for yourselves. But you have to do all the work. To play your best, you'll have to achieve a harmony between your Public Game and Private Game.

"But I'll tell you something. It's worth the effort because anything you can learn about managing your own ambivalence this week may well help you achieve harmony back home."

The three executives look at one another, beginning to wonder what they have gotten themselves into.

CHECKING OUT THE COURSE

The Nature of Executive Games

*Golf—the worst damned fun anybody
ever had!*

Cy Manier

FRANK LIGHTS A CIGARETTE. "If you want to know what I think," he says, "this Public Game–Private Game stuff is just so much bullshit. Hard work and enough time to practice is all I need."

"Frank," Larry says, "your swing is okay. It's your *judgment* that is in question. That's what the Private Game is about. At least, I think that's what the Pro is saying. Pro?"

"The Private Game is about a lot of things," the Pro says. "It's about judgment and knowledge, ambition and fear, courage and fatigue. But mainly it's about how we play the real game.

"The sad thing is that most people won't study it, really look inside themselves, until they're in so much trouble they have to if they're going to survive. A lot of the executives I see don't really want to talk about managing their games until they've become unmanageable. Sometimes I think we'd be better off if instead of talking about how people swing the club or what they do to the ball, we talked about what they do to themselves."

25

•

What *are* we doing to ourselves? Why would anyone wait until things get unmanageable to find out? It doesn't sound very productive, does it? But that may be what lots of us are inclined to do. Certainly that has been the case in the private sector in recent years. Not too long ago a group of American executives met in Tokyo with their Japanese counterparts to discuss global competition. Speaking to the Americans, Mr. M. Konosuka Matsushita, executive adviser to Japan's Panasonic Corporation, put it bluntly. "We are going to win," he said, "and the industrial West is going to lose. There is nothing much you can do about it, because the reasons for your failure are within yourselves."

Mr. Matsushita may be right: perhaps the reasons for our failure are within ourselves. We have shown an amazing capacity for discounting our own mistakes and embellishing our accomplishments. Many of us have certainly let our ambivalence blind us to the lessons of experience and success. But Mr. Matsushita is dead wrong when he says there is nothing we can do about it. However late, we *can* learn to manage our executive games. Maybe we should, for a moment, forget about what we do with budgets and people and concentrate instead on what we do to ourselves.

The Pro has said that golf really involves both a Public Game and a Private Game. Being an executive is as much a two-game process as playing golf. In business organizations, the Public Game has clear goals and objectives—to accomplish work, provide a service, make a profit, and so on. The Private Game is another matter; it is played in the head and requires different, private and inner, skills. It is geared to different purposes.

Individual executives often have different goals. Some seek advancement or security or belonging. Others want challenge or freedom or growth. Because we have different goals, we often favor different principles and ground rules. Each of us plays the Private Game differently. This is fine —as long as we understand two things.

First: *The Private Game that each of us plays directly affects how we play the Public Game.*

Second: *How we play the Public Game affects how well those in our charge can play.*

The main point is, to be truly productive, each of us must master *both* the Private Game and the Public Game. We can't separate them, so we must achieve a harmony between them. We have to notice how our personal and private crosscurrents can pull or push us from our intended course. I know executives who firmly believe people work better when they have control over their own work. These same individuals can't keep their hands off what other people are doing. I know others who profess to love people and just want to help them, but they can't bring themselves to recognize and accept other people's basic competence and need for growth and self-reliance. Something in their Private Games keeps them from applying principles they subscribe to publicly. Their games do not harmonize.

There is an interesting parallel between golf and the way we have developed executives. In both instances people want to learn how to improve their performances. In both instances there are essential teachable principles. In both cases these involve only the Public Game. And in both situations people still want *more*. This should be instructive. More often than not—be it in golf or in the functions of the executive—formal instruction *ignores* the Private Game. But that's where the real action is. We must come to terms with that if we are to play the executive game well.

Simply recognizing the existence of the Private Game can be a good starting point, and coming to grips with our Private Games can supply the missing link in our search for full potential. So our first goal might be to examine our own games. I can promise you that if each of us becomes aware enough, we can master our Private Games. This awareness will help us become better executives. As we learn to manage our private influences more effectively, we will *publicly* manage and teach and parent more effectively and productively.

RETHINKING AND RELEARNING: THE SEARCH FOR EXECUTIVE AWARENESS

If we want to realize our own potential as executives, we need to be willing to rethink our approaches to the game. We must be open to new learning. Jack Nicklaus attributed his sixth Masters victory, at the age of forty-six, to a new way of chipping and putting. Reflecting on his newfound approach, he said, "The only constant in golf is that you never stop learning it."

How do the rest of us continue such learning? Dr. Bob Rotella, sports psychologist to many of golf's superstars, says we must work at becoming aware. "You have to understand yourself and your game enough to know where you are, where you've been, and where you're trying to go."

The same is true of executives. We must focus on the Private Game—the goals, assumptions, aspirations, and fears we have as executives. And we must recognize the intricate entwinement of the Private Game and Public Game. To be truly productive, we must come to know

1. where we are
2. where we have been
3. where we are trying to go.

Moving from Public to Private

When we begin to look at executives and their management in terms of their Private—rather than their Public —Games, new possibilities emerge. Old dilemmas become more understandable. Solutions begin to present themselves. Take, for example, the inconsistencies of executive concerns and styles found in most organizations. Regardless of the setting, most executives put in some pretty long days. They go to meetings, talk on the phone, review options, talk with colleagues, make decisions, look at budgets, and try to provide some sense of direction. At least part of their time is spent agonizing. Some worry about production and how to get people off their duffs. Others fret about morale and stress. They worry about whether or not people like them. It becomes a serious distraction from the Public Game—the real task at hand.

Part of our problem lies with how we have trained our executives. Each generation has offered to the next generation of executives a peculiar mix of fundamental principles and simplistic advice geared primarily to the Public Game. The Private Game has gone untended.

Getting the job done and the quality of relationships, for example, are the perennial touchstones of most executive aspirations and frustrations. But not all executives value them equally. It is in this context that the Private Games become so important. They require attention. Let's use an example of three corporate executives and the problems of executive development as a case in point. Suppose co-workers identify one executive as favoring people-oriented caretaker practices. A second is clearly committed to production-centered autocratic practices. The third is mired in a procedure-bound bureaucratic style. All echo, "We want to change. How do we become effective executives?" If you are in charge of executive development, how do you answer?

You might be tempted to go over the functions of the executive one more time. That's what we've been taught to do. By doing so, however, you would ignore the Private Games. You would focus entirely on where the executives are trying to go, without considering where they are or where they have been.

Let's assume you are having a sales meeting in Chicago. Your sales reps from Los Angeles, New York, and Houston all call and ask for directions to the Windy City. Would you describe Chicago to them? Of course not! Neither would you give all of them the same answer. Obviously you must consider where they're starting from. You might also factor in why they are there. Only then can you give each specific directions.

So it is with becoming a good executive. While learning to apply the principles and practices of productive management, we must teach ourselves to move from our public to our private concerns. Where we are, where we have been, and where we want to go—these are what the Private Game is all about. When we begin to rethink our roles in such ways, we may discover some aspects of executive action previously overlooked. We may begin to glimpse our own Private Games in action. We may discover ours is a shared dilemma.

Now, let's return to the Academy, where the Pro is taking his executives on just such a journey of discovery.

•

"I ADMIRE YOUR commitment, Pro," says Tim. "Lord knows people need to learn to think about their games more effectively. But working with execs all the time must be a real chore."

"I love it!" the Pro exclaims. "It's what attracted me to the Academy in the first place. The opportunity to use one game to explore another can really be rewarding.

"Sure, some of the people I work with can be difficult. But when we get right down to it, they are all just variations on one theme. I try to help the people who come here discover the theme.

"We're *all* executives. Think about it. Everybody, sooner or later, has to make decisions, use authority to get things done, manage personnel. It's the same whether you run a business or a household, teach school or raise kids. We all manage something.

"But if we mismanage ourselves, it's almost certain we will mismanage other people. That's why executives are so important. Their games—especially the games within—affect how everybody else plays."

"What kinds of games within games?" Larry queries. "What's going on here besides the game of golf? I need you to get a little more specific."

The Pro chuckles. "A lot," he says. "If you tune in, you can see several games going on simultaneously. It doesn't just happen at a golf academy. But golf sure makes it more obvious.

"A favorite quotation of mine from Robert Sasserath helps make the point. 'In prehistoric times,' he said, 'cavemen had a custom of beating on the ground with clubs and uttering spine-chilling cries. Scientists call this a primitive form of self-expression. Modern men go through the very same ritual. We call it golf.'

"Golf is the context I work in, and I see a lot of self-expression. The play I've found fascinating is the games people bring to the Academy. Most people I see have pretty fixed patterns of self-expression. Golf is just an outlet for their approach to life in general.

"Everybody who comes here says 'I want to get better!' Most people *want* to realize their potential. But somewhere along the way, something happens. Some of their other games take over. They lose sight of golf and start defeating themselves by playing another game. That's the biggest problem I encounter.

"I see two basic problems with the executives I work with. The first, and by far the easiest to solve, is simply one of people not knowing what they need to do. This is essentially an intellectual and, in golf, a physiological problem. I can help with that one.

"The second is a problem of the spirit. It's one of people

not doing what they know they must do to play well. That's a tough one. It's something executives have to solve for themselves."

Frank frowns. "Are you saying the problem with executives is that they're indecisive?"

"I wish it were that simple," the Pro says. "You can fix indecision by getting enough of the right information. The problems I see are more insidious. Executives aren't indecisive—they're *predictable!* When there's a choice between doing what they know needs to be done and doing whatever their fear would have them do, most of them will go with the fear every time! That's what ambivalence does to us. It's the same with golf.

"Golf is really a simple game. Just set the physics in motion and hang on. But that doesn't mean it's *easy!* Some people just can't trust anything simple. They get scared and feel compelled to *help* it. Others feel that if something so easy can work so well, adding a little *power* will make it even better.

"Whatever the case, some kind of personal self-expression—some kind of fear—takes over and distracts people. They end up *not doing what they know how to do.* That's when they start defeating themselves."

•

We all know executives who have opted not to do their jobs as well as they might. Many simply don't know what to do to ensure effective leadership. Even more of us know but do not *do* what we know we must.

When we decide not to serve either our own best interests or those of others, something significant is going on. For example, we have seen that when Frank Fortis plays golf, he tries to force an improbable solution on the problems he encounters. Given a second chance, he will try the same thing again. We might wonder if all the Franks play their executive games using the same techniques. We might also ask why.

Why does Tim McBride place so much trust in something outside himself—his "magic" nine-iron? Is it fair to assume that in his executive game he simply picks up his ball and withdraws when his "magic" fails? Again, we might ask why.

And why does Larry Freeman approach the game of golf so dispassionately? Are such realistic and unabashed assessments of his own talents relative to the demands of the golf shot at hand also characteristic of the executive games he plays back at the office?

Maybe we can study Frank, Tim, Larry, and others playing their Private Games and garner some insight into how and why they play their Public Games. Then, if we share any of their tendencies, maybe we can learn something about how and why we play our own games as we do.

The Problem of Executive Pain

We know from experience that being an executive can be a real chore. It can even be painful. We expect executives to manage organizations—their purpose, people, performance, power, and philosophy—in active, effective, and skillful ways. If they do so, the executive job can be a source of great joy for everyone. Many executives, however, are not doing as well as they might. For too many that can be a source of great pain.

Some executives seem to wallow in pain. They feel for themselves and everybody else. Others are stoic and hide their agony. They have learned to tough it out and play hurt. Then there are those who seem virtually unfeeling. They reflect their personal discomfort by inflicting pain on others.

Regardless of the source or how people handle it, pain sets in motion our Private Games, games that distract us from the task at hand. To learn to manage the game in our heads, we must first learn to acknowledge executive pain. To that end, let's take a closer look at the pains that distract us.

Pains of purpose. Many executives agonize over the purpose of life and the personal role they were *meant* to play. "Why am I here?" they ask. They would like some clarity, some sense of reason, for it all. Others are painfully confused about priorities. Are we to show a profit? Hold down costs? Save for the future? Both leaders and followers experience anguish when the answers to such questions are unclear.

Pains of relationship. This kind of pain may take many forms. A lot of executives agonize over people. Some worry about whether or not their co-workers really like them. How can they be fair in enforcing standards and evaluating people?

On the other hand, many executives resent the people they must work with. Some females have trouble with males simply because they are male, while males sometimes have trouble with females because they won't act like males—or because they do.

Other executives fear people. They suspect co-workers are out to serve only themselves and may use them up and leave them twisting in the wind. All of us often feel put upon and vulnerable. Fear of the prospect of being left alone distracts us. And these personal pains affect how each of us plays the executive game.

Pains of performance. Directly or indirectly, performance is a measure of our self-expression. Yet some executives seem totally unconcerned about performance. This lack of concern is misleading. It masks the pain of having to judge or be judged on the basis of performance.

Other executives are clear that performance is necessary for survival. Their fear is that they might someday be found wanting—guilty of failing to measure up. It often appears that they are the only ones who give a damn whether the work gets done or not. They are lonely and, if the truth be known, scared.

Pains of power. Power is one of the more volatile and potentially painful aspects of the executive game. How, why, or whether we use power or influence can be a reflection and a cause of personal pain.

Some executives despise power. Its pressures seem intolerable. Some fear no one will take them seriously; some have apprehensions about offending people.

Other executives love power. To them, controlling what is to be done, who is to do it, and how and when it will be done is the essence of being an executive. Those who need to influence and control other people usually inflict more pain than they experience. But then the consequences of others' reactions and resistance can cause them pain.

Pains of philosophy. In the thirteenth century, St. Thomas Aquinas wrote, "Three things are necessary for the salvation of man: to know what he ought to believe; to know what he ought to desire; and to know what he ought to do." Aquinas wrote as a philosopher of theology, but he could have been writing about the executive struggle to realize potential. Not knowing what to believe, what to desire, or what to do is a major barrier to personal growth. Uncertainty about who you want to be is a prime source of executive pain.

Being an executive has, like playing golf, great potential for both pain and joy, but sometimes we feel only the pain. Sometimes we feel like Gary Player must have felt when he commented on the game of golf. As the winner of nine major championships and more than 140 events around the world, Player said, "Golf is a puzzle without an answer. I've played the game for forty years and I still haven't the slightest idea how to play." We all, it seems, could use some relief from the uncertainties of our games.

That relief may be found in *awareness*. Acknowledging our executive pain can illuminate our path.

•

"THE PAIN IS IMPORTANT," the Pro continues, "because pain triggers the Private Game. But when we're hurting inside, we tend to get more focused on performance of the Public Game. When something's not working, we make things worse by harping on how to fix it. Sometimes we literally increase the pain. We need to back off and try to separate pain from performance."

"I don't follow you," Tim says. "How do you know pain is the problem?"

"I'm sure you've noticed how easy it is for most people to groove a faulty swing," the Pro replies. "Have you also noticed it's nearly impossible to groove a good one? Even the touring professionals fight that problem. You've got two sets of moves—a good one and a bad one, one proper and one counterproductive. For some reason, the good one seems hard and the bad one comes easy. The good one feels strange and uncomfortable and the bad one is like an old friend. It's pain avoidance that encourages us toward the wrong choice."

"That makes sense to me." Larry nods. "I know I flinch or try to compensate if my hands are sore. Why wouldn't I do the same thing if there were some kind of pain going on in my head?"

Frank snorts in exasperation. "It's only a *game*, for God's sake! Do you guys really believe playing a game is painful?"

"I don't know, Frank." Larry says, grinning. "How did you feel when you dumped your two-iron into the water the second time?"

"Awareness begins with the acknowledgment of pain," the Pro says. "If you can't feel it, you can't heal it."

PERSONAL PLAYING STRATEGIES

Glimpses of Where We Are

*There're twenty million amateurs trying
to learn how to hit a draw while two
hundred pros are trying to hit a fade.
What does that tell you?*

Lee Trevino

We all have our own ways of playing the game. We may not know our strategic preferences. But because they are so consistently a part of us, everyone else knows. Many of the people closest to us can even predict how we will handle problems of the game when they arise.

•

"TELL ME WHAT YOU MEAN," Frank challenges the Pro. "How are we unwilling to do what we already know to do to play better? Nobody's more willing to grind it out than I am!"

"I'm talking about more than just effort," the Pro says. "I'm talking about the *kind* of effort each of you prefers. And *why* you prefer one kind and reject another that might be more productive.

"For example, Frank, why would you choose the same improbable shot over the lake when the results of your first try clearly indicated it wasn't in your best interest?"

"First of all," Frank says, bristling, "the shot wasn't *improbable* as you say! It was well within *my* capabilities. You just haven't seen enough of my game yet to know!"

"Maybe," says the Pro. "But I doubt it. Nicklaus wouldn't have tried that shot. Frankly, most of the people I see who keep making the same mistakes over and over think they're right. They usually *deny* that anything's wrong!"

"Come on, Pro," Tim interjects. "Frank's doing the best he can. Don't be so hard on him. . . ."

"What's *your* goal, Tim?" Larry queries curiously. "Why do you feel a need to protect Frank of all people?"

Tim reacts with hurt surprise. "I don't feel a need to protect anybody. Why would you say that? Why would he say that, Pro?"

The Pro smiles. "I think I hear a little denial going on with you, too, Tim. Denial may keep us from doing the work we need to do. You see, Private Games are all about private goals. If we get these goals in focus, we can get a glimpse of the games we're really playing. But if we deny them, we just keep ourselves confused. It's hard to know what to work on. But we can find out if we're willing to *look*."

•

When we speak of private goals, we are talking about the personal motives that trigger the Private Game. We are not referring to those external incentives to which people often aspire. More money, promotions, a rubber tree plant for the office, and the like are important to some people. They can even be a means to private, personal satisfaction. But for the most part, they are representations of the Public Games. They are simply ways of keeping score.

The goals of the Private Game are different. We may, for example, privately seek a sense of pride or desire security or yearn for a feeling of power. Goals such as these tend to be hidden and personal. They may not be clear to an observer, and even the person involved may be totally oblivious of them. Despite their hidden quality, they are central to how each of us plays the Private Game in conjunction with the Public Game. They can be a major source of pain and self-interference. This is why we must clarify our private goals before we can realize our personal potential.

Problems Reveal Private Goals

Uncovering private goals can be difficult because people are so adept at keeping them covered. An old story from my days as a graduate student makes just such a point. A famous clinician, it seems, was trying to get a patient to open up through the use of pictures. The doctor drew a squiggly line and asked, "Does this remind you of anything?"

"Sure." The patient nodded. "Sex!"

The doctor drew a square and repeated his question. Same response: "Sex!"

The process continued through triangles and circles and straight lines, always with the same response from the client: "Sure, sex!"

Finally the doctor stopped drawing and said, "Have you ever felt that you might be a little preoccupied with sex?"

"*Me?* Preoccupied with sex?" the patient retorted. "Hell, doc, *you're* the one drawing all the dirty pictures!"

There are any number of projective tests, interviews, and other measures for inferring a person's private goals. I think *problems* reveal our private goals more directly. The way we handle problems and, as a corollary, what we consider to be a problem in the first place can tell us a lot about our private goals.

Problem situations are important to our private goals because a problem—however perceived and identified—represents *a test of our personal competence.* Any test of our competence will likely trigger our private goals. Whether we perceive such a test of competence as a challenge or as a threat is, more often than not, a direct result of our private goals.

On the surface, at least, we might think that problems —tests of personal competence—will automatically activate behaviors rooted in the private goals of competence. But rather than engage the problem, we often divert and compromise our efforts because of more primitive urges. The thornier the problem, the more we disregard competence and prepare to *fight* or take *flight*. Fight, flight, or problem-solving are the available strategies in dealing with problems. Most of us prefer one or another. And the most preferred strategy for meeting tests of our competence reveals a striving for some very particular personal goals. It can tell a lot about the Private Game we are playing.

•

FRANK IS STILL PONDERING the Pro's question about why he chose to make the same improbable shot twice. "I guess I just like to *attack* the course," he says finally. "You know, sort of bring it to its knees like Seve Ballesteros and Greg Norman do, so I can taste the glory! What's wrong with that?"

"For one thing," offers Tim, "you can sure lose a lot of balls. I wish I could do what you do, Frank, but I just try to stay out of trouble. I still screw up, but it's not because I try anything risky. I've still got new golf balls from two birthdays ago. That's my game: plenty of equipment, but no glory."

The Pro nods. "What about you, Larry? What's your strategy?"

"Well, I figure each shot is like a solution to a problem. I like the challenge. I even enjoy my bad shots because, when I find the ball, it gives me a chance to try something different. I just sort of try to do my best and take what I get."

•

Larry responds to problems by attempting solutions. He sees a bad shot as a chance to be creative. His is a productive strategy.

Frank, on the other hand, opts to *fight*. He is more intent on *imposing* his preferred approach on the problem than he is in trying to solve the problem. He wants to prove himself right. His approach is, if anything, counterproductive.

Tim, on the other hand, simply takes *flight*. On the course, he first turned the problem over to his "magic" nine-iron. When this didn't work, he withdrew from the contest altogether. Tim chooses neither to adapt to the problem nor to try to solve it. His strategy is simply unproductive.

Obviously the three executives have different private goals. Neither Frank nor Tim really *tries* to solve the problem. By choosing to fight or take flight, they actually try to satisfy private goals rather than come to grips with the problem at hand. This raises an important question for executives. What are the private goals we seek to satisfy by reacting in a fight, flight, or problem-solving manner?

The Private Goals of the Fight Strategy

The fight strategy is a natural part of the human repertoire. To fight—that is, to aggress, to try harder, to subdue, to dominate, and to win—is part of our phylogenetic memory. It carries forward from a more primitive period in the history of our species. In its original form, it was sometimes necessary for survival.

The concern for survival still endures. There are executives who see their professional lives as continuous survival-of-the-fittest tournaments in which only the strong have a chance. They tell us nice guys finish *last*, and that if the meek are to inherit the earth, it will only be when the strong are through with it. Life is a contest between winners and losers.

But where we find an outward preoccupation with survival, we will also probably find a private fear of untimely demise. An apparent determination to win may signify a private fear of losing. And heroic efforts to prove our adequacy to others invariably indicate private feelings of our own vulnerability and inadequacy. This doesn't mean that a person who fights is *actually* weak or inadequate, but that he or she very likely fears weakness and inadequacy. Weakness, losing, or uncertainty are deemed by people like Frank to be public signs of inadequacy for all to see.

As long as these fears dominate the thoughts, feelings, and practices of an executive, no amount of knowledge of sound fundamentals or principles is enough to ensure success. The public problems in need of solution are left begging while the executive pursues satisfaction of private goals. This is why the fight strategy, as a part of an executive's Private Game, interferes with his or her personal potential.

Here are a few of the characteristics—or, more accurately, the defense mechanisms—of the fight strategy that make us ineffective in adapting to the demands of the executive game.

- Anger at those people who cause or bring problems that threaten our competence.
- Aggression and hostility in the hope of suppressing the problem and making problem bearers retreat.
- Simplistic and rigid thinking that allows us either to redefine the problem to bring it under our control or to ignore elements of the problem so it fits our preconceived solutions.
- A preference for certainty over accuracy. Certainty is useful in allaying any secret anxieties we might have about our competence as a result of personal confusion or doubt.
- Intolerance of questioning or testing our competence. To allow examination of our ideas and decisions may erode authority, invite attack, and risk exposure.

- No sensitivity to the effects our acts have on the problem or on any other people involved.
- No learning from mistakes. "Given the same situation, I'd do the same thing again!"
- Blaming our failure on others to avoid personal responsibility and exposure.
- Using anything, including formal power, to keep people at a distance, to protect our personal "system," and to hide our inadequacies.

Notice that all of the defenses of the fight strategy are counterproductive.

The Private Goals of the Flight Strategy

The German philosopher Nietzsche once wrote, "To live is to invite pain." He might well have had in mind people like Tim who prefer a flight strategy when faced with problems. The root of the fight reaction is a desire for survival, success, and status—mixed with a fear of exposure of self-perceived inadequacies, it is a sign of "power" pain and how to stay on top. But the flight strategy is a pain avoidance defense. And the pain it may inflict upon others is preferable to the pain of being revealed as incompetent. Tim's private goal is to *avoid* the "people" pain of looking foolish, of being disliked. And flight is his preferred strategy. The irony is that those who take flight to avoid the problems that come with playing the game often look foolish and are disliked in the process.

When we take flight, it is usually because we feel inadequate to the problem. But it is the opinions of other people—*pain of being judged unworthy*—we fear most. It seems better to do nothing, to avoid calling attention to ourselves.

Enslaved by pain avoidance, we refuse to come to grips with problems. We may even reach a point where we can't recognize them in the first place. To *know* there is a problem and consciously opt to *do nothing* is itself pain producing. As a result, we learn not to see too much.

We have all known executives who insist

"Hey, you're just overreacting; it's no big deal, really!" Or . . .

"It won't do any good, so why waste the effort?" Or . . .

"Don't make waves; you've got to go along to get along."

Then there are the twin engines of flight:

"I'm sorry, my hands are tied." And . . .

"Well, it's really not my job."

Meanwhile, problems go unattended. In our quest for the private goal of painlessness, we leave a lot of slack for others to take up. Generally, problems do not solve themselves magically. More often they fester and worsen until someone else has to assume drastic action. So, like the fight strategy, flight is maladaptive and unproductive.

Those of us given to flight may look for the following in our Private Games:
- An inability to recognize problems that other people seem to see clearly.
- Dishonesty, first with ourselves and then with others.
- Ready explanations of inaction or irrelevant effort:
     "His feelings would have been hurt if I . . ."
     "It will take so long I won't have time."
     "But she really tried *so* hard."
- Inability to recall the problem or its essential elements.
- Procrastination. If we can't ignore the problem, at least we can deny it our attention.
- Aches and pains or inordinate fatigue. Physical susceptibilities that provide a reason for quitting or doing nothing.
- Lack of sustained interest in issues or areas that pose tests of personal competence.
- Immersion in irrelevant activities—involvements that are

neither particularly satisfying nor productive—in place of problem-centered efforts.

- Cautious, self-dampened, unimaginative ways of behaving. False acquiescence so problems can be passed over and conflict avoided. Withholding negative opinions so interpersonal tensions will not be triggered.
- Passive-aggressive acts. Showing aggression by *not* doing what we have been asked, and perhaps agreed, to do.

Like the fight strategy, the flight strategy is a Private Game with a personal goal—the avoidance of the pain of being revealed as unworthy. And it, too, is counterproductive.

Fight, Flight, and Responsible Behavior

Strategies of fight and flight are both mechanisms to deny personal responsibility. But executives given to one or the other strategy have difficulty with such an interpretation because they often *feel* very responsible—sometimes too much so.

Problems are tests of competence. What we see as a problem and how we respond to it reveal the workings of our private goals. William Glasser, a noted psychiatrist and author of *Reality Therapy*, has observed that the universal private goal of virtually everyone is to be competent and productive. But no one will achieve this goal until he or she is willing to behave in a responsible manner. Being personally responsible is a cornerstone of competence and productivity.

All of us have a need to feel good about ourselves. But although it's a universal desire, we differ dramatically in our skills to satisfy such a need. We confuse *feeling good* with feeling good *about ourselves*. We behave irresponsibly.

The reason is that many of us do not understand that responsible behavior has two components—one personal and one interpersonal. Responsible behavior primarily entails working toward personal goals of self-worth. But it also includes the interpersonal goal of ensuring that one's personal efforts to achieve self-worth do not block or make it difficult for other people to pursue their own similar goals. On the surface, fight strategies may appear personally responsible, but more often than not they are interpersonally irresponsible. Executives who feel good employing fight strategies often constrain, prohibit, intimidate, coerce, and disenfranchise other people as they continue to see the world as a series of contests.

The more common instance of irresponsibility among those preferring the flight strategy is self-sacrifice—they feel good about deferring their own personal goals while placing inordinate value on others' aspirations. They let themselves down. But flight may be interpersonally irresponsible as well. If the need to avoid "people" pain is so strong personally that we impute our fears to others, it may lead to a form of palliative caretaking in which we seek to protect and require little of others. In the process we let others down by delaying their learning to respond to requirements of any kind. Finally, there is an impersonal form of flight in which avoiding pains of involvement and feeling rather than seeking competence is paramount; pains of "purposelessness" make little else than hassle-free survival matter. This is the least responsible strategy for dealing with problems.

The core issue—the real test—in responsible behavior is facing up to the game of personal choice and consequence, acknowledging that our outcomes are determined by the choices we make. Such a game is a personal matter. It is, foremost, *accepting accountability to and for oneself.* Being truly responsible entails affirming

> "These are *my* actions."
> "I *chose* to do these things."
> "No one else either made my choice or forced my course of action."

Of course, all of us feel that other people and events influence us for both good and bad. But when *we* act in ways that are not in our own best interests, it is because *we choose* to do so. We may not like some of the choices we have to make, but once presented, the choices become ours alone.

By the same token, we—not someone else—cause our own feelings. Being truly responsible entails saying and genuinely believing, "These are *my* feelings. No one can feel for me. And no one can *make* me feel other than how *I choose* to feel." Being responsible entails holding oneself accountable for one's own feelings.

Choice is a key ingredient in mastering the Private Game. Each of us has to decide what is right or wrong for us, what works for us and what doesn't. The same is true for those who share the course with us. With choices go consequences. Does our strategy work for them? If it does not, both personally and interpersonally, we still have a choice. We can go on as before, or we can alter our course.

The Private Goals of Problem Solving

Making a personal choice is one of the first tasks facing people like Frank and Tim. Each, in his own way, is irresponsible. Their strategies don't work, they *know* they don't work, and they have a choice: learn to do better, or keep on playing the same old game. But most of us are like Larry. We sometimes fight and sometimes take flight, but more often we face the problem and simply respond to its demands.

Problem-solving behavior is neither exceptional nor unnatural. Most people can overcome tendencies toward fight or flight to deal realistically with problems. This is because the private goals of competence—the need for self-esteem; for a sense of adequacy, productivity, and worth; for loving relationships; and for growth—are so strong that they propel us forward—even in the face of the discomforts that go with personal responsibility.

The following are characteristics of effective problem solving:

- Sensitivity to our personal reactions to problems. Do we tend to fight, take flight, or try to cope realistically?
- Honest examinations of why we favor one or another strategy.
- Honest assessments of our own track records. When we have chosen to fight, have we *really* been able to hide our inadequacies? When we have taken flight, have we *really* succeeded in feeling more worthy? Do we gain strength when we successfully solve problems?
- Recognition that we have a personal choice in the matter.
- Commitment to solving problems despite the perceived risks and discomforts involved.
- A willingness to explore—to collect data, seek opinions, test alternatives.
- A concern for consequences.
- Implementation. Put the solution to the test by taking the actions we have agreed to take.
- Test the results. Collect data about what happens so we can learn from our efforts and, perhaps, do better next time.

Problem solvers are also faced with choices. They learn from their mistakes and choose what *works*. Unlike the fight and flight strategies, their strategy is productive—and the best guarantee for survival and self-worth.

Games of Guilt and Shame

It's clear that problem solving is the mechanism we all should use to engage reality effectively, but often we prefer to fight or to take flight rather than respond appropriately to a test of our competence. Why? Both approaches seem illogical and counterproductive—ultimately more painful. There must be something else going on. A game within the game?

To make sense of the complex mix of goals and motives that compels people to forgo more productive and responsible strategies and opt for self-defeating and irresponsible behaviors, we have to understand the games of *guilt and shame*. They are central to the Private Game.

Guilt and shame are emotions. But they differ in intensity and personal significance. We experience guilt because of things we have *done* or *did not* do. Shame is entirely different. We feel shame because of what we have decided we *are*.

Shame is integral to the Private Game. Frank is one of those people who are ashamed of their feelings of weakness and vulnerability and thus protect themselves vigilantly against those people or events that call their strength into question. They learn to be aggressive and abrasive, tough and combative. Tim, on the other hand, is one of those people who are ashamed of their ineptness, poor judgment, and consequent undependability. They learn to skirt tests of competence lest they disappoint someone. But if they are pleasant enough, maybe no one will notice.

In seeking to hide their feelings of shame, both Frank and Tim behave in ways that satisfy their own personal needs to feel good in the short term, but they do not feel good about themselves for the long haul. Not everyone, of course, is shame-bound. People like Larry certainly make mistakes and experience their share of guilt. But they expect to make mistakes and do not equate their errors with evidence of what they *are*. Consequently they seldom feel ashamed about what they do or who they are.

Frank and Tim are still trying. Their dilemma is that their Private Games are based in shame. They play their Public Games in ways designed to hide the shame from both themselves and others. Hidden and unexamined, the shame feeds on itself and multiplies like some fungus in a dark, damp place. Eventually it becomes a spiral of shame-based emotions. The spiral keeps the game going. It generates its own negative energy field and opposes logic with all its impartial contradictions.

The shame spiral is important to understanding self-interference. It works like this. Whatever the source, shame leads to a fear of exposure. The fear leads to anger —anger at those who scare us and anger at ourselves for being afraid. Some of us become abusive and bullying. In the process we scare ourselves and become more ashamed. Others of us, ashamed of our anger, direct it toward ourselves and become depressed, less adequate, more of a burden, less pleasant to be around—and more ashamed. And so it goes.

There's hope for the Franks and Tims of this world if they can become aware of the Private Game they are playing. Working backward, all of us can locate the triggering device. And once uncovered, we can defuse it. If you are tired of fighting or taking flight, of being irresponsible, you can try to straighten out the spiral.

Look for the anger when you feel a need to control, become aggressive and abusive, or feel depressed and start pulling away from the world. What are you angry about— a threat to your status, an unrealistic demand, a disappointment that seems undeserved and unfair? At what or whom are you angry—people and events outside yourself . . . or yourself? Ask why.

Look for the fear that triggers the anger. What has happened that scares you? What are you afraid is going to happen? Why are you afraid? Look for the core aspect of yourself that you fear is about to be exposed. This is the shame that triggers the spiral of self-defeat.

Find the shame. Look at it. Examine it closely. Haul it out into the sunshine. Discuss it. You may find it has no substance. Or you may find it's so common that it isn't anything to shame you. This is something people like Frank and Tim might someday consider when they get tired of being shame-bound and unproductive.

They may find their original shame is simply of being human. People like Frank and Tim have lost sight of the fact that we are all weak and vulnerable at one time or another, that we are all scared. They don't know that we are all inept and inadequate under some circumstances.

Most important, they don't know that it is okay to feel weak and vulnerable, to be scared or inept and inadequate. What is not okay is to allow such feelings to immobilize us, to keep us from doing what we need to do. Those we consider courageous are not unafraid. They are courageous because, feeling scared and vulnerable and weak and inadequate, they still try to do what needs to be done. To believe otherwise, as Frank and Tim obviously do, is to deny what it means to be human. They have somehow learned to expect too much of themselves and too little from their fellow human beings.

We all make mistakes. We all have it in our power to correct them. But first we must recognize that both fight and flight and the shame that drives them are *learned*— motivated by the teachings of *voices from our past* or *our anxiety about the future*.

•

"WE NEED TO KNOW what game we are really playing," the Pro continues. "That means we have to stop denying reality and learn to acknowledge our true motives. The problem with unacknowledged motives is that they keep us bogged down in the past or busy anticipating the future. We must play in the present.

"One of the biggest problems players of all levels have is playing one shot at a time, one hole at a time. Some of us are so busy looking backward—reliving the missed putts and errors in judgment on the previous hole—that we can't concentrate on the shot at hand. Others are so frightened by the last hole that we try to reassure ourselves by looking up to see where the ball is going before we've even hit it. That's trying to prelive the future. In either case, we distract ourselves. Reliving and preliving destroy our tempo. We need to get focused because the real game is being played now!"

OLD SWING THOUGHTS

Echoes of Where We've Been

*What prevents many golfers from doing
their best is worrying about something
they've heard as a great tip.*
Tommy Armour

THE NEXT MORNING on the practice tee, the Pro asks the three executives to hit some shots so he can begin a swing analysis for each of them. As he walks along behind the players, he can hear them muttering.

"Just keep your left arm straight," Frank urges himself. "Just keep it straight, and let 'er rip!"

"Keep your head down this time," Tim warns himself. "Keep the sucker still for once and just swing around your spine, okay?"

Larry eyes his target and says, "I want just a little draw this time . . . so I need a smooth swing out to first base . . . just like this! . . ."

The Pro grins. He has heard it all many times before. He knows each executive is playing out a minor version of his own Private Game. He waves the three to gather round.

"Okay, guys," he says, "time for reflection. Let me ask you, does it bother you when somebody talks while you're trying to concentrate on a shot?"

"It bothers the hell out of me," Frank grumbles.

"Why?" the Pro asks.

"I think it's rude, for one thing," Frank replies. "It also

52

distracts me. Instead of thinking about what I've got to do, I start thinking about how inconsiderate some idiot is."

"Would you all agree?" the Pro asks. "Somebody talking can be a tremendous distraction?"

The three executives nod their agreement.

"Well, let me ask you another question," says the Pro. "Why do you talk to yourself while you're trying to play?"

"Aren't those just swing thoughts we use to play better?" Tim says.

"Old swing thoughts," the Pro replies, "can be a source of noise. They are like voices from the past—some good, some bad—but if we allow them to distract us and interfere with what we're trying to do, they don't help us. Sometimes we're so preoccupied with swinging properly that we set up a tension between remaining faithful to old swing thoughts from the past and performing in the present. That tension is really what the Private Game is all about."

Frank flops down on a bench. "You're losing me. I just don't follow all this Public Game and Private Game stuff. And the self-talk noise isn't helping any, either. I don't see what any of it's got to do with golf."

"Well," the Pro suggests, "why don't we start with some Private Game exercises. Larry, I want you to hit some balls for me. Grab a club—your six-iron ought to do—and set up toward the blue flag about a hundred fifty yards out. Don't try to do anything special. Don't think about *how* to swing. I want you to just feel your body *while* you swing. Just hit eight or ten shots for us."

Larry's first shot is pretty good. The second is off line to the left. The next he hits behind the ball, a "fat" shot.

After Larry hits about a dozen balls, the Pro says, "Were you aware of any particular part of your body?"

"Yeah, I was," Larry responds with some surprise. "As I worked at it, I noticed too much bend in my left arm. That caused me to drop the club below the horizontal. I felt like I was flailing to get back to the ball."

"Fine," the Pro says. "But I just want you to be *aware*

of your body. When you say your left arm was bent too much, you're *critiquing* what you felt. When you say you had to flail or hit from the top, you're *analyzing*. When we evaluate, make judgments, or try to analyze, it takes us out of the *present*. To play well, we've got to learn to stay in the present.

"Now, Larry, hit some more shots, and this time concentrate on the 'bentness' of your left arm. Try to scale it. Let zero be no bend, and five be completely bent. Okay?"

Larry addresses the first ball. He makes a pretty good swing. As Tim and Frank watch, Larry's left arm straightens with each shot. It is not stiff, just fully extended and firm. He starts to hit crisp, solid shots.

"What did you feel happening?" the Pro asks.

Larry is a little incredulous. "I concentrated on how bent my arm was. Then I felt that I was standing too close to the ball, so I moved back a couple of inches. I don't know what my arm looked like, but it began to feel like it was really extended. Like . . . you know, straight and firm."

The Pro nods. "I wanted everybody to see that you can improve your performance sometimes by just becoming aware of what's going on. There's a part of you that either already knows or can figure out what to do if you can just set it free.

"When Larry stopped thinking about *how* to swing the club and focused instead on what his body was telling him, something told him his left arm didn't feel right. When he focused on his left arm, something told him he was standing too close to the ball for his arm to extend. Some part of Larry figured all this out.

"Now, Larry," the Pro continues, "this time concentrate as hard as you can on what your right wrist is doing."

Larry's club hits the ground a full three inches behind the ball. The next ball goes dead right.

"I've just introduced you to the other half of the Private

Game, Larry," the Pro says. "What happened? You tell me."

"The damned thing felt stiff. I just tightened up all over. I got really worried about my grip. I couldn't do anything!"

"What did you do, Pro," Frank asks sarcastically, "put some kind of hex on him?"

"I took over his game," the Pro says. "I *meddled* with him. Being aware of his left arm was *Larry's* idea. The right wrist thing was *my* idea. I imposed my game on him. And he let me. That's what happens in the Private Game. Something or somebody is always trying to take over our game if we let it.

"Two parties play the Private Game. One can figure out and actually do what needs to be done. I call that the *Player*. But the other party wants some of the action, too. It wants to *tell us how* to play. I call that part the Meddler. The Private Game is played between the Meddler and the Player.

"The Player represents the natural ability in each of us. But the Meddler insists on calling all the shots, giving advice, and—especially—judging the performance of the Player."

"So how does it do all that?" asks Frank.

"It *talks!*" says the Pro. "It is constantly speaking up to make sure the Player doesn't foul up."

"You mean," Larry reasons, "like a boss who stands over a worker and tries to tell him every move to make? Even when the guy's got twenty years of experience on the job?"

"Exactly," says the Pro. "The Meddler is like an overactive caddie who doesn't play but wants to call all the shots. It just doesn't trust the Player to perform adequately. So it keeps up this steady chatter that interferes so much with the Player's concentration that it screws up! Then do you know what the Meddler says? 'I tried to tell you, but you just wouldn't listen, would you?'

"The Meddler represents all the interference we've known in the past. Parents, teachers, relatives, and our earliest bosses have programmed us with their counsel. Sometimes it is well-intended input and sometimes not. Some of us have critical Meddlers. Some have cautious Meddlers. Some have anxious Meddlers. Others have benign Meddlers. Some of us have strong parental Meddlers. Others have scared childlike Meddlers. It all depends on where we've been, what we've heard, and how we felt at the time."

Larry looks thoughtful. "It's like a team without a coach," he says. "I mean, we've got these two team members both vying for the number one position—bickering and competing among themselves out on the field while the game is going on. And nobody is in charge. Right?"

The Pro nods. "Our Public Game reflects the disarray and noise of our Private Game," he says. "So, you have a choice. You can let the Meddler and the Player fight it out to see which one will win and take charge of your Public Game. Or *you* can take charge.

"That's why I believe the *real* game most of us need to work on is the Private Game. If we want to play well, we've got to learn to take charge of the game in our own heads. But let me tell you, it can be hard work."

"I'll bet," mutters Frank.

The Real Game Is Between the Meddler and the Player

From the practice tee, the executives move on for some on-course instruction. On the third fairway, the Pro watches Tim put yet another ball in the lake guarding a short par 3. "What was going on with you on that shot, Tim?"

Tim is disgusted. "I looked at the hole like you've taught us—a hundred seventy yards, lake on the right, pin in the front, no wind. I took out what I thought was plenty of club. I was just about to start the club back when this voice says, 'Do you see the lake on the right?' And I reply, 'Sure I see the lake on the right. That's why I'm aiming a little left!'

"So I waggled the club to get relaxed again, and then this voice says, 'So, what are you going to do?' And I reply, 'Well, I'm aiming a little left, away from the lake. I think I can get on the green with this club even if I don't hit it good.' The voice says, 'Remember the last time you had a shot like this? You hooked it into the rocks and ended up taking a 6. Be careful not to look like a turkey again, will you?' "

"What happened then?" the Pro asks.

"Well, I was so damned scared of hooking that I pushed it and left it out to the right—right in the water again."

"Then what?"

"Then this voice says, 'What a dumb ass you are, Tim.' "

Frank snickers, but Tim is clearly upset.

The Pro looks at all three players. "The voice Tim heard was his Meddler. Tim's Player was ready to implement a pretty good strategy, but his Meddler couldn't let that happen. So it questioned Tim just at a critical moment. To really turn the screw, it appealed to Tim's fear of embarrassment. The result was just what it wanted—a failure for Tim and an opportunity for the Meddler to stand in judgment and stay in control."

•

It is the same with executives trying to do a good job at the Public Game of management. We step up to address a problem, the Meddler is right behind us telling us what to do, and the Private Game takes over. The Meddler is the Player's constant companion from situation to situation—from problem to problem.

•

"You know, I make decisions the same way I play golf,"
Tim says over dinner that night. "Just last week we had
one of our quarterly meetings on next year's budget. Feelings always run pretty high. We've got some real wheeler-
dealers who want to go for broke and some real conserva-
tives who would just as soon go backwards as take a risk.
I always get caught in the middle.

"I get ready to suggest something when this voice says,
'What do you think Joe is going to think? He worked six
weeks on that report, and you're going to wipe it out in
thirty seconds.'

"So I agonize about it for a minute and think, Well,
what should I do . . . do my job or keep the peace? That's
when my friendly voice says, 'Joe's not the only one you'll
have to convince. But you do what you want. You're the
one who's got to work with them. I just hope you don't
end up looking like a dumb ass again.'

"So finally I go along with a recommendation I don't
agree with. I'm not a dumb ass. I'm just gutless."

•

Tim is *not* gutless. He simply gets caught up in the mach-
inations of an overactive and controlling Meddler. And the
fact that he *chose* not to express his opinion—and *chose*
instead to leave an impression of agreement—reveals a
skillful Meddler. It demonstrates how an overactive Meddler can not only take over the Public Game from an
emerging Player, but can also encourage less than responsible behavior in the process. Tim's Meddler convinced him
that to voice his opinion would somehow harm or offend
the other people involved. Rather than risk their ire, he
chose to withhold his thoughts in the present, creating the
possibility that he might harm them—and himself—sometime later in the future.

THE MEDDLER

The Meddler emerges as a natural part of human development. It is like a tape recording of actual voices—of warnings, instructions, scoldings, rules, and the like—which each of us made in the past, during a more impressionable time. When we hear that voice, it is important to understand *what* the Meddler represents. We need to know *how* it intrudes and interferes, *when* and *where* it is likely to sound its favorite themes, and *why* it does what it does. In the Private Game the Meddler has the need to instruct and the desire to control, because it does not *trust* the Player.

The game between the Meddler and the Player is a volatile one. *It is primarily a game of authority and control.* The people who taught us and judged us, who rewarded us or punished us, who encouraged us or warned us, were *all people with authority* who did not fully trust us and in the process, may have led us to mistrust ourselves.

As executives, most of us both exercise and respond to authority in ways that correspond to our experiences with persons of authority in the past. That is why each of us must learn to recognize and understand the Meddler when it tries to take over our game.

Try Hard! Be Careful! What Will People Think?

There are three fundamental swing thoughts the Meddler uses to keep us in line. "Try hard" is geared to goals of performance and accomplishment. Such a message creates an expectancy of praise for success and censure for failure. If the "try hard" advice from our Meddler is deeply enough ingrained, we may reach a point where we equate personal worth with performance. We may become so hypersensitive that we see challenges and thinly disguised criticism in all that surrounds us. Take the case of Frank Fortis.

•

HAVING SAT QUIETLY with a quizzical look on his face as Tim described his latest budget meeting, Frank heaves a big sigh of disgust. The Pro takes a sip of coffee. "Frank, anything like that ever happen to you?"

Startled, Frank says defensively, "No. No, I don't ever hear any voices. I'm not even sure I buy all that crap. But there is something I want to say. I've got a bone to pick with Larry. I've been thinking about it ever since we finished up yesterday, Larry. I don't like your put-downs!"

Frank turns to the Pro. "Yesterday, after we finished number 18, I tried to make a little friendly joke with Larry. He cut me down. There was more of the same today."

Larry looks directly at Frank. "Are you talking about when you asked me if I was having any fun?"

"That's not all of it and you know it, Larry."

"I'll tell you what happened," Larry says. "After we'd all holed out on 18, Frank comes up with this scowl all over his face and says to me, 'Boy, you're really cautious out there. Are you sure you ever have any fun?' I'll have to confess that sounded like a dig to me. So I just said, 'Well, I got a par. That was fun. What did you get?' "

"That's it?" asks Tim, incredulous. "Gee, Frank, I don't think Larry meant anything. I mean, we're all out to have a good time, aren't we?"

"Don't kid yourself. That's just the tip of the iceberg," says Frank. "It was poor sportsmanship, pure and simple, and I can't stand poor sportsmanship. I hit two career two-irons and still ended up with an eight. Meantime Larry is rubbing it in with his four. Where does he get off making fun of my game, anyway?"

"Frank," Larry explains calmly, "I wasn't competing with you. It wasn't a contest. The real game is played against the course. I was playing the course, not you."

•

Frank's Meddler is solidly grounded in old swing thoughts of "try hard." Frank expects to be judged solely on how he performs. He is apprehensive about the exposure of his inadequacies. He tries to cover up with a Public Game of bravado and by blaming others. Although the game may be played as a contest—if that's what the participants want —Frank doesn't wait for such a declaration. He sees contests and criticisms everywhere, even where there aren't any. In response, he engages in any number of impulsive, inappropriate, and counterproductive behaviors. And although he may deny it, he hurts just as much as Tim does. While Tim suffers imagined rebuffs and lost affections, Frank is just as sensitive to signs of ridicule and lost respect. Like Tim, Frank endures a discomfort that is essentially self-induced. "Try hard" messages from his Meddler cause him to fight to avoid looking bad. He is therefore ill prepared for performing in the present, either at problem solving or interpersonally. Frank is not totally unaware of this, although he doesn't like to talk about it. Much as he hates to admit it, he is not without his doubts.

•

"YOU'RE RIGHT," Frank says to Larry. "I'm overreacting and I apologize. All my life I've been taught that if you try hard enough, you can do anything. But it doesn't seem to work with golf!

"You wouldn't believe how much effort I've put in over the last five years to master this game. So when I see you kind of lackadaisically ease your way around the course, it drives me nuts.

"It's not just golf. It's everything else, too. I preach the same thing to my kids and the people I work with. What if I'm wrong?"

•

The *implicit* message from the past that those of us who are like Frank hear is that *it is most important to do well.* Results count more than people. Frank will find this approach to the game to be both unproductive and unrewarding.

Those of us who are like Tim face a dilemma born of a different swing thought. When Tim's Meddler whispers "Be careful," it translates into *"You are not adequate to the task—no amount of trying will change that. So be careful, and at least don't hurt yourself or anyone else. Be careful not to be a dumb-ass or cause a problem or disappoint somebody."* Peace is more important than the person.

Although for different reasons, both Tim and Frank wonder constantly, "What will people think?"—the third swing thought from their Meddlers. It is in this sense that they both suffer from the same malady—a misplaced sense of self. Each bases his opinion of himself on what others think or may come to think of him. The Meddler has convinced both of them that they are but *extensions* of someone else, reflections of others' opinions, rather than executives each with his own personal identity.

In executive ranks, the implications of the Private Game between Player and Meddler are profound. We start to understand why some executives push only for results and others work only for harmonious relationships, why some love power and others fear it. When the Meddler wins the Private Game, the Public Game suffers. This is why we must learn to back the Player.

THE PLAYER

The Player is the performer. The Player does the work that needs to be done. From our Player comes the confidence to take responsibility for both our own actions and the consequences of those actions.

The Player is the centerpiece of truly productive relationships. It encourages spontaneous movement toward others in giving and receiving affection, healthy altruism, discriminative trust, cooperation, empathy, and sympathy. It personifies the joy of meaningful involvement with others in play, in work, in the shaping of mutual interests and ideas.

The Player is also capable of a healthy moving *against* others. It has the ability and freedom to assert itself. It is able to oppose, to accept and enjoy healthy friction, to exercise rational authority, and to meet challenges and threats to its genuine convictions and interests without fear, guilt, or shame.

The Player is the master of its Private Game and Public Game. The Player sounds magnificent, doesn't it? Well, the truth of the matter is that the Player is downright ordinary. It simply represents the natural competence and adaptability we all have, just waiting to be unleashed. But even the best of Players has a Meddler lurking somewhere in the background, offering advice and muttering warnings, trying to stay in control by keeping us mired in fears of the past. We can expect conflict between Player and Meddler any time we encounter a problem in need of solution.

The Basic Conflict

The messages that will eventually become the Meddler are triggered by the emergence of the Player. The whole thrust of the developing Player—both physically and psychologically—is toward self-reliant and competent behavior. The goals of our bodies and our minds are growth and realization of personal potential. We are programmed genetically for self-reliance and productivity. Each progression in this direction, however simple, is a source of personal satisfaction.

That progression, however, is often a source of concern and anxiety for the people responsible for our well-being. Some try to hold us back even when we're ready to try things for ourselves. Others push us out on our own prematurely, while we are still tentative and afraid. We get conflicting messages, and we are scared and frustrated and angry all at the same time. And we are confused. Unsure about where we want to go and doubting our abilities to get there, many of us opt to stay where we are.

Most people find this an intolerable condition and look

for creative ways of avoiding the conflict and minimizing the anxiety. Many of us become compliant in the hope of winning affection and approval at the cost of the submission and subordination of our Player. We accept "helplessness." We seek safety in the love and approval of the powerful people in our lives. We learn to base our actions and define "good" or "bad" according to the reactions of those we are trying to please.

If this fails and it becomes obvious that approval will never be forthcoming, we become aggressive. We expect the world around us to be hostile and seek safety through excelling, dominating, and gaining recognition. Shrewdness and power become coveted attributes. We try to "win" a place for ourselves. When this doesn't work, we accept the emotional "isolation" of our world and become detached. A specious "independence"—self-sufficiency and unfeeling objectivity—becomes our formula for safety.

Thus are sown the seeds of fight and flight. We may escape the pain, but the conflict will persist. We will not behave responsively, and our Private Game will be so fraught with discord and irrelevancy that we are destined to do poorly at our Public Games.

•

"SO WHAT ARE WE TO DO, Pro?" Tim sighs. "It sounds like we're all trapped by old swing thoughts."

The Pro grins. "Well, if we want out of the trap, we can take a tip from some of the finest teaching pros I've ever heard about. A couple of guys named Plato and Santayana. They were experts on trap play. Plato said something like 'The unexamined game is not worth playing,' and Santayana used to tell his students something to the effect that 'anyone who doesn't remember the history of his swing is condemned to repeat it.'

"So let's examine what we're doing in light of where we've been until we understand why. Let's take a real close look at the game in our heads and get to know the contestants better, so that we can decide who we want to prevail. That's a first step toward increased awareness. If we're ever going to take charge of our own games, we will have to become aware of our options.

"But there is one thing we must recognize and keep in mind constantly. *As long as we allow the Meddler to win the game in our heads, we will have problems of the spirit. It is the Meddler who keeps us from doing what we know we have to do.* That's why we must become more aware. Awareness can silence the Meddler so the Player can prevail."

LEARNING TO FEEL THE PARTS OF YOUR GAME

Awareness Is the Key to the Present

Remember, you must feel the force;
you can't force the feel.
Bob Toski and Jim Flick

THE PRO PICKS UP A CLUB and swings it back and forth, as if trying himself to loosen up. "The key to a good game," he says, "is *awareness*. And it's the same whether you're talking about your Public Game or your Private Game. You've got to be aware of what's going on with your swing. You've got to focus on what *you* are doing, how *you* influence the club and path, the tempo and plane, one way or the other. That's how you learn to play in the present instead of the past.

"But you have to learn to *feel* the parts. There are all kinds of important body sensations that are critical to a good game. Some people just ignore them. Others all but disown them, refuse to even think about them. But they are the things *we* do to influence our swings for good or bad."

"Like what?" Frank asks.

"Well," the Pro says, "grip pressure is one example. Hip turn—how much or how little—is another part we need to feel. Still another is the path or arc our arms make. We need to feel whether we return the club to the ball the same way, on the same path, we take it back. A lot of people take their arms back low and slow—make a big arc —and then, once they're coiled, they forget how they got there and try to move in a straight line from the top down to the ball. They aren't aware that they have to sort of retrace their backswing coming down. They get in a hurry and try to take a shortcut that can cause disaster. These are all feel checks. But the point is that all the parts have to work together for a good swing.''

''How is that the same as the Private Game?'' Tim inquires.

''Well,'' says the Pro, ''both games require good tension management. Just as you can learn to *feel* the parts of your Public Game, to separate the good tensions from the bad tensions, the same is true of the Private Game. If you're willing to acknowledge the noises and tensions you feel coming from your Private Game, you can come to understand what's going on with all the parts and why and how they interfere with your performance. Once you can feel the parts, you can even learn how to quiet the noise and reduce the tension.''

The Pro takes a few steps away from the executives and bends down in the grass.

''Now,'' he says when he returns, ''let's play another kind of game. I call it the five-ball drill. You see that ball over there I just put on the tee? Each of you gets five balls, and the objective is simply to knock the ball off the tee with as many of your five balls as possible, one at a time. How you perform can tell a lot about your game. Frank, why don't you go first.''

Frank takes five balls from the range bucket, positions himself about four feet from the target, winds up like a baseball pitcher, and lets his first ball fly. It sails a good ten feet past his target. He winds up again. Two feet short this time. He moves closer and literally slams each of his three remaining balls down at the target. The closest lands about ten inches to the left of the teed ball. ''What a dumb game," he mutters. "I thought I came here to learn about golf!"

"Tim?" says the Pro.

Tim positions himself as Frank did, about four feet from the target. But he has learned from Frank's strategy. He softly lobs his first ball underhanded. It misses by about a foot. He lobs another. Six inches short. Another. Eight inches right of target. Yet another, until his last ball grazes the target ball and knocks it off the tee. Tim grins broadly at Frank, barely able to contain his excitement. "McBride one, Fortis zero," he chortles.

Larry takes his turn, re-tees the target ball, and positions himself directly over it. Holding a ball between his thumb and forefinger, he sights down on the target, much like a bombardier, and lets his ball drop—squarely on target.

"Hey," Frank yells. "You can't do that!"

"Why not?"

"Bend the rules just enough to come out on top, right?" Frank says.

"What rules, Frank?"

Frank sighs in disgust. "The Pro said, '*Throw* five balls, one at a time, at the ball on the tee.' "

The Pro smiles and says, "Is that what you heard, Tim?"

Tim is obviously not liking any of this. "Gosh, I don't know," he says. "I just watched Frank. I figured he knew what to do."

"Larry," the Pro says, "how about you? What did you hear?"

"I thought you said the objective was to knock the ball off the tee with as many of our five balls as we could. And that how each of us does can tell us something about our game. I didn't hear *anything* about *how* we were supposed to do it. I sure didn't hear anything about having to *throw* our five balls!"

"I'd like everybody to just reflect on things for a

while," the Pro says. "If you will, I think you'll begin to see how even a simple little game can have a lot of parts to it.

"For example, it appears that all three of you heard different messages. And you each *felt* differently about what you heard. Frank heard instructions and ground rules and decided to add a little power of his own. Tim wasn't clear about what he heard, but something told him the best thing to do was to imitate Frank. Larry, of course, was somewhere off by himself again as usual. All he heard was the stated objective of the exercise. How did such a simple game get so complex so quickly? Each of you must have *added* something on your own. What was it?

"That's what I mean by learning to feel the parts of the game *while* you're playing. It may be a little hard at first, but if you'll stay with it, I think you'll be a step closer to the kind of awareness I'm talking about."

•

Awareness can shed light on why Larry hears more clearly than either Frank or Tim. Greater awareness might help Frank understand how he was distracted by imagined demands and constraints so that, somehow, he concluded that *he* must supply the power rather than using the natural energies available to him. And Tim, if he could feel the parts of his own game better, might begin to understand his own uncertainty and why he looks to others for guidance about what to think and do and feel. Such awareness can greatly enhance the Private Game. And a well-played Private Game cures many ills.

Awareness begins with the acknowledgment that both the Meddler and the Player exist within ourselves. They, and how we *feel* about them, are critical parts of our Private Game, and they influence the kind of Public Game we are playing. The effects of the Private Game between the Meddler and the Player are sometimes made subtle, and perhaps more insidious, because not everyone can hear the dialogue going on between the two. And if we can't *hear* our Meddler and recognize what it is doing and how we are feeling, we will be hard-pressed to quiet its influence.

More often than not, an inability to hear the noises of the Private Game does not mean there is no noise—no interchange between Meddler and Player—so much as it denotes an *intolerance* for such noise. Some of us find such preoccupations so bothersome that we simply turn them off. We *choose* to be unaware. Frank Fortis is like that.

It is one of the many ironies of the human experience that those of us most concerned with outward performance —with image, protocol, and propriety, with tidiness and appearance, with the impact we have, and with how much others respect us—are sometimes least aware of the parts of our games. Strangely, some people like it that way.

To become aware—to hear, much less to seek, the voice of our Meddler—is, for some of us, to open up old wounds. To acknowledge voices from the past is to risk once again opening ourselves to all the turmoil and anxiety, the feelings of dependence and helplessness, of those original basic conflicts.

We remember that all the voices of that earlier time were those of people with authority. And we knew then, as we know now, that authority is by definition linked to some mechanism of enforcement. Maybe superior size, maybe a power to reward or punish, or maybe the most insidious sanction—to approve or disapprove. Such mechanisms can make us feel helpless, and a sense of not hearing gives us an illusion of being in control.

Frank is one of those people who have very likely been "meddled" with during their formative years. Many people neutralize their anxieties by learning to agree with the meddlesome voices in their lives. Over time they incorporate the values and practices of their interfering role models. They themselves become meddlers. They reason that if a Meddler can be the source rather than a target of criticism and punishment, simply by exercising authority and exerting control, why not just act authoritatively, seize control, and *become* a Meddler? Hence, there is no dialogue. Only the Meddler is allowed to speak.

Tim McBride, of course, is a different sort. He has become a juggler, trying to keep all the parts of the game—his own and everybody else's—going at once. He hears everything and is inclined to *believe* everything he hears. Tim has been "meddled" with, too, but he has learned a different lesson. More than anything, Tim *wants to please.* His anxieties don't concern control as much as how he will be judged and evaluated by others. He relies on his Meddler to keep him likable. In many respects he is more unaware than Frank is.

Frank's and Tim's performances suffer because of interference with their potential. Frank is unaware because he has found a way not to listen. Tim is unaware because he listens to everything and, consequently, hears only noise. Frank is able to act, at least, while Tim is virtually immobilized. Neither gets the kind of valid and usable information that is the foundation of genuine awareness. To realize their potential, Frank must first learn to listen, and Tim, already listening, must learn to be less self-conscious so that he can *really* hear. Both must free themselves of voices from the past so they can take charge of themselves in the present.

The solution for Frank and Tim—indeed, the most viable path to Private Game mastery and growth for us all—is becoming more aware so that we can recognize and accept the Player within ourselves, not the Meddler, as the real source of our strength and competence.

OUR MEDDLERS AND THE DENIAL OF CHOICE

Perhaps it is time we considered the Meddlers in ourselves in their original context, in terms of those meddlesome people who served as our early role models. They taught us how to play the executive games we play today.

What was so powerful about those early experiences that so many of us obediently carry their admittedly painful lessons with us today?

Different people have different kinds of Meddlers within themselves. Individually we have patterned our personal Meddler on the particular kind of meddlesome people we have known throughout our lives. Some of us have known angry and aggressive Meddlers, some of us have known anxious and cautious ones. But regardless of style, Meddlers have all had one thing in common: *they denied us choice.*

The Meddlers in our lives have *opinions* about what we, and even people they don't know, need to do. And they are driven not only to express these opinions, but to make them ours as well. They provide information, too, but go on to tell us what they think and what *we* should think and do and feel. Having presented us the data, they tell us what to *conclude* on the basis of such data. Having advised us on a proper conclusion, they tell us how we should *behave* to be in accordance with such a conclusion. They tell us what we *need* to do, what is best for *us,* why we need to do it—and, sometimes, how *they* will feel if we don't. And then they tell us how *we should feel* if we disregard or embellish any of their advice and opinions. Left with no choices to make, no opportunities to decide things for ourselves, we never learn how to choose or decide. Over time, the prospect of having to choose or decide becomes frightening.

The Player inside us remains silent and hidden from sight, driven underground by more powerful meddlesome influences. This, of course, is not the natural order of things, and because it retards growth and is contrary to our true nature, it can become painful. It is then that some of us begin to react by railing aggressively against the Meddlers in our lives while others of us try to earn acceptance through cheerful compliance or escape through detachment. In neither case, however, are we really exercising personal choice. Our thoughts and acts and emotions—indeed, all decisions—are *reactions,* still tied to the meddlesome influences in our lives.

Ironically, some of us who have known such "helpful" Meddlers don't want to lose their support. These useful, protective people serve as a buffer between us and the pains of taking responsibility for ourselves. They make our decisions for us, and their approval provides a benchmark for assessing our own feelings of worth. Those of us who have known judgmental Meddlers—people who instruct and evaluate us, dangling the rewards of measuring up just out of our reach—don't want to lose them, either. We don't want to give up on our one last chance to prove ourselves and thereby please them—or beat them. Meddlers give a perverse kind of purpose to our lives. Some of us would miss their voices if they disappeared altogether. All of us struggle with separation, but those of us who live with a Meddler have a special fear—the fear of being left to fend for ourselves.

The Anxiety of Separation

Growing up is hard at any age. The feeling of being estranged, either physically or psychologically, from a familiar authoritative influence can be traumatic. As small children, we avoided total separation from the authority figures in our lives by carrying their voices with us in our minds. Consequently, over time we became able to take their place and began to talk to ourselves on their behalf, creating a meddling influence in their stead. Some of us continue to do that throughout our lives. But some of us are ready to grow up. We recognize the need to quiet the Meddler so we can free our Player and separate ourselves from old swing thoughts.

But let's be clear that *quieting* the Meddler in ourselves in no way implies that we must effect a final, irrevocable, separation. If we "hate" the Meddler or blame its voices for all of life's disappointments, that, too, is refusing to take responsibility for ourselves. But we can render it less active and influential so we can begin to discover the potential for growth of an unconstrained Player.

As it turns out, there are several methods for quieting the Meddler in each of us.

Distracting: Give the Meddler Another Job

Distraction is a powerful and often quick cure for an overactive Meddler. Speech teachers and drama coaches have for years known the secret of distraction. They may not have called it that or realized it was the attention of a Meddler they were diverting, but the result was the same. We can all use the device from time to time. If you are a little anxious before performing a task—on the first tee, for example—in preparation, just take ten deep breaths. Focus your attention on the number of breaths. Count them, one at a time. The Meddler, thus occupied, will forget about the shot at hand.

Or if you feel you can't look an audience in the eye, don't. Look at all the *foreheads* out there instead. Study them closely. During an interview, for example, just stare at the spot above the bridge of the other person's nose. Estimate the number of hairs it would take to fill the distance between his or her eyebrows. With the Meddler busy at another job, in no time a perfectly comfortable and capable Player will take charge of the situation.

Sometimes, however, something more than distraction is needed to quiet the Meddler. Some of us must virtually exorcise meddlesome influences. And we can begin by examining those meddlesome messages that cause us discomfort.

•

"YOU KNOW, PRO," Larry says, "I think with all this Meddler stuff going on, teaching has to be one of the hardest jobs anybody could have. I mean, it's got to be so frustrating and thankless sometimes. Why do you do it?"

The Pro laughs. "One of the things I've learned here on the practice tee is that teaching and learning are both influenced by where everybody's been—teacher and student alike. A lot of messages get filtered through somebody's Meddler. People end up saying things they don't know they're saying and hearing things nobody has said. Larry's right. It's hard sometimes. But it's not the *sending* of information that's hard. It's the *receiving* that makes it a difficult game. Sometimes there are more voices than we can handle. And that means there are more messages and more meanings than some of us care to process.

"Meddlers hear what they expect to hear. And when the Meddler takes over, you can't be sure that people hear what you're saying when you do try to share information with them. And other times, they hear stuff you're not saying, like you did with the five-ball drill, Frank."

"So what's the solution?" asks Tim. "Just tune out?"

"Maybe," the Pro says. "Or, maybe, try to figure out why we hear what we hear, what it means to us, and how we feel about it."

•

Surfacing: Connect Feelings to Messages

Each of us is bothered—we feel and react in predictable ways—by particular kinds of messages sent our way. It is our *feelings* and *reactions* to messages, rather than their source, that we must first come to grips with if we are interested in quieting disruptive influences from the past. Such an examination, honestly conducted, can raise to the surface some erstwhile ignored distracting influences.

Surfacing is an exercise involving the *what, how,* and *why* of our Private Games. Essentially, it is a question-and-answer session that we conduct with ourselves.

What? We can begin the surfacing process by trying to identify and classify *what* kinds of messages bother us. We can try to list special words and phrases that make us feel angry or scared or guilty or suspicious or sad. For example, people like Frank are most bothered by what might be considered *messages of encroachment,* invasive words that intrude on our turf, threaten our sense of personal space and freedom, or question our adequacy. Tim, on the other hand, might list *messages of disappointment,* words like ''I always thought I could count on you'' or ''I *never* would have believed *you* would do such a thing.''

How? If you are like Frank, how do you feel about messages of encroachment? Or, if you're like Tim, how do you feel upon learning that someone feels you have disappointed them?

How we *feel* is central to the way our Private Game influences our Public Game, because *painful* feelings are the major means of enforcement the Meddler relies upon to keep us in line. Some of our more inappropriate or counterproductive behaviors—our executive struggles— are best explained and understood as reactions to the pain we are feeling. Connecting painful feelings to messages is a vital part of the surfacing process. It is a way of forearming ourselves so that, more aware, we can manage our future reactions in a more thoughtful fashion.

Why? Why do messages of encroachment make some of us angry or afraid? Why do pronouncements of disappointment make others feel sad or unworthy? It seems likely that messages powerful enough to trigger feelings that entrap do so because they carry hidden meanings for us. And if we could only surface these meanings, we would very likely find them rooted in the past but reminding us in the present of a shame we are trying to forget.

Perhaps Frank is bothered by messages of encroachment because they remind him of a less happy time when he was dependent on others for instruction and guidance and couldn't get them. Whatever the case, Frank is easily bothered and could profit from knowing why.

Perhaps Tim is upset by others' expressions of disappointment because they remind him of a time when he feels he *did* let someone down. Tim, too, could profit from learning why certain messages can readily trigger feelings of guilt and shame.

Learning why may take time for people like Frank and Tim. They have become quite skillful at avoiding such awareness through their practices of fight and flight. But the surfacing process can be a beginning for them both. Just reflecting on the what, how, and why of the messages that bother us can put us in touch with some important feelings and advance the cause of awareness.

And what about people like Larry? Very likely he dislikes the same kinds of unsolicited instructive and evaluative messages that bother Frank and Tim. Most of us dislike such intrusions on our games. But Larry differs from people like Frank and Tim in that he has learned to deal with bothersome messages simply by considering the *source*. That is a mechanism we can all use to quiet the Meddler in ourselves.

Pinpointing: Consider the Source

The process of pinpointing has three steps. First, we can try to determine which part of us—the Meddler or the Player—is speaking to us in any situation. Second, if the Meddler has prevailed, we can try to trace its messages back to their original source. Then we can evaluate the credibility of bothersome messages in terms of how well they actually served those people in our past who sounded their themes. Sometimes a process of pinpointing can help quiet a Meddler by discrediting its favorite messages.

To determine whether it is the Meddler or the Player in us who responds on our behalf, we can listen to the *voice* and *tense* of the message we hear. Player messages, for example, are usually couched in a sort of *first-person declarative*. "*I* want to do this right!" or "*I* don't want to be there!" These first-person sentiments warrant our attention. After all, they come from the one who will be doing our work for us. Meddlers, on the other hand, invariably speak to us in what might be thought of as a *second-person directive.* "Keep *your* left arm straight!" or "*You* had better not do that!" or "*You* hurt my feelings."

Sometimes, locating and identifying our Meddlers can help us decide how much weight to give the unsolicited messages we receive. Toward this end, we might listen to the *themes* that characterize the meddlesome messages we are getting. Some people are as identifiable by their themes as they are by their fingerprints. Some are nearly always contentious. Others can be counted on to caution us. Still others will say, "I told you so."

If we can match today's painful themes with the people who originally sounded them for us, personalize our Meddlers in a manner of speaking, we can begin to take some of the mystery and sting out of the messages we hear. Then we can judge their validity in light of their sources. With a little honest work, we may even be able to give them names and talk to them on a more personal level. "Okay, Doris," we might say, "I hear you and I know you worry a lot. That's what I would expect you to say." "Yes, Mom, I promise not to embarrass you." "That's okay, Grandpa, I would have been disappointed if you hadn't reminded me." These are a few possibilities. So is "I know life is full of temptations, Reverend Smith."

Once we have personalized our Meddlers, we can begin to ask ourselves how well their messages served their originators. We can ponder history and decide whether we *want* to handle our lives as our parents or teachers or former bosses handled theirs and would instruct us to do now —or whether we would rather live more in the present. We might even be emboldened to experiment with the opposite of such advice.

Paradoxing: Practice, Practice, Practice— Then Do the Opposite

When we comply with the Meddler's advice, we reinforce and strengthen its hold over us. If our goal is to quiet the Meddler in ourselves, we must somehow break the cycle of anxious conformity. Instead of doing anything in order to avoid a full-blown eruption at any cost, we can try a game of *paradoxing*.

As a first step in paradoxing, instead of trying to avoid hurtful pronouncements of our worth—and thereby leaving our Meddlers' power latently intact—we can expose their patent absurdity. We can tell ourselves, over and over, "Be careful now," or "Watch the lake on the right," or "What is Joe going to think?" or "Don't say anything if you can't say something nice!" We can speak the Meddler's messages aloud at every opportunity. We can remind ourselves constantly of all the bothersome themes until they become so commonplace and boring that they begin to lose their sting. Then we may be able to assert ourselves a bit and simply say, "Thanks for the advice, but I don't agree." As a second step in paradoxing, after having practiced the Meddler's favorite themes to a point of indifferent familiarity, we may then choose to take an opposite course. We can even turn what might otherwise be an anxiety-producing risk into a simple exercise of games and wagers.

The problem with paradoxing is its potential for reigniting old conflicts we have sought to avoid. In the long term—just as surfacing and pinpointing help us become more aware—this will become less of a problem. In the short term, however, we may need a way of easing into the paradoxing process. One of the more civilized methods is to set up a contest and place a friendly wager on the outcome. The Player, much as with a friend of opposing conviction, can say to the Meddler, "Well, we disagree. Let's put our opinions to a test and bet thirty minutes of silence against thirty minutes of compliance. I'll do it my way. If I fail, I'll give you my unquestioning obedience for the next thirty minutes. If my way works and I succeed, however, you have to agree to keep quiet and let me play my game for the next thirty minutes. Is it a deal?"

Tim might have responded to his Meddler at the budget meeting by saying, "You may be right that my comments will wipe out all the work Joe has done. But you may *not* be. I'll speak my mind, and if Joe is really wiped out, I'll listen to you next time. If he finds my comments helpful, I'm leaving you at home for the next meeting!''

Now, obviously these are *mind* games, but that is where the feelings are. And that is where the Private Game is played—in the mind. Mental conditioning is a prerequisite to the third and final objective of Private Game mastery. We can learn to trust our natural capacities and skills only if we are aware enough to decide where we want to go— and willing enough to let our Player take us there.

GETTING A PEEK AT OUR NATURAL CAPACITIES AND SKILLS

The Player is the self we are looking for when we say we're trying to ''find ourselves.'' But we are so fragmented that the Player in each of us is unknown to many of us in the fullest sense of the word. Not only don't we know what it is, we don't know that we don't know. Distracted by constant reminders from a vigilant Meddler, we have a difficult time *finding* our Player, much less feeling and trusting it. But it can be done. Consider Larry Freeman, clearly the most competent golfer among our three executives.

•

OVER COFFEE AFTER DINNER, Frank Fortis says, ''Does any of this stuff make sense to you, Larry? You seem to play a decent game. Does this stuff apply to what you do?''

Larry smiles a little wistfully. ''I think it helps me understand for the first time something that happened to me a couple of years ago when my game really began to come around. But I have to go way back for it to make any sense. First of all, I always wanted to play like you do, Frank.''

''Me?'' Frank is incredulous.

''Yeah, you know, those big booming drives and all that. I was always the fat little kid who got picked last every time we had to choose up sides to play baseball. Well, even after three years in the army that image stayed with me. Even when I became the youngest VP in our company's history, to me I was still the little fat kid out in right field. Looking back, I know it affected how I did my job.

"But then I discovered golf. This was a game where you didn't have to run fast or have the body of a giant. All you had to do was execute these fantastically simple maneuvers. And I got pretty good. I was in the eighties after my first year. That's better than ninety percent of the people who play the game. Yet even though I took lessons and read books, I couldn't seem to get any better. I was still just a little fat kid trying to play golf. Except on the practice tee! It really used to drive me nuts. But after today, I'm beginning to understand what was happening. I couldn't play as well as I wanted, but I was the world's greatest practicer!"

"Do you know why, Larry?" the Pro asks.

"Yeah, I do now. On the practice tee my Meddler didn't give a damn. Nobody was watching. My Meddler took a nap and I let the Player in me have some fun. After a while, I became convinced I could play this game if I could just figure out what was keeping me from performing on the course the way I did in practice."

"So what did you do? What happened?" asks Tim, suddenly very interested.

"It began one afternoon during the summer," Larry says. "The course was empty because of the heat. I went out by myself, and to make it interesting, I decided to play two balls—as if there was a twosome going. Only I decided I would play one ball the regular way and one with only a five-iron. And I was serious. With the regular ball I could hear all the voices going. I weighed all my options and fussed over which club to use, worried about what my swing looked like, the whole nine yards. With the other ball, all I did was hit it. No voices, no decisions, just a five-iron regardless—so hit it!

"Well, when I added up my score I had an 81 with my regular ball. But what really got me was *I had an 83* with just the five-iron! Something clicked and I said to myself, 'To hell with all this agonizing and fussing around. I can *play* this game because I'm *really* good.' "

"So what happened then?" Tim says, loving the mystical quality of Larry's story.

"Well," Larry goes on, "the next day I decided to try to build on the experience. I decided to use all my clubs and everything and, this time, play for *score*. But I played a personal scramble—you know, where you hit two balls and select the best one to play your next shot. I figured I could get a *real* picture of my potential if I had a chance to play from my *best* position on every shot."

Frank looks scornful. "Hell, Larry," he says, "that's not real golf!"

"You may be right, Frank," says Larry, "but I shot a two over par 74 that day, and ever since then this little fat kid has been in the 70s consistently!"

•

Larry got lucky. He put his Player to the test by accident, found it adequate, and learned to trust that part of himself. Larry's adventure with his five-iron covers most of the major requirements for quieting the Meddler in us long enough for the Player to emerge and take charge. First, Larry distracted his Meddler by engaging in a "side game" in which the Meddler had no interest. Fooling around with only a five-iron didn't have anything to do with *real* performance on the golf course, so he didn't have to be careful.

At the same time, in playing by himself on a hot, deserted course, Larry effectively nullified the prospect of meddlesome messages and any concerns he might have about what other people would think. Rather than setting up a contest, to surmount twin barriers, he simply went around them—and consequently liberated himself into new awareness.

Having achieved a measure of freedom from his critical Meddler, Larry then managed to participate in the playing of the game while at the same time observing the consequences of his own participation. By focusing on a combination of his own involvement and feedback, he reached a level of awareness that rendered the problems of golf more clear and manageable.

Finally, in the form of his paradoxical side games, he created opportunities for himself to explore and discover. Larry had no preconceptions of how to use only a five-iron for the myriad shots required in a round of golf. Neither did he have any performance goals or expectations. He was willing to explore so he might discover. In the process, he learned his Player could play the game of golf, even under less than ideal conditions.

In a few holes of golf, Larry hit upon a formula some people spend years looking for: the way to greater productivity. He quieted his Meddler in the Private Game and located the means to rediscovering and reviving his Player so he had a chance to play the Public Game unencumbered.

•

"YOU KNOW," says the Pro, "what I like about Larry's story is that it illustrates one of the real puzzles of Private Game mastery. Sometimes we have to explore the *wrong* way of doing something before we're ready to discover the right way. It's almost as if we have to overcome our own intelligence to really understand some things. I'll give you a personal example.

"Golf is a game of opposites. The hardest part of trying to teach golf is having to overcome people's common sense. Some people—especially beginners—want to 'help' nature. They try to scoop the ball to get it airborne. And that makes 'sense.' Right? If you want something on the ground to go up, you have to pick it up first. Or if you want it to go farther, you hit it harder. Right? And it's nearly impossible to get them to stop—even when they can *see* that what they're doing doesn't work.

"I try to get them to experiment. I say, 'Try the *opposite* of what you think you ought to do. If you want the ball to go up in the air, don't scoop it; try hitting *down* on it. If you want it to go left, try swinging out to the *right*. If you want it to go farther, try swinging *easier*, not harder. Just spend ten minutes doing the *opposite* of what experience says you should do."

"And what happens?" Frank questions.

"It works better with some people than others. Some won't even give it a try, even though they're standing on a practice tee paying me good money to teach them golf. Others try, but halfheartedly—as though they really want to fail so I'll give up and let them do things their own way. But a lot of people are like kids in a candy store. They really get caught up in finding out how many different things they can do with a golf club. I call it discovering the 'hidden nature' of golf . . . and that's really what it is, discovering the hidden energy so you can use it."

•

Self-deception—misunderstanding the "hidden nature" of things and rushing to impose our commonsense meanings and premature judgments—may well be at the core of our dilemma. The dominance of a Meddler and the subordination of our Player are very likely due to our notions that there's something "wrong" with the Player in us and a reluctance to accept its emergence as a natural event.

So we must begin our search for the Player in ourselves by remembering that we are dealing with a natural process, playing a game of "opposites." We are looking for a part of ourselves that will unfold naturally and reveal itself to us—provided voices from the past are not allowed to color and obscure it. This means, if we are to have a successful journey, we must look for what *is* rather than what *ought to be*. And if we have patience and courage, we will arrive at a marvelous place—a place where most of us have never been before.

THE ADVANTAGES OF A LIGHT GRIP

To Release, We Must Be Willing to Let Go

*If a lot of people gripped a knife and
fork like they do a golf club, they'd
starve to death.*

Sam Snead

In pursuing the third objective of Private Game mastery—that is, freeing our potential so that it can play the game for us here and now—we are faced with a choice. We must decide whether to trust reality—what *is*—or the conventional wisdom of what *ought to be*. Choosing reality is a critical step on the road to awareness.

For some guidance, let's return to the Academy, where morning has brought with it pouring rain. Larry, Tim, and Frank are taking advantage of the time indoors to talk further with the Pro about the Private Game.

•

"You know," the Pro says after a sip of coffee, "sometimes if you look away from golf, at life in general, it helps to understand the Private Game better. You're all top executives, right? And one of the things each of you has to do in your work is see that the right decision gets made at the right time.

"So, my question is this: When you're faced with a really critical issue—one maybe affecting the whole organization—and a decision is called for, what do you do?"

Larry speaks first. "If I want a good decision, *plus* the commitment and support of the people who have to implement it, I get the people together who are going to be directly affected. I explain the problem as I see it and try to lay out the general objective. Then I ask for their help— their ideas and interpretations. The bottom line is that for a decision as critical as you describe, I try to bring as many resources to bear as possible. I guess you could say I use a team approach. But the team changes depending on the issue and who's most affected."

"Okay," the Pro says. "Frank, what do you do?"

Frank looks at Larry as if he can't quite believe his ears. "First of all, I don't usually have as much time as Larry apparently does. But if I'm going to earn my salary, I have to be willing to make the hard ones. I study the issue in depth. I make sure I'm clear on the objective, analyze my options, then I make the decisions. Decision making is one of my strong suits. And I have to say that while my decisions are not always *popular*, they're always fair. I don't mind the heat. That's what I get paid for!"

Tim shifts on his chair. "I'll be honest with you. I don't *like* making those kinds of decisions. I always worry that I'm going to overlook something or let somebody down. I envy Frank, I really do, and I wish I were more decisive. But, like I told you, I make decisions the same way I play golf. So, I've set up a system sort of like Larry's. I encourage my people to make their own decisions whenever possible —as long as they're careful to stay within existing policy, of course, and keep me informed so I'm not taken by surprise."

"Now, let me ask another question," the Pro says. "Do any of you see similarities between the way you play golf and how you make executive decisions?"

The three executives sit silently for what seems like ten minutes. Finally Tim volunteers. "It sounds to me like Frank is the only one of us who knows what it means to be an executive. He's willing to take *control* and devil take the hindmost. That's what it takes to get things done. I wish I could do the same thing."

"Why can't you?" asks the Pro.

Tim stumbles over his answer. "I don't know. I sort of back off. The fact is I don't want to impose my will on a bunch of other people who can't do anything about it. Things don't always go the way I'd like, but I think my people know they can count on me and they appreciate that."

The Pro says, "Tim, did you ever work for anyone like Frank?"

"Yeah, about ten years ago."

"Did you like working for him?"

Tim gazes down at the floor for a moment and then looks directly at Frank. "I hated his guts! It was because of him that I decided to go into administration."

Frank shrugs his shoulders. "Tim, that's the way you're bound to feel if you let other people chew you up and digest you. Hell, sometimes I don't like it any more than you do. But being willing to take charge and make the right things happen is a lot better than putting your fate in the hands of a lot of people you may not be able to trust. It's a dog-eat-dog world out there, and if anybody is going to make me look bad, it'll be me!"

"Larry," the Pro says, "you haven't said much. What do you think?"

Larry grins at Frank and Tim. "I'll tell you one thing. I wouldn't want to work for either of you. Between Frank's giving me orders so I won't screw up and Tim's trying to help me while I do all the work, I'd be a basket case.

"If there's a decision to be made, the objective is to get the best solution you can. Everybody's going to foul up sometime. But I think you can minimize error by calling in the experts—and those are the people who do the work in question every day of their lives. If the decision is a good one and people make it work, we'll get the job done. I don't think a leader's job is to solve problems. I think *leadership is seeing that problems get solved.*"

"Is this a golf academy or a management seminar on executive decision making?" Frank says curtly. "I'm not even sure what we're talking about!"

"I think," the Pro says, "we're talking about our needs for control and our apprehensions about how other people might judge us if we fail. I think these are two major sources of Private Game noise. They affect how we make decisions—on the golf course *and* in the office.

"My main point is that all of us have some pretty basic hang-ups about controlling or being controlled, and about other people's judgment of us. I don't know where they come from, but I do know they can destroy a golf swing.

"Most of my students ask me one of two questions— 'How can I lower my score to a respectable level?' or 'How can I get to playing well enough not to embarrass myself?' I think they're asking the same question—that is, 'What can I do to gain enough control over the outcome of my shots that people will either be suitably impressed or, at least, not think I'm a klutz?' My answer is, 'Nothing! You can't control the future, and the outcome of a golf shot is a future event. You can't control what goes on in other people's minds. The only control you really have is over what you do—right here and right now—and what goes on in *your* mind. And the two feed off one another. That's why getting the Private Game straightened out is so crucial.'

"If you're the kind of person who's hung up on authority and obsessed about being in control—who feels like it's up to you to *make* something happen—you can't help but tighten up. You'll probably overcontrol things and make poor judgments at inopportune times. You get hung up on 'ought' and 'what if' to the exclusion of 'what is.'

"Frank, that two-iron of yours over the lake is a good case in point. If you hadn't been hell-bent on trying to impress the rest of us, you wouldn't have tried to force that shot. Your tendency was to fight the problem—regardless of wind or distance or water—and try to impose your will on the outcome. From what you've told me, you do the same thing at the office—and maybe elsewhere as well."

"What about me, Pro?" Tim asks, not sure he wants to hear.

"Well, Tim, in a lot of ways you're like Frank. You try to control things, too."

Tim is dumbfounded. "Me?"

"Yeah. You're not nearly as direct about it as Frank, but you too focus on the future instead of the present. Frank wants *insurance*. You want *reassurance*. While Frank's inner noise says, 'I've got to *make* the right thing happen,' your inner noise tells you, 'I've got to *find* somebody—or something magic—to make the right thing happen.' Frank *fights* and you take *flight*. Your attention is diverted from what you're *doing* to what you *want* to happen.

"My point," says the Pro, "is that you control by withholding. Frank tries to control by adding power, oversupplying—ideas, decisions, directions, you name it. But you try to control by holding back, by making sure people don't have information or opinions or whatever you're uncomfortable with. Whether you intend to or not, I think you try to alter the situation and influence the outcome just as much as Frank does. On the course, you try to guide the ball by holding back your natural motion. In a way, you do the same thing at the office. I call that control. What would you call it, Tim?"

"I'd call it control, too, I guess," says Tim. "I just don't know if I do that. It sounds like me, but it doesn't feel like me."

Tim looks to Larry for help. "Larry, aren't you and I doing the same thing? Don't you worry about control—about how people are going to feel, what they're going to think?"

"I think everybody does," Larry says. "Maybe it's a

matter of degree. But if I do my best to take care of the present—you know, those things I really can influence directly—the future will turn out okay.''

The four men sit quietly for a moment. Frank ends the pause. ''You're saying Tim and I have to learn to loosen up somehow. To overcome our need to control things. To just let go.''

''The Private Game is like a game within a game,'' says the Pro. ''Playing is natural and spontaneous and fearless. And when you try to relax and just play, the Meddler loses control. Control is a Meddler's game; being playful is a Player's game. But the control game is played by the irrational, fearful part of us.''

''Well, I sure don't like being irrational,'' Tim declares. ''If what you say is true and we're all bound up in our own underwear worrying about whether people are going to like us or obey us or whatever, how the hell did we get that way?''

''I don't know,'' the Pro says. ''Each person probably has a different reason. All I know is that it's not in our best interests. That's enough for me to want to fix it if I can.''

•

There's the rub. If we don't understand it, it's hard to fix. So let's begin by reiterating a basic point: A preoccupation with control is a major barrier to the kind of personal awareness needed for successfully discovering the potential of our Player. Invariably a concern for control is linked to our personal attempts to ensure that future events and outcomes will not reveal our personal inadequacies. Our ultimate concern is what other people will think of us should events expose us as inadequate. This is a real, virtually palpable, problem for those of us like Frank or Tim because we don't trust ourselves. People like Larry, on the other hand, are not immune to such concerns so much as they have learned to *manage* them more effectively.

But if we can't trust ourselves, how on earth can we

trust anybody else to behave adequately and appropriately? And that means we are now concerned, as well, with having to control other people. We can become aggressive and try to force others to behave as they "should" (read "as we want them to"), like Frank. Or we can become compliant, so undemanding and cooperative that we exert subtle pressure on others to do the same for us, like Tim. In either event, the core concern is the same: if people really *knew* us, they wouldn't respect us or take us seriously. They might not want us around.

ABANDONMENT: THE LOSS OF CONNECTION

At the center of all our attempts to protect and defend ourselves through control is a *fear of abandonment*. It comes in many forms. Some of us experience it when it appears we might lose the *respect* of other people. We fear failure. Others equate abandonment with lack of *affection* from other people. We worry about not being included, we fear being rejected, we are bothered about not being taken seriously, or we're too self-conscious to risk playing at all.

Some of us avoid abandonment by avoiding closeness —whatever the cost. Others avoid it by courting closeness, working to delay the inevitable as long as possible. We resolve next time around to use *more* control or to be *more* ingratiating. We set ourselves up for a self-perpetuating cycle of unproductive behavior. But if we can begin to recognize our fears of abandonment for what they are— the emotional consequences of our overactive and irrational Meddler—we can take steps to drag them into the open and rid ourselves of their influences.

•

"PRO," FRANK SAYS, "you said control is a Meddler's game, but I don't think trying to control the things you're responsible for is necessarily all that bad. Knowing how to direct and control is what being a good executive is all about.

Maybe control is a problem in golf—I don't know yet—but *not* controlling is the problem I see for executives!"

"I think the control issue is the same for executives as it is for golfers," the Pro says. "I think it's a matter of *what* we're trying to control and *why* we're trying to control it. We're usually trying to make sure that we and others see us as living up to our *ideal* notions of ourselves. We get caught up in what I call the *Scratch Ideal.* We all want to play a scratch game, where we shoot par and don't need any strokes, and we're always evaluating ourselves—and expect to be judged—according to scratch.

"The problem is that our notions of the ideal seldom correspond with what's real. We can learn what we think is the ideal swing—how to look good, feel fluid and powerful, and all the other stuff—but the reality is whether it works for us or not. What's real is what the club face is doing at the moment it hits the ball and whether the ball goes where we want it to go."

•

Reality vs. the Scratch Ideal

The Scratch Ideal is the only thing acceptable to the Meddler in us. It encourages us to do something—anything—to satisfy the ideal. If we let it, it can drive us nuts! Concentrating on what is real is a more productive focus because becoming truly adaptive and responsive to life's demands requires us to see reality as clearly as possible so we can understand and come effectively to terms with it.

The problem is that some of us can't let go. We *grieve* over giving up our ideal notions. And we are not the only ones with ideals. Other people have them, too. Many of our problems with other people stem from the fact that their mental images and illusions of the Scratch Ideal differ from our images and illusions. And that adds to our dilemma.

•

"HOW THE HELL do we get into this Ideal vs. Real bind in the first place?" Larry asks with a worried look.

"We *learn* it," says the Pro. "Let me put it another way. What we call 'release' in the golf swing is a squaring up of the club head at impact. It's a natural product of the centrifugal force built up during the swing. But most of us interfere with this natural sequence of things. We try to control with our hands and wrists a piece of equipment that's traveling one hundred miles per hour.

"We don't trust the club or the physics to deliver the swing we want. We feel we have to *help* it if we're going to satisfy the ideal image we have in our heads. If we don't satisfy the image, we can't play a scratch game! It's real simple.

"Now, a lot of students who come here are already equipped with some ideal notion of how to swing the club. They are not only caught up in the Scratch Ideal, they are committed to an ideal swing to get them there! It becomes the standard for measuring their personal performance. And it becomes their definition for what is *normal*, for what everybody *should* do!"

To understand our tendencies to control, we have to understand the "Scratch Ideals"—our conceptions of what ought to be—which we are trying to hold on to. And we have to examine how we feel about the gap between our ideal and the real. This is because, in the final analysis, *our efforts to control are an attempt to make reality conform to our ideals of how things should be.*

An ideal, by definition, is "a mere mental image, existing in fancy or imagination only." It is an illusion, the product of fanciful thinking and unexamined mandates from voices in the past. It is an old swing thought without verifiable substance to which we are nevertheless faithful and committed. Some ideals can lend valuable direction to our efforts. But others can be sources of our frustrations, wasted effort, and discontent—especially when they don't jibe with reality. Misused, rigidly clung to, they sow the seeds of disillusion and disappointment. But we hold on to them because it is painful to become disillusioned.

If the gap between ideal and real is intolerable to us, it becomes a source of distraction and unhappiness. Yet the Meddler in us holds on to the ideal and torments us about the gap between ideal and real. We respond in different ways. Some of us get angry when things don't go the way they "ought to," and we try to close the gap by force. We are overtly controlling. Some of us are overwhelmed by the discrepancy between what we want and what is. We feel helpless, become melancholy and depressed about the unfairness of it all, and hope someone will take pity on us and change reality for us. This is covert control. Others of us simply refuse to see the gap; we deny that the real differs from our ideal. We pretend that we are scratch players. This is control by self-deception. But regardless of how we react, we remain focused on our ideal and seek ways to maneuver what is real while holding the ideal intact. We set ourselves up for chronic disappointment.

We have a choice when the ideal fails the test of reality. We can fault reality; we can deny it and try to control events more to our liking. And because we don't like a reality that leaves us feeling confused and somehow un-worthy, we can cling all the tighter to our mental images of what ought to be. We can fear what will become of us if we lose our illusions. Or we can turn loose and give up illusions about ourselves. We don't have to lose control of our aspirations or standards because we simply transfer them from our idealized view of what ought to be to a more reality-based acceptance of what is.

•

CAN WE CONTROL ANYTHING?

The only thing any of us has any real influence over is *ourselves*—what *we* think and feel and do. If we really need to control things, most of us need look no farther than our own contributions to the game. Believe me, this is enough to keep most of us busy. And it is the only productive control any of us really has.

•

"I DON'T LIKE any of this," Frank grouses. "I believe you have to have something to shoot for, some principles to guide you."

The Pro smiles. "The test is what happens to the ball. Consequences! That's the reality. I see you trying so hard to live up to your ideal that you destroy your own swing. Your ideal is power and distance. You swing so hard that the club head gets out ahead of you and is facing left by the time it gets to the ball. That's why you're hitting all those pull hooks that are driving you crazy. In your zeal to satisfy the image you have of yourself as a power hitter, you're self-destructing.

"As weak as it may sound, you'll make a more realistic swing if you concentrate on swinging the grip. Forget about the club head and let your left arm lead the swing so that the club head lags behind and squares up when it wants to. That may not jibe with your power ideal, but it will give you power shots!"

"What about me?" Tim asks.

"Your ideal seems to be to make as few mistakes as possible. So you lock your wrists so the club can't release. Your hands are out in front, the club face can't square up, and you make mistakes. If you want to get rid of those pushes and sick dying quail shots to the right, try *throwing* the club head at the ball for a change."

Larry is listening closely to all this. "We have to be able to adjust, don't we? Regardless of what your old swing thought is—regardless of what seems normal and ideal—you've got to test it out against the realities of the game and learn to accept what is. Isn't that what you're saying, Pro?"

"You bet!" replies the Pro.

Larry nods. "Now I see why you had us talk about how

we make decisions. I was struck by how different we three are, all with different priorities. Now I see why. Frank's executive ideal is to bite the bullet, take charge, and make the hard decisions himself. Tim here just wants to avoid making life harder for anybody. And I see my job as simply doing what I can to see that the problem gets solved. It doesn't do any good to argue about strategies because consequences are the reality checks—our only way of knowing if we made the right choice. At least I think so."

•

Like Larry, we can accept reality on its own terms, free of preconceptions and distracting voices. And we will be better for it. Our energies will go toward solving the problems at hand rather than trying to control the present according to images from the past. And we will refocus our efforts toward a more productive and rewarding outcome—on what *we* can do to play a better game.

•

TIM IS FROWNING. "Pro," he says, "you just said we've *got* to do a bunch of things. What's the difference between 'got to' and 'should' or 'ought'?"

"The difference lies with getting what we want," the Pro answers. "I have trouble with 'should' and 'ought' because they're just ideas. But if we really *want* something, there are some things we *must* do to even have a chance of getting it. Unlike 'should' and 'ought,' 'must' is tied to consequences.

"If I live in San Francisco and really want to be in Pinehurst, I *must* do something to get what I want. I can't *wish* it so. To get where I want to be I must take action—leave the house, buy a ticket, board a plane—and I must take productive action. I can't get to Pinehurst very well by heading toward Seattle.

"If you guys really want to get better at the game, then there is some work each of you *must* do. That's just reality.

Remember that we're talking about a game of *response*. It's not a game of control or anticipation or reaction. It's a game of responding to the particular demands of each shot, one shot at a time.

"If you can turn loose of your need to control things and release the natural energy of your Player, you *will* be adequate to the task. I guarantee it. But you *must* work at it. *You* must supply the effort!"

TOWARD A FREEDOM OF MOTION

We Can Beware or Be Aware, But Not Both

*The mind messes up more shots than
the body.*
Tommy Bolt

"IF IT'S A GAME of response, why can't we stop reacting and just respond?" Tim asks.

The Pro thinks a minute. "Most of us are so tight that we completely lose the freedom of motion it takes to be truly responsive. We're afraid of being personally accountable—responsible for what does or does not happen. That's what makes us reactive—anticipating being held accountable. Players make gorgeous practice swings and then become so tense over the real shot that they can't take the club back.

"But you've got to stay loose. You can't waste your energy worrying about what's going to happen. You've got to just swing away. Be willing to take what you get, knowing that whatever you do get, you can handle it! You've got to stop playing a *beware* game so you can learn to play an *aware* game."

•

Irrational Beliefs: A Cause of Bewareness

What we believe about things—ourselves, other people, and events—pretty much dictates how we feel and what we do. We are influenced by two sets of beliefs. One is rational and reality-based. The other is irrational, based not in reason so much as in our emotions and extreme worst-case fantasies. Which set of beliefs we use to define and interpret events makes all the difference in our lives.

Too often, acting on impulse or out of pain, we choose the irrational. Some of our worst fears and most self-defeating practices can be explained—that is, make any sense at all—only in terms of what turn out to be completely irrational beliefs and assumptions.

Irrational beliefs take many forms. The Scratch Ideals the Pro spoke of often lead us to irrational conclusions. We "deserve" something, we believe, because we have been faithful to the ideal. Or, having abandoned it, we believe we will be punished—and set about finding our just punishment. We heap blame on ourselves or become wary because of any number of unreasonable demands our beliefs place on us and others.

Blaming can become a way of life. So it is that many of us go through life feeling somehow guilty and apologetic, tormented by situations we think we caused or failed to prevent or fix. Or we may blame others who we think let us down. These are harmful connections to the past, favored by the Meddler in us, working to control by guilt or anger. And over time we let our painful feelings about things obscure the facts. We become more and more beware—of ourselves and others.

We are all losers in such a game. We lose our spontaneity and authenticity. Above all, we lose the ability to acknowledge and accept—to rediscover and release—the fundamental competence that is naturally ours.

Responsibility: A Rational Alternative to Bewareness

Choices based on irrational beliefs, more often than not, are rooted in our reluctance to acknowledge and accept full responsibility for our own feelings and actions. It is our preferred mechanism for letting ourselves off the

hook. Although more rational beliefs may better correspond with reality, many of us find comfort in the absolu-
tion granted by the irrational beliefs promoted by our
Meddlers. If we can blame someone else, then *we* are not
responsible.

Yet most of us *want* to be responsible, to break out of
the trap of our own irrational beliefs. But how can we go
about it? We might dispute the logic of both our irrational
beliefs and our irrational feelings. We might challenge each
and every one of our irrational conclusions on purely logical grounds. This means we must dispute the Meddler within us and the process of bewareness itself. The payoff comes
when, having silenced an irrational Meddler, we gain a
new perspective and see more clearly that we do have a
choice in the present—to beware and believe the goblins
of our own inventions or be aware and engage reality.

Awareness and bewareness are both mind-sets, just
like rational and irrational beliefs. One is responsible and
one is not. We can choose which path to take, particularly
if we know what each entails and where each might lead
us. As it turns out, the very best way to dispute irrationality
is to *understand* it for what it is. In this spirit, let's consider
the steps bewareness would have us take.

THE BEWARE MODE

Bewareness is an irrational mode of living and playing
the game. It is rooted in unpleasant memories from the
past and fueled by irrational fears of the future, diverting
us from the present and distorting our perception of the
task at hand. It shows up in many aspects of the executive
game—strategic planning and budget sessions, personnel
decisions, evaluation, and leadership. Whether we are
bosses, teachers, parents, or just staff members, we operate
from bewareness because we do not trust our natural competence to handle the consequences of natural events.

Consider the dynamics of bewareness, step by step.

THE PROBLEM

B

Beliefs about our limitations
that are irrational, and
equally irrational beliefs
about other people—how
they feel about us, who is
trustworthy and who is not,
who is critical to our well-
being or not.

E

Escape from responsibility
and *easing* of the pain and
discomfort of uncertainty
and anxiety, at least for the
moment. The resulting relief
reinforces the whole
BEWARE cycle and makes
it more likely next time
around.

E

Exposure estimates based
on the irrational feelings
we have about the risks
involved in putting
ourselves on the line—and
how people will judge us.

W

Warnings that are triggered
by the combination of our
irrational beliefs and
emotions. Voices from the
past begin to sound all the
themes of what might go
wrong and make the
prospects of personal
accountability frightening.

R

Reactions designed not to
deal rationally with the
problem, but to prevent the
occurrence of our worst-
case scenarios and the
likelihood of personal
accountability.

A

*Apprehensions and
anxieties* about the worst
that can happen if things
go wrong and who will be
blamed if they do.

Some of us are characteristically timid and cautious. Others can be counted on to force the issue, while still others try to hide. All of us are motivated by fear. All of us, at least at first, operate from a BEWARE mode. If when faced with a problem or a test of competence we choose to remain on a path of bewareness, we will find our efforts channeled by the influences of fear.

There are two noteworthy characteristics of the BEWARE mode. First, it is entirely self-serving. There is no attention to the problem at hand or to other people's needs, only to the personal risks and emotional consequences involved. We are busy protecting ourselves. Second, if we successfully avoid the problem by coming up with a skillful defensive reaction, we garner for ourselves a sense of relief, an easing of tensions, which amounts to a "pleasant" outcome.

Pleasant outcomes reward, verify, and encourage the whole BEWARE sequence so that we will be even more inclined to react the same way again. All of us caught up in the BEWARE mode waste our energies in a Private Game of self-protection.

•

"IN MY OPINION," the Pro says, "the main reason people do not play golf as well as they practice is that they try to keep something *bad* from happening. They go about it in different ways, but the objective seems to be the same. *Beware!*

"When some of my students get on the course, they tense up and act as though they can prevent calamity—the loss of a hole or a loss of face—by *forcing something good* to happen. Nine out of ten times they end up trying something really dumb.

"And then there's the guy who wants to guide the ball. He's so afraid something awful is going to happen that he can't trust himself, his golf clubs, his ball, or the golf course architect. He swings like he's trying to carry the ball by hand and lay it down where he wants it. But he's so cautious, he screws up his natural rhythm, and the result is physics gone haywire. No club-head speed, no square contact, nothing.

"I'll bet over eighty percent of the golfers I see fall into one category or the other. And I sometimes wonder if their golf games are just an aberration or if they lead their lives the same way."

•

If we let it, bewareness can indeed become a way of life—on the course, at the office, and even at home. In general, two major concerns trigger the BEWARE mode: fear of failure and/or fear of rejection.

BEWARE Failure: "Forcing" an Appearance of Success

By now we know Frank to be a results-oriented, production-centered executive, more concerned that he be judged not on how well liked he is, but on how well he makes something come out the end of the tube. But where we find a preoccupation with a show of strength, we will usually find a fear of weakness. Where we see an insistence on perfection, we will usually find a suspicion of inadequacy, and so on.

Frank, as an executive, believes personal effort—force and overt control—is the key to not looking bad. He has little trust in other people, although he's not sure whether it's their competence or their intent he distrusts. In any case, showing dependence or asking for help are sure signs of a weakness he cannot tolerate. He is as hard on other people as past authorities were on him. His own Meddler tells him this is what a boss *should* do. He personally makes the decision in order to keep the warnings and apprehensions of his Meddler from coming to pass. And although he doesn't admit it, he escapes anxiety.

Upon examination, we might find Frank's BEWARE mode, as revealed by his own comments, to look something like the chart shown opposite.

FRANK'S BEWARE MODE

B
Irrational Beliefs
"If you try hard enough,
you can do anything."
"Decision making is one of
my strong suits."

E
Escape from Responsibility
"Being willing to take
charge and make the right
thing happen is a lot better
than putting your fate in the
hands of a lot of people
you may not be able to
trust."

E
Exposure Estimates
"If anybody is going to
make me look bad, it'll be
me!" "Where does he get
off making fun of my game,
anyway?"

R
Reactions
"I make the decisions."

W
Warnings
"It's a dog-eat-dog world
out there." "That's the way
you're bound to feel if you
let somebody chew you up
and digest you."

A
Apprehensions and Anxieties
(Inferred) People lose
respect for someone who
won't take a stand. If I turn
it over to anybody, they
may foul it up and it will
reflect on me. So . . .

For Frank, autocracy is better than the uncertainty of turning his fate and reputation over to people he can't trust.

Most of us have a little of Frank in our makeup, some more than others. But what of Tim? What does his executive BEWARE mode look like?

BEWARE Rejection: "Helping" Ourselves to Acceptance

Tim's approach to both golf and the executive game flow something like the chart shown opposite.

We can see a number of contradictions in Tim's BEWARE mode. Like Frank, he doesn't want to look bad. He engages in a form of covert control that at best gives a false impression and at worst makes him look bad and feel worse. Then he rationalizes the relief he achieves by telling himself people appreciate the fact that they can count on him.

On the surface it appears Frank and Tim are poles apart —but both suffer the constraints of bewareness. Tim is openly apprehensive and inclined to take few risks. In truth, Frank maintains so much control that he also takes few risks. Both use denial to minimize risks.

At some point, because of its self-defeating logic, the BEWARE mode will boomerang for both of them. Then they will have a genuine option to pursue awareness. But if they are like most of us, the Meddler in them will have them opt to stay in the BEWARE mode and simply try different ways of acting out its dictates. This is because bewareness blinds us, both to what we are doing and to our options for doing better.

•

"A LOT OF THE BEWARE players I see," says the Pro, "are not happy with their games, even though they've chosen to play the way they do. So they try to disguise their inadequacy by trying to be something they're not.

"They try to compensate for one extreme by trying the

TIM'S BEWARE MODE

B
Irrational Beliefs
"I'm not a dumb-ass. I'm just gutless!" "I'm always caught in the middle." "I don't like making those kinds of decisions."

E
Escape from Responsibility
"Hey, this ain't the U.S. Open." "Everybody thinks I'm in total agreement." "Things don't always go the way I'd like, but I think my people know they can count on me and they appreciate that. . . ."

E
Exposure Estimates
"Be careful not to look like a turkey again." "What should I do . . . do my job or keep the peace?" "Who's to say I'd be right?" "I don't want to make life any harder for them than it already is."

R
Reactions
"I don't say a word. . . ." "I end up going along with a recommendation I don't agree with." "I encourage my people to make their own decisions."

W
Warnings
"Remember the last time you had a shot like this?" "What is Joe going to think?" "Joe's not the only one you've got to convince."

A
Apprehensions and Anxieties
"You're going to wipe out six weeks of work in ten seconds." "I always worry that I'm going to overlook something or let somebody down."

opposite extreme. The cautious guys start swinging hard, while the hard swingers start swinging so slowly that they don't even complete their backswings. But compensations are contrived and unnatural. You've got to be willing to work on the whole swing."

•

Boomerang Effects:
Bewareness and the One-Dimensional Executive

As the Pro pointed out, bewareness changes our perception of the problem and causes us to lose our flexibility of thought and sense of current purpose. We become unidimensional and deal in opposites.

So it is that we find in some organizations flight takers who decide to toughen up and fight and fighters who see a need to lighten up and humanize their management by becoming passive and taking flight, rationalizing it as "good human relations." When this occurs, we find executives with constricted vision. We find Tims masquerading as Franks—blustering, decisive, and aggressive-sounding —until such time as their competence is tested, at which point they quickly crumble and resort to type. And we find Franks emulating Tims—suddenly nice guys intent on giving the store away—until both production and morale unexplainably plummet and the pendulum swings back once again to the old autocracy.

As long as Frank and Tim persist in the BEWARE mode, they will not fully be able to recognize problem solving as an alternative to fight or flight. They will be unable to see such things as joint effort and collaboration as viable options. And they will find it difficult to think of their own jobs in terms of doing what it takes to release and encourage competence in the workplace, or anywhere else, rather than when to give directions and exercise control or when to ask questions and provide support.

BEWARE Life: "Hiding" from the Pain

Those of us like Frank and Tim are fortunate—although we lack awareness, we still are capable of movement and growth. We can still achieve that freedom of motion that comes with awareness because we have chosen to stay engaged—if not with problems, at least with life. Not everyone makes that critical choice. For some the pain is too much; they disengage entirely and stop playing altogether.

•

"PRO," TIM SAYS, "I've gotten more out of the last couple of days than I did on either the practice tee or the course. But don't a lot of people just shrug it off or run from it? I mean, it seems like you'd have to be ready for it, open to it, for it to do any good?"

"You bet," the Pro says. "First of all, I don't really get into it unless people want to. And every once in a while I get a student who doesn't want to do anything. I don't know why they come in the first place."

"Like Fred the Fed," Larry says, laughing.

"Who?" Frank asks.

"Fred Angstra," says Larry. "That guy with the government who was supposed to be our fourth player but went home in a huff on Tuesday."

"Boy," says Tim, "was he weird!"

"He was different," the Pro agrees, "but with a little work, he could have been a hell of a golfer. I think his handicap was down around 3 or 4 at one time. Either he wasn't really interested or I just didn't have anything to offer him."

"Yes, but you couldn't show him anything or get him to try anything," Larry says. "It was like he signed up and paid his money to come to the Academy to practice what he was already doing. He just stayed to himself, pounding balls way down at the end of the practice tee."

"The guy was a good golfer," the Pro says. "Sometimes the better you are, the harder it is to learn something new. It's really hard to risk what you've got in order to try something different."

"What I want to know is, why did he leave?" says Frank. "What was he mad about?"

Larry shifts on his chair. "He wasn't mad. I think he was hurt. And I think *I* had a hand in it."

"How so?" questions Tim.

"Well, he was riding with me Tuesday morning. He had hit his tee shot on number 6 right next to a ball washer on the adjoining hole. And he says, 'This is an artificial obstruction. I get to drop two club lengths away from it, right?' And I said, 'I think you just get one club-length relief, Fred.' He wanted to argue about the rules. So I told him to do whatever he wanted. But he wouldn't leave it alone. He called the Pro over."

"I gave him the rule of thumb," the Pro says, "that if it costs you a stroke penalty, like in a hazard, you get two club lengths, but if it's a free drop, you only get one."

"So, Larry, how were you responsible for him leaving?" asks Tim.

"I said, 'Fred, it's just a game.' And he says, 'Maybe to you it is, but to me it's not. And, dammit, I at least ought to know my rules!'

"And then this gremlin seized hold of me and I said, 'I thought the whole point in being an expert on the rules was to keep you *out* of trouble.' He looked at me like I had pronounced him DOA or something. He left that night."

•

Most of us, when we're hurting, seek a familiar space. Whatever the real reason for Fred's departure, he chose to *leave*. We can wonder how often in his life he has dealt with discomfort or challenge by leaving.

One problem for Fred, and for those of us like him, is in feeling victimized—let down and abused by the people around him. He expects too much from life and, neglected and abandoned, feels helpless before the unfairness of it all. This is a particularly debilitating form of bewareness. And Fred opted for a particularly debilitating solution—retreat into the loneliness of his own private and orderly world, secure from the capriciousness of life events. He is afraid to live.

•

"I GUESS I CAN TELL you guys something," the Pro says. "I called Fred's club Thursday to check on him. I talked with the assistant pro. He told me that Fred never plays; he just practices.

"And I said, 'That does seem strange. He could be really good. Doesn't he *ever* play?' The guy says, 'Not since he lost the club championship six years ago.'

"I said, 'You mean he just quit? Period?' And he says, 'It was the embarrassment more than anything. He and the guy who had been champion the last three years were going head to head. Fred had the guy down two holes. All he had to do was tie 17 and he was the new champion.'

"That's when it gets weird. The guy says, 'Fred teed off first and hit right down the middle. We have those little cement jobs that show yardage, and Fred's ball *landed* on the hundred and fifty yard marker. The ball bounced dead right and came down in the roots of a tree in the rough. The best Fred could do was declare his ball unplayable, take the penalty, and try to get on in three.' A real disaster."

"Boy," says Tim, "it makes you wonder why they call it the *fair*way."

"Yeah," the Pro continues, "but it seems Fred went berserk. He demanded a ruling, claimed he got to hit over, he tried everything. He was completely unnerved."

"But," Larry says, "that sort of thing is just the rub of the green, right? That's just the nature of the game. Couldn't Fred accept that?"

"I guess not. He lost 17, 18, and the first playoff hole. He hasn't played since. But the sad thing is he still loves the game!"

•

Fred's BEWARE mode is so extreme that even though he still practices, he refuses to play. He has given up on the game. If there is hope for Frank and Tim, is there any hope for Fred?

•

THAT NIGHT, the phone rings in the Pro's room.

"This is Fred Angstra. Did I wake you?"

"No, I'm still up," the Pro replies. "What can I do for you, Fred?"

"Well, I need to talk about a refund," Fred says.

"I don't follow."

"I figured it up. I left Tuesday evening, so I calculate I only used thirty-eight percent of the time I paid for. I'd like to get a refund for the sixty-two percent I didn't use."

"Fred," the Pro says, "you'll have to write the academy registrar. But I would encourage you to sign up again and use your credit. That way you could still get the instruction you wanted."

Fred hesitates. "I don't know, Pro. It's hard for me to get away. Believe it or not, a lot of senators depend on me."

"I can appreciate that," the Pro says, "but you could also be a fine golfer with the right kind of work. Your pro told me you played for your club championship. I'd like to see you do that again."

"Did he also tell that he cost me the match?" Fred retorts.

"No."

"I guess he wouldn't. I got a screwy bounce and he ruled I had to play the ball anyway. He didn't even have a rule book with him to be sure. I was so mad at his lack of professionalism that I couldn't do anything right after that. But what really got to me was that a guy with half my talent walked off with all the glory. I've put up with that all my life—worked my butt off and watched some guy who couldn't carry my briefcase get jumped over me to the job I was waiting for!"

"That can hurt," the Pro sympathizes.

"It's not the hurt, it's the unfairness—and the stupidity," Fred continues.

"Well, I wish you'd give my invitation some thought," says the Pro. "I'd really like to see you enjoy the game again."

PLAYERS AND SPECTATORS

Deciding Which Game to Play

*Golf, in my view, is the most rewarding
of all games because it possesses a very
definite value as a molder and developer
of character.*
Bobby Jones

THE FOLLOWING MORNING it is still raining. Over coffee the Pro relates his conversation with Fred. "That's weird," says Larry. "Who would take the time to compute the refund he wants when he left voluntarily? And then blame his club professional for losing his match. What *is* it with that guy?"

"I think," says the Pro, "Fred is like most of us when our Private Games get in turmoil. He's struggling. And like a lot of us, he sees things and recalls things in whatever way will cause him the least pain. He's caught up in a constant state of bewareness. Until he breaks out of it, he won't be able to play the game. None of us will. You've got to be aware!"

•

To begin this leg of our journey to awareness, we need to remind ourselves of the direction in which we will be traveling. Direction is more important than objectives. If we want to master our Private Game, if one of our goals is to learn to trust our natural capacities, we must first move in a direction of understanding ourselves and our game enough to know where we are, where we've been, and where we're trying to go. There will be distractions and unknown terrain, but the AWARE mode can be our map and compass.

PREPARING FOR THE AWARE MODE

Because the Meddler's irrational game of bewareness encourages us to be so self-centered, we need something to neutralize its warnings so the Player within us can be free to do what needs to be done. We must get to the core, and in doing so, we will find ourselves confronting and coming to terms with the very issues and concerns our Meddler and its games of bewareness would have us avoid.

Old bewareness dies hard. But have heart; the sturdiest among us has had the same problem. Rocky Marciano, who retired in 1956 as the only undefeated Heavyweight Champion of the World, used to tell an interesting story about himself. Marciano, to many experts the most relentless and savage competitor boxing has known, recounted that as a child he would walk the long way home from school to avoid a neighborhood bully who was intent on beating him to a pulp. Even Marciano knew what it meant to beware and took evasive action to escape the confrontation. Then, years later when he was a world champion, that same bully—now a fan—walked into the gym to watch him spar. When Marciano saw him, he said, he was "absolutely petrified. I was that frightened."

No matter how strong we are, we can expect to contend with old bewareness even as we work for awareness. It is the anxiety of inadequacy—not the danger—that really plagues us. And that anxiety will stay with us, even when we become champions and *know* we are adequate, until we *confront it* and learn to manage it instead of letting it manage us.

Moving into an AWARE mode allows us to focus our energies on *solving the problem* of our self-defeating feelings and learning to manage them, rather than on *defending* ourselves from the devils and goblins we have invented. Only when we are AWARE can we begin to appreciate how our concerns about adequacy and abandonment and our inclinations to fight or take flight have distorted our perception of problems. Only in the AWARE mode can we begin to know and trust ourselves.

•

AFTER A LONG PAUSE, the Pro continues his discussion of Fred Angstra. "A peculiar thing about people like Fred is their capacity for self-deception. Fred can admit he doesn't handle pressure very well, but he can't admit that *he* lost."

"I do that sometimes," Larry says, "but sooner or later I have to accept the fact that I'm the main man. Mostly because the people I play with won't let me get away with it!"

"Well," the Pro says, "it really helps to have somebody who will keep you on track. It seems to me that a lot of the problems most of us have would be easier to handle if we could see them more clearly, and sometimes the only way we really have of checking on ourselves is through other people."

"We're getting away from golf again, and this time it's going to be human relations," Frank interjects.

"Sooner or later," Larry says, "everything ends up in relationships. Golf was meant to be played with other people. How we relate to people on the course is as much a part of the game as how we putt. And it even shows up in management.

"I was thinking how some people let themselves get so beware that they can't reason straight anymore. I've got this VP at the office who, every time we try to discuss a problem, tries to *state the problem in terms of the solution* he prefers. Now it occurs to me that maybe he's just anxious that the outcome be okay.

"Maybe we're falling behind schedule on the development of a new project and he'll say something like 'The problem is we've got to raise more capital.' Invariably that'll take us off on a thirty-minute discussion of how to raise more money when capital isn't even the problem!

"I was beginning to think the guy was getting progressively dense, but now I think he's just anxious. If I complain about something, bewareness takes over and he thinks I'm asking *him* to fix it."

"You know," the Pro says, "not too long ago I worked with a woman pro who was in a real slump. So I had her hit a few shots. I couldn't believe what I was seeing! She had completely changed her swing from the last time I'd seen her. So I said, 'Tell me what you're working on.' And she says, 'Well, my putting has gone sour, so I'm working on my accuracy so I won't have so many long putts.'

"She was in a classic BEWARE mode. Then she went on to describe what I call the *ripple effect* of bewareness. Her problem was putting; but she figured that if she was accurate enough with her approach shots, it would take the pressure off her putting. That meant she had to be in good position off the tee, so she was working on driving the ball more accurately.

"I mean, she was thinking about the last stroke of the hole every time she teed up and hit the *first* shot! Her real problem directly affected every aspect of her game. She really had a bad case of 'paralysis from analysis.'

"So I told her, 'Look, there are two ways to approach a golf shot. You can *think* your way through it or you can *feel* your way through it. You've been thinking too much. Now I want you to try to go out and play 18 holes without thinking. Start *feeling* your game. I don't want you to think about putting or yardage or anything. I want you to use your *senses*. I want you to hear, see, smell, touch, and taste the game.'

"I told her, '*Visualize!* Look at the spot where you'd like the ball to land and visualize it happening—actually *see* it in your mind's eye—going off your club, through the air, and to that spot. Don't think about how to get it there—swing, grip, or anything.'

"Then I said, 'When you select a club, I want you to estimate your yardage—just *sense* how far and what club—strictly on your gut feel for the shot. Just look at the hole—let your eyes take it all in, feel the wind—and I guarantee, you will know what club to use.' I wanted her to *feel* the parts of her game."

"Were you trying to distract her Meddler so her Player could make decisions?" Frank asks. "Was that the point?"

"Part of it. But I was also trying to break the chain of negative thoughts that were leading to poor results, and then to give up all her plans of compensation that were leading to more negative thoughts."

Larry leans forward and asks, "So how did she do?"

"She shot a 67. So I gave her my favorite lecture about not interfering with her own potential and how her natural performer would do the job if she would just let it. But the main thing was that I was able to get her away from trying to *think* her way through the game. I got her to let her Player do what needs to be done."

•

The Pro tried to bypass his student's irrational, intellectualizing, trouble-making Meddler by appealing to her senses. If we are to achieve awareness, we must learn to do the same. We must escape the ripple effects and convoluted thinking that go with Meddling games of bewareness. The Pro took a shortcut with his student. But for lasting results, we will have to look deeper. To achieve true awareness, we will have to learn some new Private Game skills.

•

THE SKILLS OF AWARENESS

"Boy," TIM EXCLAIMS, "this game is too serious for me. We need to lighten up a bit. Tell me something, Pro. What's the funniest thing you've seen on the golf course?"

The Pro ponders Tim's question for a moment. "I can't think of any single incident, but Pro-Am tournaments have sure given me a few chuckles over the years. Any of you guys ever played in one of those things?"

Frank says, "I've played in several, but I've never thought of them as being funny."

"I've played in a couple," says Larry, "and I agree with the Pro. They can be hilarious. You get a couple of top-level executives, a Hollywood celebrity, and a big-name tour professional together for a tournament, and put them before a huge gallery, and it's like something out of *Alice in Wonderland*.

"The celebrities are fun, but some of those executive types go bonkers! I played with a guy one time who was in such a state of shock that he teed the ball up on the first tee, aimed at the 18th green, and was about to hit it over the gallery. The pro caught him just in time. I talked with him later and he confided that he had been taking tranquilizers for three days just getting ready for the tournament. What was funny was that this guy's name and picture had been all over the newspapers a week before because of a multibillion-dollar deal he had engineered. I mean, he was considered a genius in the business world. But put him on the golf course and you'd never know it. It was like he forgot who he was. All he could think of was that he was a high-handicap golfer and he was scared to death to be playing with a tour pro in front of hundreds of people. I actually felt sorry for him."

"Well, why did he enter the competition, then?" says Tim. "I know how he must have felt. I feel the same way. That's why I decided a long time ago simply not to enter those things. Why torture yourself that way? It's easier just being in the gallery."

"I guess," says the Pro, "it all depends on why you play the game. I think a Pro-Am is like an exercise in personal awareness. And you can really tell whether a person has the skills for awareness or not."

Larry looks intrigued. "What do you mean by 'the skills for awareness,' Pro? I thought from what you've said that awareness was mostly a kind of outlook, a sense of being in touch with yourself. Are there skills for that?"

"I think so. First of all, you have to be open to the experience and willing to perform. That requires skills of openness and involvement. If you aren't open and can't get involved in something, you can't become aware of it. Then, to get the most out of it, I think you have to be able to observe and learn from what you're doing. That's difficult because it requires skills of authenticity and receptivity. Real awareness comes only from a combination of honest, spontaneous effort combined with an openness to feedback. The really good golfers I've known have all four skills. They are aware of their games."

•

To achieve personal awareness and mastery of the Private Game, we must first take a closer look at how we approach our Public Games: whether we are intrigued by the experience of tournament play or would prefer to stay in the gallery; whether we try to avail ourselves of opportunity with all its demands or would rather stay within our personal range of comfort. We need to determine whether we learn anything from the games we play so we can improve or whether we insist on playing them a certain way regardless of outcome. These are the core issues of awareness. Each requires a special skill.

Opening Up: The First Skill of Awareness

Expansion, not insulation, is the goal of growth. So openness, the first skill of awareness, is essential to avoid *narrowness*, the unnecessary and unproductive restriction of thought, feeling, and action that prevents growth. Like other facets of Private Game mastery, openness is largely a matter of personal choice.

Many times we don't want to change. We are satisfied with what we have; we're not about to trade it for some unknown commodity. We sense that loss of control is the first step toward unwanted change. But contrary to what our Meddler might have us believe, a willingness to listen and explore commits us to nothing. Indeed, such experiences can confirm and strengthen us. If our premises are sound, our practices effective, and our emotions genuine, they can stand the test of experience. And if they are not, don't we want to know it? We are dealing with a growth cycle. The stronger our sense of self is, the less threatened we are by new experiences. The more open we are, the stronger our sense of self can become. Opening up simply puts us in touch with the information we need for making choices.

Becoming Actively Involved: The Second Skill of Awareness

In the Talmud it is written, "In the world to come, each of us will be called to account for all the good things God put on earth which we refused to enjoy." We are encouraged to celebrate, to use and enjoy, the life we have been given.

Most people want to be users of life. The need to experience is a conscious urge, even when experience constitutes a challenge. We explore, extend, and invest ourselves and our energies. Others of us, however, listen to our Meddlers and choose not to act out our needs for experience. But we will be discontented and feel unfulfilled much of the time, because even though we have lost touch with our needs for stimulation and variety, they will still be with us.

In short, some of us play in the tournament and others prefer to stay in the gallery. But, as the Pro said, unless we can be truly involved with something, we can't become aware of anything. The type of involvement—physical, intellectual, or emotional—and the object of involvement—work, play, service, or personal learning—are relatively less important than the *act* of involvement. Uninvolved, we have nothing to work with—neither energy nor information about the world around us. As a result, we remain unaware.

The energy we need for involvement is, for want of a better term, *psychic* energy. It is a true mind-body state in which feelings of "want to" and "can do" power us intellectually, emotionally, and physically. Energy comes primarily from one's sense of self, and it is replenished or depleted by how this sense is expressed. It is renewed by involvement and experiences and weakened by disuse and indifference. Moving through the AWARE mode can strengthen our sense of self and energize us; but we will then need a vehicle for expressing this energy.

The activity required for involvement is a basic tool for feeling better about ourselves because it allows the release of the natural performer in each of us. Passivity is an enemy of involvement and, therefore, of awareness. Our Player, the performer in us, is by nature active. But our Meddler, a nonperforming authority on all matters, encourages us to be passive and await instructions. But as long as we choose to ignore or not to respond to the stimuli around us—much less seek them out—we cannot form connections or establish any feel for cause and effect. We will not learn.

If we are truly caught up in the BEWARE mode, we will very likely find that our favorite posture is one of four possible active-passive/fight-flight means of avoiding real problem solving and awareness.

Some of us, like Frank, are *active fighters*. We are aggressive and energetic in our attempts to force our wills on the problems we encounter. We do not learn much from our experiences. We may play in the tournament, but we seldom learn anything new.

Others of us, like Fred, are *passive fighters*. Inactive, we are also uninvolved. We obstruct, refuse to cooperate, fail to do what is expected of us, and generally deal with life by hostilely rejecting the experiences and opportunities presented to us. Usually we avoid even the gallery and stay home to sullenly watch the tournament on TV. Uninvolved, we really know very little about ourselves or anyone else.

Some of us are like Tim, in flight and vacillating back and forth between activity and passivity. In either event we are running from awareness. As *active flighters* we are willing to immerse ourselves in any task or project that will take us away from our problems. We like to play the game, but not under tournament conditions.

If we are like Tim, we may be guarding against becoming *passive flighters*. If that happens, we will be less involved and even more unaware. We lose our sense of self and its energy and retreat to the security of the gallery to wait, passively and dependently, for the crowd to show us the way and move us along.

Whatever our life posture, we are where we are *by choice*. We are not victims of circumstance. Of course, there may be pressures on us and limitations on our options. But these never *compel* us to move in the directions we do. We can still choose whether to beware or be aware, whether to be active or passive, whether to fight, take flight, or respond adaptively to the tests of competence we encounter—whether to play in the tournament and be users of life or not.

Learning to Watch What We Do:
The Third Skill of Awareness

There are two functions implicit in the third awareness skill: participation and observation. For some reason, many of us seem inclined to one or the other, but not both.

If I whisper to a person who is hard of hearing, my efforts to communicate will probably not be very effective. I will need to adjust my volume. But if I am so intent on getting my message across that I cannot see the other person leaning forward, straining to listen, watching my lips, or frequently asking me to repeat myself, I will not only fail to raise my voice and adapt to the realities of the situation, I will fail to achieve my goal of communication.

In other words, some people are so preoccupied with their personal goals that they are blind to the effects of their personal practices. In management seminars, behavior like this may be labeled "poor listening," "talking too much," "being insensitive," "aggressive," and the like, but it is grounded not so much in bad intentions as in lack of attention. When we are so caught up in the importance of our own objectives that we pay little attention to the means we employ to reach them, we run roughshod over other people and their equally important objectives.

Others of us may be inclined to observations alone. We may, in fact, have developed substantial skills in apparent support of observation. We may be quite adept in making people feel comfortable, for example, skilled at drawing them out and encouraging *their* participation. But do we know how others are affected by our lack of involvement or, for that matter, by our passive efforts to lend support and appear receptive? And if we don't, how do we know how accurate our observations really are? Frankly, the more removed we are from the action, the less trust we or anyone else should place in our conclusions about what we *think* we have observed.

True awareness is based on firsthand experience subjected to the twin tests of reality: reliability and utility. The third skill is one of participation *and* observation. We must learn to function as *participant-observers*.

Becoming a participant-observer is, for the most part, a matter of successive trial-and-error learning, and we can begin to acquire and nurture participant-observer skills simply by *questioning* ourselves.

- What am I *trying* to do? What am I *actually* doing? *Why* am I doing what I'm doing?
- Are the results of my actions reliable and useful? If not, what might I do differently?

Participant-observers have a threefold advantage. They are willing and able to play in the tournament; they have the ability to watch *how* they play; and they are able to take note of what effect their game has on other players and spectators alike.

•

"PRO," LARRY SAYS, "what do you like best about the game of golf?"

"That's easy," responds the Pro. "The *integrity*. There are just a handful of rules, but they're all relevant and they apply equally to everyone.

"But what I really like is the way each player is responsible for the game. If you see an infraction, whether it's somebody else's or your own, you're supposed to call it. I don't know of any other game where players call penalties on themselves. There is no room in golf for dishonesty."

"What about handicap hustlers?" Frank says. "Some of the people I've played with just flat lie about their handicaps to give themselves the edge. That's cheating, isn't it?"

"It is in my book," says the Pro, "and it's a real shame. The handicap system is one of the things that makes golf such a fair game. The purpose is to 'equalize' things so you can play *fairly* with *anybody*."

Larry nods agreement. "And the sad thing about it," he says, "is that sometimes the worst offenders don't deceive anybody but themselves. I worry about the players who think they're going to be judged according to their handicap. They're trapped by the Scratch Ideal. They purposely misrepresent themselves by turning in only their *low* scores so they can claim a low handicap. They know sooner or later they've got to play the game and their handicap won't hold up. But until the moment of truth comes, they take some kind of weird pleasure in having people think they're great.''

"How we present ourselves is all wrapped up with our Private Games," the Pro says. "I guess I'd like to see people have a chance to get their Private Games in line with the integrity inherent in the Public Game.''

•

Presenting an Authentic and Spontaneous Self: The Fourth Skill of Awareness

If we can't be honest with other people, it's usually because we haven't learned to be honest with ourselves. Awareness is geared to self-understanding. A failure to involve ourselves in an authentic and genuine fashion frustrates awareness because any feedback we obtain applies more to a "pretender" than to ourselves.

Some people believe that such misrepresentation is due to forces beyond their rational control. Perhaps this is true in some instances. However, I believe the vast majority of deceptions and false fronts to be not only conscious, but planned in advance. We *know* when we misrepresent ourselves to others and why we do it. We do it to compensate for a faulty sense of ourselves and our own potential for productivity. We're still worried about what people will think.

Our Meddler is again at work, and when we allow it to win the Private Game, we lose our *authenticity* and *spontaneity*, our capacity for natural adaptation to the events and tests we encounter. We lose our flexibility and our creativity. That is why it is axiomatic that the stronger the

Meddler in us becomes, the less spontaneous and authentic we will be—and the less creative and adaptive we are in playing our Public Games.

How, then, do we acquire authenticity and spontaneity in our Private Games and our Public Games?

We can strive to operate in the AWARE mode, open to and actively involved in new challenges and experience as a participant-observer. We can *trust* ourselves. And we can refuse to let our Meddlers dictate what we see in ourselves or how we present ourselves to others. Challenge them, distract them, ignore them—and we will be free to be both spontaneous and authentic.

It will not come easily at first. Voices from the past and fears about the future will admonish us about the destructive consequences of such impulsive behavior. But the authentic and spontaneous Player in us does not seek largesse or immediate gratification. It yearns only for release.

9

BUNKERS, HAZARDS, AND OTHER LITTLE DEATHS

A Time for Creative Play

*The golfer very soon is made to realize
that his most immediate, and perhaps
most potent, adversary is himself.*

Bobby Jones

Bob Toski and Jim Flick began their best-selling book, *How to Become a Complete Golfer,* on a somewhat whimsical note. "Golf may be a game played by intelligent people stupidly," they wrote, "but it doesn't have to be. . . ."

Toski and Flick were making a very telling and, for our purposes, fundamental commentary on how the game is played, for it is one of life's true puzzlements why intelligent people persist in getting in their own way and making choices that are bound to be self-defeating and counter-productive.

•

THE PRO TAKES A SIP of coffee. "Golfers," he says, "are a mysterious breed. You'd think the real pros have it together better than anybody, but they're human, too. Sometimes the really great ones provide the best examples of how a noisy Private Game can affect the way the Public Game is played. Sometimes even the most successful let a desire to do their best take a backseat to more private concerns. I'll give you an example.

"Cary Middlecoff tells a story about Ben Hogan having trouble with his putting. Preparing for the Masters, he tried a split-grip technique. It was unorthodox and looked funny, but it worked for him. Hogan shot 65 with that grip in his practice round at Seminole. Then, the next week, on the very first green at Augusta, he set his old conventional grip on the putter. He went on to shoot an undistinguished round with a lot of missed putts. When he finally holed out on 18, Middlecoff asked him, 'Where's your split grip?' Hogan said, 'I can't do it in front of all these people.' He didn't want to look foolish!"

"You mean," Larry says, "as great a player as Ben Hogan was, he was more concerned with what people would think than he was with putting the best he could? Even if it meant losing?"

"That would seem to be the case," says the Pro. "The story illustrates what I consider the great trap of the game: *ambivalence.*

"A lot of people are troubled by an almost unbearable tension between a desire to do well and an equally strong fear that doing what's required to do their best will mean giving up something of great personal value, like the appearance of style and grace. It's a collision between a desire for gain and the fear of loss.

"In my opinion, learning how to handle the pain and the joy—the gain and the cost—at the same time is really what the game's all about. If we can't do that, we find ourselves in a trap we'll never get out of."

•

Self-Trapping

Are we victims of some evil process beyond our control? Or are we simply ambivalent, faced with choices and decisions we really don't want to make because we are afraid of the costs? We do have control of our choices and decisions. Maybe, as the Pro says, we trap ourselves—in a trap of our own making.

•

"TRAPS ARE FUNNY THINGS," the Pro continues. "A lot are natural, but most are man-made. Golf course architects go to great lengths to locate them in the right places, make them the right size and shape, to add a special kind of challenge to the game. But did you know that the first traps were created naturally?

"Most of the old courses—like St. Andrews and Carnoustie—were built along strips of land between the beach and farms. At night, when the cold wind blew, sheep would look for a place to get out of the cold. When they found a little hollow or depression, they all gathered in it and hunkered down. With all those hooves tromping around and digging in, they wore the grass away and reached sand. All of a sudden, we had sand traps!

"Then later, when course architects studied the original layouts, they said, 'Hey, we've got to have traps and bunkers.' So that's the way the courses were designed. I think it's the same with the traps of ambivalence. Most of the traps that make the game difficult are *man-made*!"

"Ambivalence," Larry says. "That's what that up-and-down exercise was all about the very first day, wasn't it?"

The Pro smiles. "I guess."

"I remember that exercise," Tim says. "The staff used it to select the foursomes for the week."

"That's no way to team people up," says Frank. "They told us to put a ball down in four-inch rough, then we had to hit it over a sand trap to a small green that sloped down to water on the other side. We all thought they were going to put the best together in the same foursome, and the next best and so on, so everybody tensed up and we all looked like a bunch of beginners.

"They were trying to make us look like a bunch of fools!" Frank says. "It was sadistic."

The Pro looks at the three executives. "The exercise brings out a lot about people that we want to know up front so we can do our best job with them all week. Because the ball is sitting down in heavy rough, you've got to put enough arm swing into the shot to get it out of the rough and over the trap onto the green. If you try to force it and swing too hard, or catch too much of the ball, you'll get over the trap but land in the water. If you get cautious, you'll either stay in the rough or dump it in the sand trap, in which case you'll still have the same basic problem to solve. What a person elects to do can be very revealing. Frank here chopped down on the ball and sent it clear over the green into the water."

"Yeah," Tim says, "and he hit three more just like it before he was willing to throttle back any. But that was better than what I did. I was so scared that I made two patty-cake swings and stayed in the rough, then another one into the trap. It took me two more patty-cakes before I finally got so embarrassed that I knocked it over the green into the water."

"Anybody remember what Larry did?" the Pro asks.

"I do," Frank says, "because he explained it while he was doing it. He hit it into the trap on purpose. Then he says, 'A sand shot is easier to control than one out of heavy rough,' and he proceeded to fluff it up on the green, made his putt, and got up and down in three. He's got to be the luckiest guy I've ever played with. I'm clear on that!"

Larry looks thoughtful. "It's beginning to make sense to me, Pro. I remember you saying, 'Fear of the trap is no worse than ignorance of the trap. Ignorance is just fear covered over so we don't have to acknowledge it. But either way, you can't do your best. Sooner or later you'll make the wrong shot and get yourself in trouble. Then you'll overcompensate and just make things worse. There are a lot of different traps on the course, and any one of them can spoil a good round. Enough of them can spoil the whole game.'

"Then you said, 'We're going to look at a lot of traps of the game, take the mystery out of them. We'll try to come to grips with the things that make us fearful and keep us ignorant and unaware. We're going to learn about *arrogance* and how it can blind us, about *frustration* and how it can make us play angry and afraid. We'll examine our feelings about *perfection* and how each of us tries to *compensate* for our imperfections—why some of us fear self-reliance. And we're going to explore how all these feelings can really be opportunities for more creative play.' ''

"You've got a good memory," the Pro says. "I was introducing you to how we victimize ourselves."

•

THE ANATOMY OF AMBIVALENCE

To one degree or another, we are all victims of our feelings when we are faced by a problem or decision, trapped by our own ambivalence. We can fight it or flee from it—suppress or run from awareness—but if we do, we will only embrace bewareness and all its counterproductive self-defeating maneuverings. We trap ourselves, and in trying to get out, we dig the trap deeper still. Some of us will even become addicted to our self-defeating pursuits to the point that we defeat the other people in our lives as well.

We also have the option, however, of accepting our mixed feelings, the collisions of desire and fear, as natural and healthy experiences to be used in our own growth and development. If we can accept responsibility for our own game and court awareness, we can respond more effectively to those events that test our competence. We can free ourselves of many traps and get on with the game.

•

"IT AMAZES ME HOW WE can take a perfectly natural and wonderful experience and figure out a way to screw it up," says the Pro. "There's no doubt that most of this game is played between the ears, and that the mental side of the game is sure a lot harder to master than any of the physical moves required.

"The whole game is an exercise in mixed emotions. And how we handle our own mixed feelings is probably the single most important factor in how well we play. Fred is a good example. He loves the game but hates the risks involved. So he has chosen to handle his mixed feelings by practicing but not playing.

"But love versus hate isn't all I'm talking about. There are all kinds of mixed feelings in this game. The backswing is a good case in point. Everybody can see that to get in a proper position to make a golf swing you have to turn your back to the target. But turning away from where you want to go really gives some people problems. They feel like they're losing control. Usually they will forgo the good results that turning their shoulders would bring in favor of keeping the target in view. When push comes to shove, they would rather feel in control and stay in the trap."

"But people like that won't ever play a decent game," Larry says. "Can't they understand that getting in the proper position allows not only for a better swing, but for more productive control at the same time?"

"That's what's so insidious about ambivalence," says the Pro. "If Hogan had gone ahead and used his split-handed grip and putted lights out, half the golfers in the world would have started using a split-grip the next day. He was *Hogan*! He was the standard for everybody else, but he couldn't satisfy himself—or his Meddler—so some things he just wouldn't do. The point is, to do well you don't *have* to give up anything that's really in your best interest. The thing you're holding on to is what is defeating you. But if you *think* you have to give up something you just can't live without, too often you can't even try.

"Here's another example," says the Pro. "The *yips*— that absolutely mind-numbing inability to take the putter back to stroke a three-foot putt."

"Are you kidding?" Frank asks in amazement. "A tour player can't make a three-foot putt? Come on! What are you talking about?"

"Human frailty, Frank," Larry says. "Ever hear of it?"

"Well, you can call it what you want," says Frank, "but as far as I'm concerned, that's just a cop-out. Hell, all you've got to do is think positively, just *will* it into the hole! I expect every putt I hit to go in. The only time it doesn't work for me is when the greens are bad."

"I know, Frank," Larry says. "You're one of those unfortunate guys who spend their lives stroking perfect putts on imperfect greens. . . ."

Frank's eyes flash. "Now wait a minute . . ."

Tim is uncomfortable with the anger he sees as imminent. "Okay, come on, guys. Pro? You were talking about the yips. Guys get the yips because they're ambivalent? Is that what you're saying?"

"That's what I think," says the Pro. "And it only shows up with *short* putts. Nobody expects you to make the long ones all the time. If you miss, you don't look foolish. And that's the trap. On short ones you know that the only way to get the ball into the hole is to take your putter back and stroke the ball. But that's also the only way you can *miss*!

"Some guys can't handle the prospect of missing the putt and looking bad. So they literally freeze. They are completely immobilized by simultaneous desire and fear. When they finally do stroke the putt—as they know they must—there's no way they can make it. Their fear takes over and they overcompensate. If they're afraid of leaving it short, they'll hit it two feet beyond the hole; if they're afraid of being long, they'll leave it six inches short. When it all gets to be too much, they just give up playing. That's what ambivalence can do to you. It can ruin your game."

"Not only on the golf course, Pro," Larry says. "It's the same at work, too."

•

At work or play, whenever we find people failing we will invariably find ambivalence as well. When faced with a problem or a test of our competence, we are ambivalent, but most of us figure out a way of coping. We learn to fight or take flight, to seek comfort or endure distress, to sidestep or to engage the problem. Whatever our course of action, if it seems to work, it becomes the model for managing all of the cross-purposes and mixed feelings we encounter in playing the game. We dig our own trap.

The trap of ambivalence is rooted in a self-centeredness common to us all, which is geared originally to learning to do what is required for healthy and productive living. But its energy is easily misdirected into an obsessive pursuit of perfection and compensation, into arrogance, aggression, or a compulsive flight from judgment. Above all else, ambivalence is a natural human process in need of management. So as executives—as managers of our own experience and that of others—let us familiarize ourselves with the elements of the process we both govern and are governed by.

•

"FRANK," THE PRO SAYS, "you started to say something about your approach to putting. About positive thinking. Tell us how that works for you."

A crack of thunder rattles the windows of the clubhouse and a flash of lightning splits the gray drizzle outside. "That does it!" explodes Frank. "I kept thinking we might still get out and hit the ball a little. But not with lightning in the area.

"I don't *deserve* this!" he continues. "I planned this damned trip six months in advance just so I could be assured of decent weather."

In the face of Frank's anger Tim gets a sheepish look. "Yeah, and it's probably my fault," he says with a halfhearted smile. "My wife says all I have to do is take my golf clubs somewhere and it'll rain. She says I must have been a rainmaker in an earlier life."

Larry chortles. "You guys kill me. Frank thinks the

weather is a personal insult from God, and Tim thinks he's God and needs to apologize. I love it!"

The Pro smiles. "Well, most ambivalence is a sign of some kind of arrogance. Disappointment is a natural part of the game. But how we *handle* disappointments determines how well we play. Too often, disappointment brings out our arrogance—our feelings of being special. That's a mighty deep trap!"

•

Adventures in Arrogance and Speciality

Each of us has known a time in life—in infancy and early childhood—when feelings of power and control were a dominant focal point of our existence. (Ironically, it was a period when we were as dependent and powerless as we would ever be.) We hadn't really learned to be powerful in any systematic fashion yet, but we had *feelings* of power and acted accordingly. Most of our needs were magically met. All we had to do was show distress, and as if by magic, our diapers were changed or we were fed or cuddled.

This feeling of power formed one of the earliest models any of us has to use in deciphering the mysteries of the game. It formed our first knowledge of *personal significance and influence,* of feeling special. And years later some of us still take comfort in our specialness, as if we possess some magic power. We hold to the magical idea that we can make things happen. What little disappointment it takes to send us into a temper tantrum at not getting what we want! Others among us feel special obligations and are a little frightened and troubled by the notion. We are afraid our magic might backfire. How little it takes, a failure to praise a suggestion or an expression of disappointment, to send some people into a tailspin of guilt and hurt feelings.

Either way, we are caught in a trap of self-reference. We are self-conscious because we really believe at some primitive level that we are special and have some magical influence over our own lives and those of the people around us. This belief betrays a peculiar kind of personal arrogance.

Mistrust: The Root of Arrogance, Anger, and Despair

Unfortunately, sooner or later reality intrudes. Hard on the heels of our early experience of omnipotence follows another experience. We meet consciously, perhaps for the first time, with Meddlers. Not only do the people we count on most for gratification stop gratifying us, they begin to make demands of us.

All of us have known disappointments. But the early ones are significant. They threaten our specialness. They are the first of many tests of competence to come and influence, even years later, how we handle setbacks and challenges. Most of all, we learn to *mistrust.* We begin to doubt our own power and question the good intentions of those around us. Afraid, we compensate by demanding that people acknowledge that we are special.

•

"ONE OF THE BIGGEST OBSTACLES a teaching professional has," says the Pro, "is overcoming a student's misconceptions of the golf swing and the inevitable attempt to compensate when you tamper with a swing thought. As badly as they play, some people actually *defy* you to help them change their swings. They don't know how to trust.

"I've had guys make the best swing of their lives, hit the ball forty yards farther than ever before, then tell me it didn't work for them because their problems were unique!

"I've also had students who really took me as some kind of authority on the golf swing and wanted to *please* me so bad they would get depressed when I pushed them. Some of them would actually apologize for hitting a bad shot. And the ones who were skeptical, not quite ready to accept that I knew what I was talking about, would get angry. They seemed to resent my expertise.

"It became clear to me that not only were there various

authority-figure noises going on, but there was something more important to these people than playing better. And, apparently, I was a threat to whatever that was. I was scaring them.

"Then it finally dawned on me that the anger and depression I was getting were different attempts to get me to back off. People were trying to get me to leave them alone—to leave them with whatever they were trying to protect intact."

•

When our speciality is challenged and we get our first taste of disappointment and frustration, we are frightened; but we sense that we must try to figure out how to handle the fear. Many of us react with anger. We pout and throw tantrums in righteous indignation. Or, at the other extreme, many of us simply withdraw and give up in despair.

Let's look at anger and despair as tools of self-protection, for not only are they at the center of our decisions to fight or take flight, they are both mechanisms for resisting awareness.

•

LARRY NODS IN AGREEMENT. "I think you're right, Pro," he says. "People do use anger and despair to get other people to back off and leave them alone, especially when they have a problem they don't want to deal with. Executives are notorious for that kind of behavior."

"Yeah," says Tim. "I had a boss once who would throw regular temper tantrums if you questioned his judgment or pointed out an error he had made. He just had to believe he was right about everything, and none of us was willing to tell him any different."

The Pro responds, "That's exactly what people like that want. They want to keep their opinions and approaches safe from review and evaluation. On the course, they want to swing the club the way they want to and, ideally, have you compliment them on a great swing, even when they hit lousy shots. But if they can't win your approval, they'll settle for your silence—which they then take as approval. They're surprised when they find out, usually too late, that they've been operating in an informational vacuum.

"When people get angry on the course, they're usually angry at themselves. But they just can't say, 'Boy, I really screwed up.' So they get angry at whatever or whoever is around them. Rather than acknowledge the fact that they made a poor swing and try to figure out how to fix it, they curse the foursome in front of them for not replacing their divots or raking the sand trap properly—as if the people in front have caused their problem rather than their own lousy swing."

"That lets them off the hook," Larry says. "Whatever they do poorly is always because somebody else didn't do their job and leave the course in good shape for them."

Tim jumps in eagerly. "Or somebody distracts them," he says. "Boy, I know those guys. I play with a doctor who is a pretty good putter most of the time. But when he misses one, he goes nuts! I've seen him yell at a maintenance man two hundred yards away for making too much noise with his mower. I'm scared to death to play with him because my caddie rattled my clubs one time while he was putting. Actually, it was after he had stroked the ball, but when he missed he came down on that poor kid like a ton of bricks. You would have thought it had cost him the U.S. Open. It was clear to everybody that the caddie hadn't done anything, but he was humiliated anyway. We figured if he could treat a caddie that way, it was just a matter of time before he would do the same to us. He made us all victims of his anger!"

"Bullshit," Larry says. "You're not a victim. You're a willing participant. That guy's a bully. But bullying only works if people decide to accept it and yield to it. The only way you're a victim is that you have chosen to go along with the abuse. And then it's you, not him, who has made you a victim.''

"But, Larry," Tim says, "the guy's a wild man. He's ready to blow any minute. I think if any of us pushed him, he'd come completely unglued.''

"Not necessarily," the Pro says. "One of the strange things about the people I've seen like that is they really do control their anger. I mean, they might attack a caddie on impulse, but they're a lot more restrained when it's somebody on an equal footing with them. Unless you really get close to the bone. Then they fight dirty!

"When people like that feel cornered, anything goes. Not long after I left the tour, I was working with this lady amateur. She was pretty good, but she wouldn't turn her hips properly and pulled a lot of her shots. The more I worked with her, the madder she got—really at herself. But finally she said, 'Listen, if you know so damned much, why aren't you still on the tour?' She was trying to hurt me any way she could, so I'd back off. And it did hurt.

"If I had given up on her, she would have been left to flounder and I wouldn't have learned anything. For example, I never would have learned that anger and hostility are just misdirected energy. At times like that I think it's the teacher who can really learn the most. So I hung in there. I realized that *my* reality was not *her* reality and that for whatever reason, she wasn't going to trust what I had to say until she had a chance to discover it for herself. So I got her to join one of my discovery groups on Tuesday mornings.''

Tim is intrigued. "What's a discovery group?''

"It's part of my approach to getting people to experiment," the Pro answers. "This one was entitled 'How to Hit Bad Shots Consistently.' By getting a group of players to try hitting *bad* shots, you get rid of performance anxiety. People discover some real basic cause-and-effect principles that can be applied to practicing good shots. It can even be a lot of fun. Anyway, experimenting with the 'wrong' way worked for her. She found the awareness she needed, and although she still doubted my teaching ability, she wasn't angry anymore."

•

We justify our anger and aggression in many ways. It is not our children, extensions of ourselves, who behave badly, it is the *teacher* who caused it. And it is not we who are wrong to be angry, it is those who provoked our anger.

For every aggressive act there is a target. Passive, apprehensive, and powerless people like Tim or Fred make the best targets. They avoid confrontation. But although they may choose to walk on eggshells, they don't like it. They too are angry. They are most angry at themselves for failing to come to their own defense; but they are also angry at the Franks in their lives for putting them in untenable situations. Someday they'll get even.

As it turns out, one of the major differences between executives like Frank and those like Tim or Fred, between people who fight and those who take flight, is how they handle their anger when they are frustrated or disappointed. Executives like Frank turn their anger outward, spew it on all available targets, extort what compliance they can, then move on to the next encounter. Those like Tim and Fred, on the other hand, hold their anger and turn it inward, where it ferments and bubbles until it begins to damage the container itself. Neither approach is productive or healthy.

Executives like Larry are different. They are not immune to frustration, disappointment, and anger. But they have learned to handle such feelings differently. They are less self-centered—less bogged down with feelings of specialness. Therefore they are free to be more concerned with the problem to be solved.

•

"LARRY," TIM SAYS, "you've hit some ugly shots and gotten some bad bounces. Don't you ever get angry?"

Larry chuckles. "Sure. But I try to keep focused on getting the job done."

"But what about when somebody screws up and it really costs you?" Frank asks.

"Then I try to be philosophical—usually by poking fun at myself. I'll say, 'How can this be happening to *me?* I'm special!' It sounds so ludicrous to my own ears that I have to laugh at myself. Then I remind myself of something I really believe: 'I am unique, but no way am I special!' I can't declare myself special. That's for someone else to decide, based on how *they* feel. It may not work for everybody, but there's one thing I'm sure about. The more personally I take things, the more I'm trapped and can't respond appropriately."

•

Executives like Larry trust themselves. And because they are able to remain problem-centered rather than self-centered, they typically convert their anger into resolve.

•

"I'VE HAD A LOT OF opportunities to observe how people react to critique or swing exercises that seem risky to them," the Pro continues. "I've decided golf is a game of little deaths. It scares some people and that's what makes them angry.

"Timothy Gallwey talks about a poll he once read. It was a survey of what executives worry about most. Dying —the Big Death—was way down on the list. The biggest fear was *making a speech.* And I think that fear has to do with being judged, being evaluated as less than perfect. A *little* death.

"If we don't give a perfect speech, hit a perfect shot, or make the perfect decision, it's like dying a little at a time; and we have to live with the memory. Some people can't stand to be found wanting or inadequate because they equate their performance with their personal worth.

"The striving for perfection is driven by a fear of being imperfect. It's the *fear* that gets in our way and interferes with our potential. But you can't separate the striving from the fear. They're a package deal. If you let them get blown all out of proportion, your life is going to be full of 'little deaths.' And that can be torture.

"You have to understand that you don't have to be perfect to be *good!* Did you know the touring pros estimate they execute fewer than six percent of their shots, less than one out of ten, the way they want to? They're a long way from perfect—but they're damned good!"

•

The Game of Little Deaths

There is good reason to believe that aiming for perfection is a major culprit in our games of ambivalence. To strive for perfection and set your sights on unrealistically high goals means that by any realistic criteria, you can't help but fall short. True achievers, those who seem to accomplish more than their apparent potential would indicate is possible, simply try to do their best. While they aim high, invariably they focus on realistic and attainable goals. And they reach them. They're not perfect, but they're uniformly good at what they do.

Having to perform, to constantly measure up to a collection of subjective criteria, is like dying a little at a time. Most of us would rather do something else. So we either learn to avoid as many little deaths as we can, or, when we must perform, we compensate so that our imperfections are less apparent.

•

"THE PROBLEM IS NOT our desire to do well," says the Pro, "as much as it is our desire to please. A lot of people seem to think they've got to be perfect for other people to like them, or respect them, or listen to them. If we let it, that can screw up our games by making us give more thought to what people are going to think of us than we give to playing the game the best we can. If we want to put an end to all the little deaths of the game, we've got to ignore the Meddlers that tell us we've got to be perfect. And the main problem with chasing perfection is that it probably doesn't even exist. It's another of those man-made concepts that don't jibe with nature."

•

Perfection may be an illusion. We may be judging ourselves and others according to a standard that doesn't exist. There are no parallels in nature. The beauty of a ruby or sapphire is a case in point. They are identical in every way except for the chromium impurities that give them their distinctive colors. Without the impurities, each is an unattractive gray crystal suitable only for industrial purposes. Imperfection is the key to their beauty.

A golf ball is another example. A perfectly round, perfectly smooth golf ball would not stay airborne. The earliest players discovered that scuffs and abrasions—things to mar the perfection of the sphere—were needed to give it the aerodynamic characteristics necessary for flight. Today we call such imperfections dimples, and manufacturers spend great sums of money to come up with a better pattern of intentional imperfections.

Maybe the Pro is right. Maybe perfection doesn't exist. But if it does, it would seem that the standards of perfection are mostly subjective, more a product of our minds than a reflection of fact. Maybe that's why a preoccupation with perfection serves to distract more than it motivates. Perfectionism is a favorite game of Meddlers.

•

"TAKE JACK NICKLAUS," the Pro continues. "He's compiled the best record in the history of golf, yet there are still people who fault him for an imperfect swing. But when he first came on the tour, the purists—Meddlers, all—really gave him a hard time about his 'flying right elbow' at the top of his backswing.

"But Nicklaus knew his own game. He knew letting his right elbow move away from his body was what gave him his prodigious power and distance. He also knew it almost doesn't matter where your right elbow is as long as your first move back to the ball is to drop your right elbow down to your right hip. That takes the hands out of the swing.

"My point is, people who didn't know any better tried to talk Nicklaus out of a swing that worked for him. But Nicklaus knew who he was, and he stayed with it. He knew that he had to play his own game. That's the key. We all have to decide who we are and whose game we're going to play."

•

THE PRIMAL TRAP

Am I Me or Am I an Extension of You?

Each of us has a need to be dependent from time to time. We all need to be able to rely on someone else for emotional and physical support. By the same token, each of us sometimes has an equally human need to be free from others' influence and demands, to be independent and self-reliant. Indeed, a natural progression from the totally dependent state of the infant to the more self-reliant state of the mature adult is a critical part of healthy human development. It is a transition that *must* occur for us to be truly healthy.

It is during the move from dependency to self-reliance that many of us have been most mismanaged by other people. If we are well managed, it is here that some of us first learn to manage both ourselves and those in our charge in a manner that promotes self-reliance and the full realization of personal potential. If mismanaged, it is here that others of us learn to manage ourselves and those in our charge in a manner that promotes dependency.

•

LARRY LOOKS AT THE PRO thoughtfully. "Playing your own game is what the pros talk about on TV, isn't it? When they're interviewed before the last round, I hear them say things like 'I'm just going to go out and try to put my best swing on every shot. I can't worry about catching so-and-so.' They're talking about a kind of self-reliance, aren't they?"

"Exactly," replies the Pro. "Most players on the tour will tell you the worst thing you can do in a tournament is to let the other guy's game influence yours. If somebody's outdriving you, you can't get trapped into swinging harder. If the other guy is struggling, that doesn't mean you can let up. You've just got to bear down and concentrate on playing *your* game and doing what you know how to do."

•

The Meddler in each of us is a remnant of earlier authority figures who put pressure on us to play our games the way *they* wanted us to play. Many of us have learned to play the game from an essentially dependent stance, too attuned in our play to what other players do or think or feel and too ready to adjust our game accordingly. As it turns out, mismanaged dependency needs explain a good deal of the ambivalent fight and flight tendencies we have observed in Frank, Tim, and Fred.

Mixed Signals and Mismanaged Transitions

Although Frank and Tim appear to play the game in entirely different ways, each is a victim of the early mismanagement of the same basic process. The transition from dependence to self-reliance is a process which *must* occur for people to realize their true potential. It has its own natural timetable, but too often it is either delayed or speeded up at the hands of some meddlesome executive. People like Tim, Frank, and Fred carry the effects of such mismanagement with them long afterward.

Tim's ambivalence, it would seem, is rooted in an unwillingness to give up the apparent comforts of being dependent in return for the risky but rewarding turmoil of self-reliance. Protected and cautioned to be careful by the authority figures in his life, Tim was encouraged to stay dependent. He never learned that it is all right to be independent, that self-reliance need not lead to self-centeredness and its risk of abandonment. He used to feel guilty about such yearnings, until the pain led him to give them up.

People like Frank usually have been forced to "grow up" and be self-sufficient too soon. They have experienced demanding authority figures in their lives toward whom they rarely expressed hostility. They felt hostile but knew expressing their anger and resentment would not yield pleasant consequences. Thus denied, dependency needs became frightening prospects. It was "bad" or "weak" to show dependence. Adult aggressiveness on the part of people like Frank can be interpreted as a reaction to earlier frustrated feelings of dependency. Frank feels the need for that healthy form of dependence that is satisfied by approval, reassurance, and devotion, but to achieve it, he fears that he will have to give up his appearance of self-reliance and rugged individualism. Frank never learned that it's all right to feel dependent from time to time.

But what about Fred, our detached loner? As it turns out, individuals like Fred have in common the same experience of a mismanaged transition from dependence to independence, usually at the hands of some neglectful or, perhaps, abusive authority figure in their lives. Most have known a depersonalized, dependence-stifling indulgence, a neglectful laissez-faire approach wherein physical wants were satisfied but emotional supports were in short supply.

Such people are ashamed that they are not lovable and have failed in their efforts to be self-reliant. Consequently they retreat from feeling. Fred's ambivalence has caused him to do just that. As an escape from the pains of frustration and uncertainty, he has retreated into himself. But in the process he has realized what he fears most: he has lost part of himself.

Too many authority figures have sent too many mixed signals for Tim, Frank, and Fred to be able to make sense of their own needs for dependence and independence. Tolerated but not valued, allowed but seldom encouraged, they have developed a distrust of themselves and their need to rely on others.

•

"THE REAL PROBLEM for all of us," says the Pro, "is that the game is one of reconciling opposites. Almost every game I know about requires a balance between what appear to be opposing concerns. A lot of us don't know how to achieve a balance, so we end up choosing one and trying to compensate for the other. That's when we get a 'hitch' in our swing. Getting hitches out of swings is the toughest job I have.

"A sound game always requires a good balance. It can be balancing a good offense with a good defense, the running game with the passing game, combining jabs with power, whatever. There's always an implicit need for balance if you want to play your best.

"Golf is a game of distance and accuracy. And that can be a real bind for most players. Distance and accuracy look like almost opposite demands. It's hard to get distance without the risk of sacrificing accuracy. And if you strive for accuracy, you usually have to give up some distance. That's just reality.

"The problem for a lot of people who come to me is that they feel inadequate to play the *whole* game, so they split it in half and concentrate on the part that makes them feel the best. Splitting is our way of numbing our pains of ambivalence. But it keeps us fragmented. Some guys put all their energy into knocking it a long way, and other guys devote themselves to keeping it down the middle. They put all their eggs in one basket and think nobody will notice the empty one. That's compensation. And compensation doesn't fool anybody forever.

"The reality is that long knockers don't make many pars from the bottom of a lake or out of bounds, no matter how far they hit it. And short knockers don't, either. Hitting it straight just isn't enough on the par fours if it takes three shots to get on the green.

"But once the compensation is really grooved, it *feels* so good and so right that people don't want to mess with it. The more satisfied people get with themselves, the less aware they are that their game is not really productive. They just redefine the game in terms of what they *think* they do best. They'll never play a really good game because they won't try to play the whole game. But they are the last to know what they're really doing."

Tim turns to Larry. "You've been awfully quiet. What are you thinking?"

"I'm just wondering how all this plays out in our other games," Larry replies.

•

The Whole Game

Most of our other games also entail achieving some kind of balance—between our needs for dependence and independence, our feelings of pride and shame, a zest for life and the fear of little deaths, between our Public Games and our Private Games, a Scratch Ideal and reality, and between the Meddler and Player in ourselves. By definition, most of our other games are also fraught with the traps of ambivalence. Unable to decide between these apparent conflicts, we choose to play half a game. We split off the bothersome part as if it is of no importance. But we only fool ourselves.

The proper management of ambivalence is essential to playing the whole game. Ambivalence opposes the balance necessary to play the whole game, and the key to achieving balance is the proper management and reconciliation of the tensions of ambivalence.

Proper management requires, first and foremost, an *awareness*—an acceptance and acknowledgment—of those tensions. Once acknowledged for what they are, we can begin to take productive action to reconcile them. We can forgo dependence for the sake of self-reliance and take charge of the game in our heads. Only then can we begin to play the whole game.

•

"SO WHAT'S THE SECRET?" Frank asks. "How do we learn to play the whole game?"

The Pro smiles and says, "It's no great secret. You already know what you have to do to get out of the ambivalence trap. But to actually get out, you have to give yourself *permission* to do what needs to be done."

10

BE YOUR OWN STARTER

Getting Permission to Play

You're on your own in this game—no
one blocks for you, no one covers up
your errors—and you have to play out
your foul balls! But you can be as good
as you want to be.

Arnold Palmer

"PERMISSION IS THE KEY to getting out of the trap," the Pro says. "Most of us spend our lives waiting for permission from somebody else before we're willing to do what we know needs to be done. A lot of us are like people looking at an empty golf course and refusing to play until the starter gives us a tee time. But sometimes there is no starter. We have to be our own starter—or not play at all."

•

One of the most poignant situations ever shown on television was a clip from Alan Funt's "Candid Camera" in which a young man waited patiently outside a door on which hung a sign reading "Other People Only." It soon became clear the young man wanted, perhaps needed, to go through the door. But he didn't even try. His agitation and frustration became more and more apparent as he watched "other people" blithely push the door open and walk inside. Once, he edged tentatively toward the opening but backed away when one of the other people looked at him. The door was clearly marked for someone other than him. He didn't have permission to use it.

We can wonder about just who taught the young man to wait for permission before doing what he needed to do. We might even wonder about ourselves in the same way. Although few of us are as extreme in our need for permission as the young man outside the door, all of us have spent an inordinate part of our lives seeking permission to do what we want, perhaps need, to do for ourselves. Why? Is there another game within the game?

PERMISSION SEEKING:
GAMES OF AUTHORITY AND OBEDIENCE

If we look closely, we will find our needs for permission linked to our feelings about authority and obedience. The way we conduct ourselves as executives and managers is, in a number of respects, a re-creation and a reliving of our own relationships with people in authority.

Hardly any of us is indifferent to authority. It is exciting and frightening, necessary and resented, all at the same time. Some of us love authority; we relish the personal influence and sense of control that go with being in charge. Others of us are scared to death; we worry continually about making mistakes or displeasing someone. Still others of us are ambivalent about authority; we are attracted to it and resentful of it at the same time. The implications of our *feelings* about authority are enormous for those of us who are executives.

Issues of authority and obedience color virtually all human relationships to some degree. The most definitive thing we can say about executives in general is that they administer *the authority* of their organizations. The primary job of executives is that of building and managing authority relationships for the purpose of getting the job done as productively as possible. Authority is the source of permission; and how we have learned to feel about it directly affects how productive we feel, how productively we work, and how we play our daily games of permission. Authority relationships are also one of the most mismanaged of executive transactions.

If we have been mismanaged by the authority figures in our past—as most of us have been to some degree, in our homes or schools or churches or formal organizations—we are almost certain to mismanage ourselves in the present. Few of our old authority figures are around to give us the permission we seek. Yet many of our acts are still geared to pleasing them, only now, it is *we* ourselves, the Meddlers in our own heads, who speak on their behalf. We deny ourselves permission. We trap ourselves. Why can't we just as easily grant ourselves the permission we need to get *out* of the trap? Most of us know how to do what must be done. Still, we refuse ourselves permission to do what we know how to do.

•

IN ALMOST A CHORUS, Frank and Tim say to the Pro, "What do you mean, 'give ourselves permission'?"

"Turn off your Meddler," says the Pro. "Be yourself instead of an extension of somebody else. Stop telling yourself what everybody will think about you without ever bothering to ask them. Give yourself permission to use your own judgment and do what is best for *you*. You'll be surprised how well it works."

"That's not easy," observes Tim quietly. "Sometimes I want to do things that scare the hell out of me. Are you saying I should go ahead and do them?"

"No," answers the Pro. "Because *I'm* not the one to give you permission. You have to decide for yourself. But you might ask yourself a simple question: 'What's the *worst* that can happen if I do, and what happens if I don't?' Choice and consequence. If you're honest with yourself, the answer can reveal a lot."

•

Look to Yourself for Permission

If giving ourselves permission to act in our own best interests were easy, there wouldn't be so many screwed-up
games. Learning to give ourselves permission is difficult
because we've been taught so well to withhold it. We mistrust ourselves and fear the consequences of our actions.

Giving ourselves permission means we will accept responsibility for ourselves and our actions. To *be* ourselves.
That's hard to do, too. But it allows us to do what is necessary to be productive, to realize our own potential without our actions standing in the way of other people's efforts
to do the same.

•

"I READ AN INTERESTING article the other day," the Pro says,
"about Ben Hogan, Byron Nelson, and Sam Snead on the
occasion of their seventy-fifth birthdays. They were three
of the greatest competitors the game has known. But what
fascinates me was how different they were as people.

"Nelson is considered the father of the modern swing.
He was a great talent, a fine man, and a great thinker. But
he was so eaten up by the impossibly high standards he set
for himself that he retired to his ranch in 1946 when he
was only thirty-four years old. He had won twenty of the
last thirty-two tournaments he played in and didn't see
how he could keep that up.

"Hogan was different. He was consumed with succeed-
ing. He spent almost all his time either playing or practicing, sometimes in great physical pain. He had what many
people consider the perfect swing. But few can copy it
because there was an unnatural quality to it. He worked
hard to develop his own approach, and he was never willing to share his secrets with anybody.

"But old loosey-goosey Sam, who may have been the
fiercest competitor of the three, did as little as possible to
interfere with his natural talent. His swing was a model of

simplicity, based almost entirely on 'feel.' To Snead, natural rhythm and feel and simplicity were everything. He used phrases like 'feeling oily' and 'effortless power.'

"But the really interesting thing to me is how they all ended up. At seventy-five, Nelson was retired and Hogan continued to practice. But old Samuel Jackson Snead was still playing in tournaments.

"Snead comes as close to trusting the natural Player in himself as anybody I can think of. He'd do whatever he had to to get the ball in the hole. Unlike Hogan, he didn't care how it looked. Snead differed from the others in that he gave himself permission to do what needed to be done to keep on playing. At seventy-five, he routinely shot better than his age on the Seniors Tour."

"You make it sound awfully simple," Frank says. "Sometimes I would really like to believe it's as easy as just doing one job and going on to the next. Maybe I try too hard."

"Maybe," Larry says, "you just need to give yourself permission to relax, Frank—learn to play as hard as you work. Or let somebody else do things for a change."

Frank smiles ruefully. "Tell that to my shareholders. Or to my competitors."

"Frank," the Pro says, "you've just proved my point. The reason we have to learn to give *ourselves* permission is because we can't depend on others to do it for us. Some people won't and some are afraid to. As long as we feel that we've got to look to somebody else, we're going to stay trapped. We've got to be our own starters. It's as simple as that.

"If it's just a matter of giving ourselves permission," says Larry, "why don't more of us do a better job?"

"Because," the Pro says, "most of us deny the reality of our game and refuse to take responsibility for improving it. We don't listen to the noise."

"Noise," Frank says. "What kind of noise?"

"The noise that tells us something is wrong," the Pro

says. "The really good players listen to the noise all the time. And they *use* it.

"You've seen pros walk away from a setup that didn't feel right and start over. Some of them can even stop in the middle of a backswing and abort a shot. They are sensitive to the noise, but they're not afraid of it. They turn their sensitivity into a *rational* process. They've learned when they're not comfortable over a shot, it *means* something. They don't try to deny it or change their swing to compensate for it. They just step away to give themselves time to decide how they want to *respond*."

●

Listen to the Noise

For most of us, the biggest barrier to the creative resolution of ambivalent feelings is our desire to avoid the tensions and uncertainties—the noise, if you will—of conflicting points of view or competing needs. Very likely, somewhere along the way, an authority figure taught us not to assert ourselves and face differences, telling us—or perhaps demonstrating—that conflict is destructive. Thus, we learned to ignore, flee, suppress, and rationalize the tensions so we are no longer aware of what they may mean.

We must learn to listen to the noise. Instead of letting it send us into an emotional tizzy, we must learn to acknowledge the fact that the noise itself is trying to tell us something important for playing the game. It may be just an argument between the Meddler and the Player within us. Or it may be the sound of a conflict in the real world.

Reality is full of noise. And the value of listening to that noise is the recognition that a *real* conflict exists that must be resolved. The crucial next step is to evaluate conflicting concerns, each on its own merits and in as rational a way as we can. Then we must come to appreciate the conflict as a necessary part of problem solving. Chaos, as it turns out, is but a prelude to creativity.

•

Acknowledging the Game Within:
Reconciling Our Inner Realities with Outer Reality

"PRO, IT SOUNDS TO ME like you're encouraging us to doubt ourselves," Frank says. "To second-guess our own games. I have real problems with that."

The Pro nods. "I'm not suggesting you *doubt* anything," he explains, "especially not yourselves. Self-doubt comes primarily from a lack of self-understanding. I'm simply encouraging you to check your own feedback, to question it so you can understand what it's saying."

Larry chuckles. "I'll bet Frank is one of those guys who won't stop and ask directions in a strange town. He'd rather spend two hours driving around 'on instinct.' "

Frank grins. "You've got my number. I *hate* to ask directions. Hell, half the people you ask don't know either."

"So you've got a fifty-fifty chance," says Larry. "That's better than staying lost."

The Pro laughs. "You guys remind me of a caddie I used to have. I called him Point Man because he was so good at checking the course out for me before a tournament. He was a character, but he really did save me time and hassle over the years. I learned that it pays to take the time to check out your impressions for accuracy. Until I teamed up with him, I just estimated my yardages. But Point Man measured them off and kept a yardage book for us to use. That was years before Jack Nicklaus made it a science. Point Man called it my reality check!

"But, at the same time, Point Man was driving me nuts. I actually resented his 'reality checks.' I just wanted to play —until, one day, he told me a story about the old Silver Scot, Tommy Armour.

"It seems that Armour was playing in the Shawnee Open. He had just won the U.S. Open the week before and he was really confident. He felt he could make the ball do anything he wanted it to. Anyway, he came to the 17th at Shawnee and decided the best way to play the hole was to hit a long draw off the tee. The problem was, if he hooked the ball instead of just drawing it, he was out of bounds. And that's what happened—seven times. Armour was so sure he could hit the shot, and so stubborn about proving it, he just ignored the realities of the course. He took a 21 on the hole.

"After he told me that story, Point Man said to me, 'Armour thought he had the shot. But, you see, Pro, there were two realities: Armour's and the course. It's the same with you. Sometimes there's such a fine line between the two, you don't have to worry. But the other times, when your reality is way off the reality of the course, you can get in big trouble. That's why I measure everything for you. I want you to know the real distance—where the warning stakes for the hazards are, and what's on the other side— so you can at least compare what is real with what you *think* is real.'

"And then he said, 'Let me give you another measurement. You're not as good as you *think* you are. But you don't think you're nearly as good as you *could* be if you'd just learn to acknowledge the realities of the course!'

"I've thought about Point Man's reality checks a lot. And how I can screw up—fail to adapt—when what I think and feel and do don't correspond with what the course requires of me. No matter what I may *like* it to be, I realize now that I *need* to know the reality of the course. I *want* to know the distances and hazards and what all the warning stakes mean. How else can I rely on myself if my game is not based in reality?

"That's what I'm talking about when I say we can learn from the noise if we just pause to sort it out. When we're confused, the best thing we can do is make ourselves check on the reality of what we *think* is real."

•

Remember, *what we believe and how we think causes how we feel.* But if we're not careful, at some point our *feelings can override our thinking.* By sorting out our rational from our irrational thinking and feeling, we can learn to base our feelings in reality, thereby putting them in a less fanciful and potentially less harmful perspective. We can check out the course to determine if and when *our* reality lies out of bounds. We can learn to question whether our own beliefs and feelings are based on reality.

The first step in the reality-check process is to become alert to signs of our own irrational thinking. On the golf course, there are colored stakes that signify trouble. We can use the same sort of warnings in studying our own mental terrain. Here are descriptions of some of the important warning stakes to look for in determining where our inner reality departs from outer reality.

Stake #1: A ME Focus
Irrational thoughts and feelings are invariably *self-referencing.* The focus is on "ME" and what "I" want or need or deserve or don't deserve, and how other people or outside events have been unfair, hurtful, callous, or demanding. For example, when someone is ill I think about what an inconvenience that is for *me* instead of what is best for the person who is sick. Rational beliefs take the thoughts and feelings of others into consideration.

Stake #2: Past-Future Time Frame
Irrational thoughts and feelings ignore present realities. They reflect either obsessions with *past* events and how they continue to influence us beyond our control or apprehension about *future* events beyond our control. Rational beliefs put past, present, and future in a proper perspective.

Stake #3: Untestability
Irrational thoughts and feelings—usually born of fear or anger or both—cannot be put to a test and either verified

or proved. Rational beliefs address realities that can be tested and verified.

Stake #4: External Locus of Control
Irrational thoughts and feelings invariably reflect a sense of little personal control. Problems are always someone else's fault or their responsibility to solve. Rational beliefs focus attention on self-reliant solutions to problems.

Stake #5: Exaggerated Words and Actions
Irrational thoughts and feelings invariably invoke hyperbole and reflect varying degrees of hysteria. They encourage us to do inappropriate things. Rational beliefs are expressed by word selections and actions that are appropriate to the situation.

Stake #6: Disproportion
Irrational thoughts and feelings lead to conclusions that are disproportionate to the situation. The predictions of dire consequences lead, in turn, to disproportionate reactions. Rational beliefs lead to appropriate and adaptive responses to problem situations.

Reality tests are the primary means for us to begin reconciling our inner and outer realities. With such information available, we can begin to think about how to play a Masters Game.

•

Playing a Masters Game
LARRY HAS BEEN LISTENING intently. Now he says, "Okay, Pro, let's say that we're ready to acknowledge—confront the noise and start examining how well our inner realities correspond to outer reality. Now what? Exactly what kinds of permission do we need to give ourselves?"

The Pro chuckles. "You're gonna love me," he says,

"because that's another of those questions I can't answer for anybody. We all need to give ourselves permission to be healthy, as I've said, but you may need something different from what Frank needs. And Frank may not need the same thing Tim or Fred needs.

"I can tell you what I need. I try to give myself permission to play a Masters Game."

"A Masters Game," Tim says. "What's that?"

"It's an approach to the game," says the Pro, "that I've patterned after some great players who have all won the Masters. I've studied all the winners and I've concluded *I* want to *train* like Gary Player, *think* like Jackie Burke, Jr., *play* like Sam Snead, and *savor* it all like Jimmy Demaret. If I can give myself permission to just do those things, I think I'll get all I could ever hope for out of the game."

Permission to Train Like Gary Player: Balancing Mind and Body

"Gary Player is one of the finest gentlemen to ever pick up a golf club," the Pro says. "But he's also one of the most dedicated and courageous. He overcame physical limitations—a lot of people said he was just too small to play with the big boys—through sheer dedication, hard work, and self-discipline.

"Gary won the Masters *three* times—in 1961, 1974, and 1978—over a seventeen-year span! And his 1974 win came after major back surgery. He accomplished what he did in large measure because of the way he *trained* for the game. He believed in Gary Player. He went to work on his body and his mind to get them both in peak condition and keep them there. He demonstrated that stamina and mental toughness were every bit as critical as sheer physical power or talent. He won over one hundred forty tournaments around the world. That's pretty convincing to me!

"Gary is a realist. He recognizes his limitations and trains accordingly. He works on strengthening his assets.

He taught me that golf is a mind-body game. Everybody who has ever played it has had setbacks and limitations and doubts. The warnings and scoldings and dire predictions of bewareness can get downright obsessive. We keep feeding on that stuff until it dominates our games. The key to success is to create a balance by minimizing the influence of both the physical and mental negatives.

"I learned two things from watching Player. First, I think when I start a lot of negative obsessing that it's my body's way of telling me I'm overworking my mind and neglecting my body. I've found I can achieve better balance at such times by some kind of physical activity—pounding balls on the practice tee or taking a walk, anything to give my body equal time.

"Second, I learned to be careful about what kind of thoughts I feed myself. A lot of people gorge themselves on junk food because of the short-term pleasure it gives them. But a steady diet of that stuff can kill you. It's the same with feeding ourselves junk thinking. We can poison ourselves emotionally by feeding on screwy irrational beliefs.

"I see guys on the tour today get down on themselves and stay down. They need to stop and consider what they're feeding themselves. They could learn something from Gary Player."

•

There are actually three Masters Game lessons to be learned from Gary Player. First, we might all learn something about the value of ignoring the voices of Meddlers. Second, we might get a glimpse of what can happen when we make a total commitment to realizing as fully as possible our innate potential. And, third, we might come to appreciate anew the importance of self-discipline and, like Player, train our minds and bodies accordingly.

Permission to Think Like Jackie Burke, Jr.:
Defining the Problem in Terms of
"Doing Something" Instead of "Being Done To"

Situations and problems seldom define themselves. That job is left to us. We are the ones who decide what is good or bad. We define outcomes as desirable or undesirable, various courses of action as critical or inconsequential, and jobs as doable or impossible. We can, if we choose, define situations and problems in such a way that we can do something productive about them. And, in the process, we can define ourselves as adequate to the task. That's what Jackie Burke, Jr., always did.

•

"WHAT EXACTLY DO YOU MEAN by 'learning to think like Jackie Burke'?" Frank asks. "What's so hard about thinking?"

"Thinking is half the game," the Pro says. "There are a lot of talented, well-trained, and well-prepared people who still don't trust themselves to do what they need to do. The Masters Game lesson I learned from Jackie Burke, Jr., is that 'thinking you can' may be the difference between success and failure.

"Burke won his Masters in 1956. He was eight shots down after three rounds—trailing Ken Venturi—but he *thought* he could win. And he did! His eight-shot comeback in the final round is still a Masters record.

"One of the things I learned from Burke is to define the problem in a way that leaves me free to act—not only to take the action required, but to do so *when* it is required. How we define the game determines how hard or easy it is for us. And that affects our willingness to act, to do something when we need to. I learned from Burke that the key to productive action is learning to view the problem in a way that allows us to manage it. A lot of people fume and fuss about things they don't control in the first place. I learned on tour that if I'm going to be really productive, I have to focus my attention on those things I *can* do something about. It's another technique for minimizing self-interference.

"Jackie Burke told me once that when he had a long tee shot down a narrow fairway, in his mind's eye he just saw an aluminum chute. Even if he missed the shot, the ball would hit the aluminum sides and bounce back in the fairway. Or if he had a lake between him and the green, he would just turn the lake into grass in his mind and take it out of play—and hit his shot.

"Burke believes that taking productive action is its own reward. He said, 'The idea is to *play* baseball, *play* football, *play* golf. A pitcher can't worry about whether the batter hits the ball, he just throws his best pitch. Same with a putter. You just size up the putt, hit it the best you can, and if you make a long one, you jump up and down with the rest of the crowd.' Burke always defined a situation in terms of what he could do about it."

•

One of the problems the Tims and Freds among us have is that we define situations in terms of risks of failure and rejection. We never learned just to *play*! We define ourselves as inadequate to the tasks we encounter. Thus we are immobilized and, by definition, unproductive. The irony is that we must look to others for what we want, and because we are so dependent, their good opinions are critical to our self-esteem. But our inaction serves no one and therefore precipitates the loss of the very security and acceptance we hoped it would ensure. Only some sort of productivity can earn such comforts. And productivity requires action.

For those of us like Tim and Fred, action can be its own reward because it triggers possibilities. If, like Jackie Burke, we can learn to define our problems as solvable and define ourselves as capable of solving them, we free ourselves to act and become our own starter. We might even learn to play the way Sam Snead did.

•

Permission to Play Like Sam Snead: Separating Technique from the Objective

"THE LESSON I LEARNED from Sam Snead," says the Pro, "was to *stay focused*. Snead was always clear about his true objectives. Play the game and get the ball in the hole! He taught me the value of keeping things in proper perspective. For example, preoccupation with technique is one of the biggest problems I see. It's amazing how often people get so caught up in doing something a certain way that they forget what they're trying to accomplish in the first place.

"We get wedded to doing something a certain way because we're afraid of what will happen if we don't do it that way. We have to overcome our fears of looking bad or being uncertain. That's what really separated Sam Snead from his peers. He didn't think of himself as being on display. He was clear about the objective of the game, and he was willing to try whatever it took to get it done. Sometimes he got downright creative. Like with his putting.

"Snead's eyesight got to where he couldn't see the line of his putts from a conventional setup. So he just invented a different approach and a new putter. He straddled the line croquet style so he could see the hole better, and he held the putter with his left hand so he could work the stroke with his right. It was ingenious. But the main point is he wasn't distracted by how it looked or the fact that no one had ever putted that way. He wanted to play as best he could, and he simply created a way to do that.

"Not long afterward, the USGA ruled Snead *couldn't* straddle the line of a putt. He didn't fight it. He just came up with a different putter and his 'sidesaddle' approach. Snead stayed focused on his objective and then figured out a way to pursue it."

"I know we're talking about the game of golf," Larry

says, "but in my office there's one guy who can be counted on to tell everybody why something can't be done. Then if he's forced to move, he takes three times longer than necessary getting all his ducks in a row, maneuvering people around, just generally orchestrating events until he's comfortable. He acts like he's more concerned with how he does the job than he is with getting it done. He drives everybody nuts with his doom and gloom."

The Pro smiles. "I agree, Larry. There's an old Chinese proverb that says, 'Those who always say something can't be done might at least have the good manners not to interfere with someone who is busy doing it.'"

•

The tendency to divert our attention from *what* we want to accomplish to *how* we want to do it can become a serious barrier to both personal and collective productivity. Not only can debates about how, who, when, what—all the ingredients of "proper" technique—prove to be time-consuming distractions, more often than not they are reflections of our own "compensation hitches," and we are wasting energy that might be invested in getting the job done. If Sam Snead had approached his putting woes the same way some of us approach our daily tasks, he would have had to stop playing in his forties! If we lay aside our preoccupations with technique, we free ourselves to start getting the job done. We might even free ourselves to enjoy the game.

•

Permission to Savor the Game Like Jimmy Demaret: Perspective and Applying the Four-to-One Rule

"PRO," SAYS LARRY, "you said you wanted to savor the game like Jimmy Demaret. What do you mean?"

"That," the Pro says, "may be the most important Masters Game lesson of all. Demaret won the Masters three times—in 1940, 1947, and 1950. He was a natural, one of those consummate shot makers who seemed to play with no effort or fuss. He was also flamboyant and loved to entertain the gallery with wisecracks and even songs when he was playing with Bing Crosby. He was the first to wear color-coordinated outfits—shirts and shoes and stuff. He *loved* what he was doing.

"Demaret worked at being nonchalant, but he was serious about the game. He and Jackie Burke got together when they retired and built Champions Golf Club in Houston, Texas. That was Demaret's favorite spot. Champions has one of the most famous locker rooms in all of golfdom. Demaret loved to stand around the bar there at night and regale people with his stories. When he died, they put a brass plate at the place at the bar where he always stood. It reads:

Jimmy Demaret
1910–1983
ENJOY!

"That sums up the Masters Game lesson I learned from Jimmy Demaret. A permission to *enjoy* the game may be the greatest freedom any of us can ever give ourselves."

"You bet!" Tim says. "Nobody likes to laugh and cut up on the course more than I do. I'm out here strictly to enjoy."

Frank disagrees. "Having shared a cart with you for three days, Tim," he says, "I can sure vouch for the laughing and joking. But I don't think you're really enjoying things that much. The laughing and cutting up is just your way of avoiding the real game. You're afraid to take it seriously because if you did, you'd have to commit yourself to a lot of hard work and frustration and pain. I think all the joking is just a 'compensation hitch' you've developed to make everybody believe you're having fun. Actually you're keeping everything at a distance."

"Well, I'll tell you one thing," Tim says petulantly. "I enjoy things a hell of a lot more than you do, with all of your 'striving for perfection.' Is that enjoyment? Did you ever stop to think that you guys just might be *too* involved?"

"I couldn't agree more," Frank says. "I'm as bad as Fred is when it comes to being hard on myself. And if I don't learn to loosen up and enjoy things more, I'm going to end up like Fred—off on a practice tee somewhere just hitting balls by myself, not really playing and not enjoying it very much, either."

"Let me ask you a question, Frank," the Pro says. "After you've played a round, you have trouble recalling the good shots, right? All you can remember are the handful of bad shots that cost you."

"Yeah," Frank mumbles. "And it's hard to enjoy anything if all you can think about is the bad stuff."

"A lot of people do that," says the Pro, "in a lot of places other than the golf course. People put themselves under a lot of stress when they come here. They really want this to be a worthwhile and successful experience. But the more they want and expect, the more they set themselves up for frustration and disappointment. When I see that happening, usually that's when I stop everything and introduce the four-to-one rule. I tell them we're going to do a little work on *perspective*.

"I ask them to take out their daily logs and on one page draw a line down the center. Then I ask them to list in one column all the things they're really upset about and have to fix before they can enjoy the game. Some list putting and chipping; others put down driving and distance and accuracy—all the usual stuff.

"Then I ask them to list in the other column all the things they are pleased with and enjoy about their game. Some list putting and chipping and driving and distance and accuracy, the same stuff that's driving somebody else nuts. Then I let them think a while, and they start adding things like 'outdoor exercise' and 'good health' and 'opportunity.'

"Then I tell them to add up their columns, and I bet them dinner that their 'enjoy' column has at least four times the entries in their 'upset' column. Then, since I'm usually working with executives like you guys, I say a few words about one of the real anomalies of corporate life— the eighty–twenty rule. How eighty percent of your business comes from twenty percent of your customers. How eighty percent of your production comes from twenty percent of your workers. How we give eighty percent of our attention to the twenty percent of the people we know who cause us problems. Or how some parents overlook four A's on their kid's report card and focus on one B! Then I say something like 'There seems to be a four-to-one rule at work. And it's the same with enjoyment. More than anything else, enjoying the game is a matter of proper perspective.

" 'I want to make a deal with you,' I say. 'In the interest of proper perspective and a fuller enjoyment of the game, I want to encourage you to think about the things that bug you, but *only* if you're willing to do it in relation to the things you enjoy. That's the four-to-one rule.'

"If you want to worry about setbacks or disappointments or frustrations for ten minutes or an hour or all night, do it. But *please* give at least four times the thought —forty minutes or four hours or four nights—to what is right and gratifying for you. I guarantee you a change in focus will make for greater enjoyment.' "

"And does the four-to-one rule work?" asks Larry.

The Pro shrugs. "It sows the seeds for a more proper perspective. It invites people to define the game in terms of its potential for enjoyment rather than as a source of frustration and disappointment. But my best experience was with a guy who didn't even do the exercise. I thought he was doing it. He was sure writing stuff down. But when we broke for lunch, he comes up to me and hands me a page from his log book.

"I looked at it, and he hadn't done the exercise at all.

But he sure got the point." The Pro takes a paper out of his wallet and begins to read aloud. " 'One thing I'm clear about,' he wrote, 'the game is a *gift*. It comes wrapped in beautiful blue skies, sunshine, and fresh air. It is delivered in marvelous green places with lakes and streams, where the smell of fresh-cut grass is everywhere. When you look into it, you find it alive with opportunities and possibilities just waiting to be explored. It has taken me to places and put me with people I would otherwise never have known. It has teased me and tested me so that I might taste pure exhilaration from time to time. And like the truest of gifts, it has required nothing of me other than a capacity to savor and enjoy.'

"And at the end, he added, 'P.S. Today, I three-putted four greens, knocked one in the lake on number seven, and barked my shin getting in the cart. I even lost six bucks to Doc Fuller. Now did this upset me? Damn right it did! But today's setbacks just make me look forward to tomorrow and a chance to do it all better. I'm just grateful for the privilege of playing at all.'

"That guy," the Pro says, "had the proper perspective."

The four sit quietly for a moment, then Tim breaks the silence. "If I could just give myself that kind of freedom," he says, "I might get to where I feel really good about myself."

"Or maybe," says the Pro, "if you felt really good about yourself, you could give yourself that kind of freedom."

LEARNING TO PLAY FROM A FIRM FOUNDATION

A Setup for Dynamic Balance

The game is played from the ground up.
Ben Hogan

In 1988 hundreds of thousands of lovers of the game celebrated the hundredth anniversary of golf in America. The publishers of *Golf* magazine hosted a centennial dinner honoring one hundred golfing greats who helped shape the game over the years.

In a particularly touching and symbolic moment, Sam Snead was called to the podium for some much deserved recognition. Ben Hogan was seated just to his right. Snead looked at Hogan and began to tell his audience a story. "When I drove up tonight," he said, "this fine-looking young man came bounding out to my car, and before I could even come to a complete stop, he says, 'Mr. Hogan, if you'll wait right here, I'll park your car for you and bring you your keys.'

"Well, that sounded like a good deal to me, so I said, 'Sure,' got out of my car, and stepped up under the verandah. In a minute or so, the young man was back and he says, 'Mr. Hogan, I can't tell you what an honor it is to meet you in person. I've heard my dad talk about you ever since I was a little kid. Wait till I tell him *I* met Ben Hogan!'

"Now, I was a little bumfuzzled. I was wearing my

171

straw hat, as usual—with the fancy colored band and all—
but I figured, even in a tux, I didn't look as good as Hogan.
So I said, 'Son, I'm sorry to disappoint you, but I'm not
Ben Hogan.'

He looks at me as though he doesn't want to believe
me. Then, sort of in desperation, he says, 'But you *are*
somebody, aren't you?'

"I just smiled at him and said, 'Yes sir, I *am* somebody.' "

THE VALUE OF FEELING LIKE SOMEBODY

One of the things that distinguished Sam Snead most
throughout his career was that he knew he was somebody.
He not only knew who he was, he liked the person he
knew. He played from such solid footing—emotionally
and physically—that although in motion, he was always
in balance.

There is an interesting parallel between the emotional
and physical aspects of the game. Both are best played from
a firm foundation. That's what the Pro had in mind when
he suggested to Tim that if he felt better about himself, he
might find it easier to give himself the freedom needed to
play well.

•

TIM PONDERS THE PRO'S comment. "Pro," he says, "what
makes you think I don't feel good about myself?"

"I've formed an impression that you hold yourself
back, Tim," the Pro says, "sort of keep yourself under
wraps, because you're unsure of yourself. I don't think you
really give yourself enough credit.

"I think we all do that. Most of us sell ourselves short
one way or another, then we alter our games somehow to
either compensate or try to hide what we think is wrong.
I'm convinced that how each of us feels about who we are
directly affects what we're willing to do. Consequently, it

also affects how we play the game. Working from a shaky sense of self is like trying to swing a golf club from a faulty setup position. You can still play, but not very well. And you sure can't have much fun.

"Let me give you an analogy. Almost everybody agrees the game is really played from the ground up, even though the arms swing the club. Footwork and placement, leg action, ball position, are critical to how well everything else can be accomplished. Establishing a proper foundation at setup is the most critical step in the golf swing. Developing a healthy sense of self does the same thing for us in *all* our games. Having an appreciation of our own potential and confidence in our personal competence is like having a good setup.

"Feeling good about ourselves, Tim, is the foundation that gives us the confidence to do what we know we need to do, no matter what the test. Bad feelings, self-doubt, or fear of inadequacy distort our perceptions and interfere with our performance just as much as a faulty setup restricts our golf swing."

"You can *learn* a proper setup," says Tim, "but there's not much you can do about your self-esteem." His voice trails off.

The Pro shakes his head. "That's my whole point, Tim. It's still a matter of taking charge of the game in your head. Once you understand the basics of either one—setup or self-esteem—you can work until you build a good one. Nobody can give you self-esteem any more than they can cause your setup. It's up to you."

•

SELF-ESTEEM: THE SETUP FOR ALL OUR GAMES

The Pro may be right. Whether we call it self-esteem or self-acceptance or some other name, it is clear that how we feel about ourselves—how we judge and evaluate ourselves, whether or not we have a sense of personal worth, of style and grace and competence—lays the foundation from which we operate. It is the confidence we have in our own adequacy that supplies the base for our transactions with the world around us.

Strong and steady self-esteem, like a good setup, prepares us for effective performance and enjoyment of the game. Weak and shaky self-esteem, like a poor setup, renders us less able to perform as well or enjoy as much as we might. For example, we know from various studies of self-esteem that

> People with low self-esteem are much more dependent on things outside themselves for direction and reward than are people with high self-esteem. Those with low self-esteem are easily influenced by what others think or do. Those with high self-esteem tend to be more self-reliant and behave according to their own dictates. They are less dependent on positive group support for good performance, have greater tolerance for stress and a willingness to attribute both successes and failures to their own efforts rather than to events outside themselves.

> People with low self-esteem have less positive expectations about their own performance and life in general than do people of high self-esteem. Those with high self-esteem expect 1) that their career choices will bring the satisfaction they desire, and 2) that they will have or be able to develop the skills required for career success. Those with high-esteem are more productive when faced with a challenge.

> People with low self-esteem are more likely to be shy and cautious in dealing with problems. When faced with a difficult task, people with high esteem prepare more for the challenge while

low-esteem individuals do just the opposite, making greater preparation for the easier tasks confronting them. In short, people with personal confidence seem much more willing to take the risks and exert the effort necessary for creative problem solving than do individuals of low self-esteem.

On the basis of such research findings, it seems clear that our self-esteem—our subjective evaluations and judgments of personal adequacy and worth—is a prime influence on how we approach and play the game.

I'm Just a Duffer! Who Would Want to Play with Me?

Low self-esteem is the score we get when the Meddler in us is winning the Private Game. We may feel that we are bad or incomplete or phony or inadequate. In any case, low esteem is a conclusion based in shame. By reminding us of our shame, making us doubt ourselves and devalue our own potential, the Meddler can maintain control and keep us dependent. By constantly reminding us of our most basic fears, an overactive Meddler can even lead us to abandon ourselves.

Having given up on ourselves, we behave in ways that encourage others to give up on us as well. We become suspicious and vigilant. We become cautious and retreat into ourselves. Because we feel so alone, we become increasingly self-centered. But we can still choose to take charge of the game in our heads, rise above the constraints, and avoid the pitfalls of low self-esteem.

As the Pro said, we can do as much about our own self-esteem as we can about our own setup. It is never too late to learn a more proper approach. We are only victims of our past experiences as long as we refuse to take responsibility for ourselves in the present. From this point onward, each of us can begin preparing ourselves for better and more rewarding play in the future.

•

"PRO," TIM COMMENTS. "I don't see how I've got the same kind of control over how I feel about myself as I do over my setup."

"They're both just products of our *learning,*" says the Pro. "If we want to fix either one, all we've got to do is lay the bad one aside and learn a new one.

"Over my years of teaching," says the Pro, "I've become sensitive to what a critical role self-esteem plays in how people approach the game and how easily they learn and enjoy the experience. I'm convinced it's the same with everybody—not the level of self-esteem, but the necessary ingredients.

"The practice tee here seems to take everybody back to zero. It doesn't seem to matter how well someone has done elsewhere, on the practice tee most people sort of regress to an earlier, less certain, and more fragile time in their lives. And you can just see their self-esteem emerging piece by piece until it's right there with you on the practice tee. And if you want a good outcome, you can no more ignore the key elements of self-esteem than you can the elements of a good setup."

"And what," Frank says, "are the elements?"

"That's where I'm headed," the Pro says. "Ben Hogan once said that a good setup was like a tripod with the two feet and the club head as the three points of contact with the ground. I think the same is true of self-esteem. It's like a tripod, too, except it's a system of psychological supports. In place of two legs and a golf club, you've got three different needs to be addressed and satisfied if you're to have a well-developed, sturdy self-esteem.

"I know it's a little imprecise," he continues, "but try to picture a three-legged support. Think of your judgment of yourself, of your capabilities and worth, how much you like yourself—in other words, your basic self-esteem—as resting on the top of the tripod. So your view of yourself rests on three legs, okay? Now, each leg is a need you have that, if satisfied and strengthened, supports your self-esteem. The more the sense of satisfaction, the greater the support. The more all three seem satisfied, the sturdier the whole system.''

Larry picks up the simile. ''And if only one or two legs get satisfied, you have a shaky unstable system, right?''

''Exactly. And that's what I see all the time, guys with shaky self-esteem because they've only worked on one or two supports. Not only are they unaware of the support they really need to feel good about themselves, their self-esteem is so shaky they'd be too afraid to do the work required if they did know.''

''So what can we do if we've got lousy self-esteem?'' says Tim. ''Are we just stuck with a shaky setup for the rest of our lives?''

''That's one option,'' the Pro says. ''Or you can choose to take charge of the game in your head and commit yourself to working on the supports, commit yourself to satisfying the needs a sturdy self-esteem requires.''

Frank and Larry speak at the same time. ''And what are the supports? What kinds of needs are we talking about?''

The Pro answers slowly and precisely. ''It's been my experience that a really healthy self-esteem rests on an equal sense of *confirmation, mastery,* and *growth.* And the more these three needs are satisfied, the sturdier the whole system will be.''

•

A Need for Confirmation

Self-esteem—good or bad, strong or weak—is a by-product of our efforts to participate, to become part of the world around us. To feel good about ourselves, one of the earliest needs each of us seeks to satisfy is that of *confirmation.* From the moment we are born, we all need some form of acknowledgment that we not only exist, but have value. The critical issue for each of us in seeking a confirming support for our self-esteem is where to look. Do we seek confirmation from other people or do we look to ourselves?

Our initial confirmation depended on people external to ourselves, the authority figures in our young lives—our parents, grandparents, aunts, uncles, siblings, and teachers. For a time, our view of ourselves was a reflection of others' opinions of us.

Not all authority figures do a good job of confirming the young. Some are demanding and overcritical. Others go overboard in their praise and encouragement and reassurance. Still others resent the task and disavow both its importance and the child. If we never received the confirmation we sought as children, our self-esteem is low and we remain dependent today—worried about what other people think of us. Our personal sense of worth is contingent upon the good opinion of others.

•

THE PRO CONTINUES. "One of the greatest sources of interference I see, especially with my less skilled players, is their concern with what I'm going to think of their swings. And they all are ashamed of how embarrassed they are. You can just feel the self-consciousness in the air.

"They could say, 'I don't know a thing about this game, but I'm here to learn and I can't wait to get started!' Instead, they're looking over their shoulders to see if anybody is watching or doing better. Half the time they're so distracted they can't even hear the instruction, much less try to execute it.

"I try to reassure them that I believe they have everything they need to learn the game and to play it well enough to enjoy it. I share some of my own travails with them so they can see that everybody who plays the game has had to struggle—and still is. And I promise them they will reach a point where it is more than worth all the effort involved.

"But I don't back off. That would be a disservice to them. And I'm sparse with my praise. That can be a disservice, too. It gets in the way of the realities of the situation. It sends a false message that only reinforces the struggle. It sure doesn't help them swing the club any better, and *that's* what they've come to learn. But the main problem I have helping someone build self-esteem is that even valid praise usually has to come from somebody else."

"But people need guidance or something," says Larry. "How do you provide that without reinforcement?"

The Pro nods. "You just said it. I try to reinforce *them*, not evaluate their games. Take the golf swing itself. You know how result-oriented and ball-bound some people can get. But sometimes they can make a good swing without the ball necessarily doing what they want it to do.

"When they make a good pass at the ball, regardless of where the ball goes, I'll ask them, 'How did that feel?' When they tell me, I say something like 'That's how a good swing feels. Work on getting that feel every time.' Now, maybe I've given some guidance. But I've also tried to focus them inward. Now they can critique themselves instead of depending on me or somebody else. They learn to be self-confirming."

"Pro," Tim says, "when you say you'd like people to be more self-confirming, are you talking about guys like Frank here? Somebody who's able to evaluate and like himself independently of what other people might think?"

"Frank's not independent," Larry comments.

Frank stiffens. "What do you mean I'm not independent? Self-reliance is my major strength. I don't have to *depend* on somebody else for confirmation!"

"I don't mean you're not confident, Frank," Larry replies. "It's just that you're still pretty sensitive to what other people think of you. You want to be the 'best.' In whose eyes? You admittedly were trying to impress the Pro here with that two-iron over the lake. You even got bent out of shape when you thought I was making fun of your game.

"All that sounds to me like you still rely pretty much on confirmation from other people. You may just want them to confirm your own opinions. But sometimes it sounds as if you're trying to *extort* confirmation. And that ain't independence."

The Pro turns to Frank and says, "We all need confirmation from others, Frank. It's no disgrace to want approval or encouragement or recognition. Even Jack Nicklaus got misty-eyed when his peers voted him the best player of the century.

"But it's like a balancing act. Independence is not the issue so much as *un*dependence. Being extremely dependent on others to help us define ourselves can keep us in constant pain and immobilize us completely. But being totally independent of others' opinions, to the point that we're impervious to either influence or the pain, is just as bad. It not only isolates us, it cuts us off from reality.

"If we really want to secure a sturdier and more self-determined support for ourselves, we have to develop a sense of *mastery*.

"Maybe, Tim, what makes Frank appear more confident is that he's begun work on the second leg. He wants to be good at the game!"

•

A Need for Mastery

Confirmation alone does not suffice as a total support for one's self-esteem. No matter how much we are loved and appreciated, no matter how strong our sense of confirmation, sooner or later our basic competence will be put to the test by life's events. Nothing is so confirming at the purely personal level than meeting such tests successfully. Indeed, many of us learn to seek out opportunities for demonstrating our mastery so we may reward ourselves.

•

"I BELIEVE SELF-ESTEEM evolves on the practice tee," says the Pro. "People start off wanting reassurance and confirmation. But as soon as that eight-iron sends the ball out there a hundred forty yards with a four-foot draw, they get a different look in their eyes. The self-consciousness sort of melts and they get this riveted hungry expression. It's like they are saying, 'Wow! *I* did that. I want *more*!' Now people start wondering about how to master the game so they can feel good about themselves."

•

The Pro is describing the emergence of what some mental health experts consider the most powerful of human motives. It is competence motivation, the desire to master a task—any task—so we can demonstrate our mastery for both ourselves and others. Mastery is its own reward.

•

"WELL, PRAISE BE, PRO!" says Frank. "You've finally spoken my language. All my life I've been trying to master whatever I've undertaken."

The Pro grins. "We still have to be clear about *why* we want to master something. But the important thing is what *you* think each time you perform well, don't you agree?"

"I sure do," Larry pipes up. "Some of my best feelings about me, some of my most memorable moments, have come when I've finally solved a problem or gotten a move perfected that I've really struggled with. But it's a real private kind of satisfaction. It stays with me and sort of carries over to the next task. Do you know what I mean?"

"Yeah," says Frank, "I do. Sometimes after a really good shot, I can hardly wait to get to the ball and do it again."

Tim shakes his head. "I wish I could say that," he

admits. "The best I ever felt was the first time I put on a pair of golf shoes and heard the sound the spikes make when you walk. I still love it. I feel like Greg Norman or somebody. But I've never placed much value on showing off or trying to be the best at anything. It probably sounds funny to you guys, but I've just always tried to be a good person. That's been enough for me. Is that weird?"

The Pro answers. "I think we all want to be good people, Tim. But we're talking about what it takes for us to feel like we are good people. Probably where we differ most is in what gives each of us value, how we define the good person each of us wants to be. Some people value only confirmation, but when they discover it's not enough, they're lost. A lot of times, what we value depends on how we've gotten where we are.

"I believe the need to be good at something is a natural follow-up to feeling confirmed. But some people get it out of sequence, especially if confirmation is denied them or used only as a reward for performance. On the other hand, not everybody gets an opportunity to master something. Some have the opportunity but no encouragement. Others are denied the opportunity altogether; they're simply not allowed to develop their competence. As important as it is to the natural growth of self-esteem, there's an awful lot of noise around the issue of mastery and competence. Most executives are pretty ambivalent about it."

•

The Pro has touched on a pivotal issue in the development of self-esteem: the degree to which competence and mastery are valued as either sources or indicators of personal worth. In childhood, a desire for mastery and competence is associated with independence and the pursuit of autonomy. A number of studies have shown that children who are encouraged to become self-reliant at an early age develop higher levels of achievement motivation later on. This is true even of those who are pressed too soon.

Unfortunately, the converse is also true. When self-reliance is discouraged—perhaps prevented altogether—and dependence is reinforced and prolonged, achievement motivation and its accompanying need for competence and mastery are blocked. Those to whom opportunities and encouragement for developing mastery have been denied appear to lack both curiosity and ambition.

The mismanagement of needs for competence and mastery is one of the major ways in which the authority figures in our lives have let some of us down and failed to prepare us for realizing our true potentials. But that doesn't mean such fundamental desires can't be resurrected and satisfied. Those of us who decide to take charge and get good at something—whether early or late in our development—will discover new sources of energy and come to know private, more profound kinds of personal satisfaction. Rather than fearing or resenting those who might attempt to teach and guide us, for example, we will form a positive identification with people who *know* things and know how to *do* things. We will no longer be threatened by, or resentful of, the competence of others.

We will find both comfort and self-respect in our abilities to master various life events. Most of all, we will discover that the exercise of competence is its own reward.

•

"YOU SEE," SAYS THE PRO, "the desire to master the game is just as important as wanting to play it in the first place. It's a naturally evolving process. When people develop some confidence in their iron shots, for example, it's only a matter of time before they're going to start working on their tee shots and their short games.

"As I've already said, a sense of growth is the third element. Knowing we can be good at something provides the momentum. It's like expecting to be adequate gives us the confidence and curiosity to reach out, to take the risk to explore and discover. Growth, more than anything, is a matter of attitude. But a sense of growth is sure good for self-esteem.''

A Need for Growth

Larry speaks. ''A lot of things come to mind when you say 'sense of growth,' Pro. How do you get it?''

''It's hard for me to explain,'' the Pro says. ''I know it when I see it—I can even spot the people at the academy who are going to grow the most—but it's hard to describe. It's sort of like an outlook, an expectancy, a need that gets translated into action.

''The kind of growth that strengthens self-esteem requires a sort of ongoing curiosity, a genuine desire to explore and discover that doesn't have anything to do with anybody else. Growth is an individual and personal kind of process, but how people feel about it—whether they value it or fear it—depends a lot on the company they keep.

''I think it's a permission kind of thing. A lot of us have looked to other people to tell us whether or not it's okay to branch out. Some of us are told 'No.' But if we're going to take charge of our game, we have to tell ourselves it's not only okay, but the healthy thing to do.''

•

As with competence motivation and the need for mastery, proper management of exploratory and discovery needs is a crucial juncture in the development of a strong and healthy sense of self. Mismanagement can stunt our growth and weaken our self-esteem. When the authority figures in our lives discourage, forbid, or punish the natural curiosity that is necessary for us to connect effectively with the world around us, they deprive us of a major support for self-esteem. Most of us carry the lingering effects of our earliest experiences. Yesterday's lessons dictate today's play.

Growth, initially at least, requires permission. Once we

have been encouraged or denied permission to act on our curiosity, we will approach most new opportunities as we learned to handle them in the past. Ultimately the permission to grow must come from ourselves.

•

TIM IS CLEARLY INTRIGUED by the Pro's observations. "This is all new stuff for me," he says, "and I'll have to admit it really does open up some doors. But what I'm not clear about, Pro, is what I do with it. How is knowing all this going to help me feel better about *me*?"

"It's the same old executive dilemma," the Pro says. "Knowing what to do and then being willing to do what you know needs to be done. The point is we *can* do something! In golf, if we want to fix a faulty setup, we can learn the fundamentals of a good setup and go to work on ourselves. We can build a habit of approaching the ball in a certain way. We can learn to check our target to get proper alignment for our feet and shoulders. Once we know the ingredients, we can consciously work on them until they're part of our routine. The payoff is a dynamic balance that improves our chances for long straight shots.

"It's the same with how we feel about ourselves. A lot of people spend a lot of valuable time agonizing over 'Who am I?' But the real question is 'Who do I want to be?' If we can answer that, we can learn the elements of solid self-esteem and go to work on ourselves. We can commit ourselves to working toward equal measures of confirmation, mastery, and growth until they become part of our routine.

"Take confirmation. If that's what you crave, what do you do? It's one of those little quirks of the game that if what you really want is confirmation, the best thing you can do is forget about confirmation and focus your energies on achieving *mastery*. Getting really good at something—anything—is one of the most confirming experiences possible.

"On the other hand, if mastery is your great consuming need, chances are you'll try so hard you'll get tunnel vision and end up getting in your own way. So if you really want a sense of being good at something, commit yourself to *growth*. Explore the novel and untried."

After a moment Frank queries, "And what if personal growth is the goal?"

"Growth," says the Pro, "is the journey toward wholeness of mind and body and emotion. All you can do is open yourself to the possibilities. And the possibilities for personal growth are best found in the quest for confirmation and mastery. But not necessarily *personal* confirmation or *personal* mastery. I know I feel best about myself when I've had a hand in someone else getting more out of the game. I think each of us grows most when we give something back to the game."

"Like Chi Chi Rodriguez," says Tim.

"Or Jimmy Demaret," Larry adds.

The Pro nods. "But the truth is most of us forget to give much back to the game. Once we get what we want, we just move on to the next desire. If we want to grow, we have to realize that it is through our contacts and relations with other people that we really come to know ourselves. That's the critical step in becoming who we want to be."

The sky darkens outside, the last rays of the afternoon sun prematurely muted by heavy clouds. The four men sit quietly, each caught up in his own thoughts.

"Another thing occurs to me," Larry says. "Guys like us not only share the course with other people, we're like the Pro here. We affect how other people get to play. As executives, each of us is in a prime position to influence a lot of other people. Maybe, with a little work, we can help get that game solid from the start!"

The Pro smiles. "Guys," he says, "that's what the *real* executive game is all about."

THE REAL EXECUTIVE GAME

A Loving Chore

*It is not the capacity to make great shots
that makes champions, but the essential
quality of making very few bad shots.*
Tommy Armour

Being an executive, as Larry suggested, is a lot like being a teaching pro. Both are professionals, and in a manner of speaking, both are teachers. And although both are concerned with performance, both share the course with other players and must contend with issues of morale. As the Pro has observed, how people feel about themselves and their performance intertwines with both performance and commitment to the game itself. How they think and feel about the executive chore can also affect how well other people are able to play and how rewarding they find the game. How they approach their responsibilities has widespread and profound implications for all of us who are trying to play the game.

What is the executive job? Ask several different executives and you will get several different opinions. "Production!" "Seeing that people perform at their maximum capacity." "Seeing that things run smoothly." "High morale." "Seeing that people have the resources and opportunity to do their best."

We can all agree on one thing: there seems little clarity where the executive game is concerned. It's almost as if different executives define their jobs and select their styles reactively, according to their own priorities and preferred playing strategies rather than as a studied response to the realities of the executive game as a whole.

In Search of an Integrating Premise

The executive chore may be a classic example of discord between Private Games and Public Games. Perhaps, faced constantly with tests of our personal competence, too many of us have been so busy playing our Private Game that we have mismanaged the Public Game to the detriment of ourselves and others. To avoid that, maybe we can find a common thread that will tie our games together.

•

"Pro," Frank says, "are you agreeing with Larry? That, as executives, we should concern ourselves with the self-esteem of the people around us? You said that's the *real* executive game. But I've always believed taking care of my own stuff was my main job."

"Taking care of other people is the main executive job," Tim interjects. "I don't believe looking out for number one is the answer. A lot of self-sacrifice is involved in being a good executive."

Larry shrugs. "I don't think being an executive has any more to do with taking *care* of people than being a teaching pro does."

"But, Larry," Tim says, "you've got to take care of people! Don't you *care* about the people you work with?"

"Yes," Larry says quietly. "But I think there's a big difference between caring *about* and caring *for*. It's the old philosophical dilemma: Is it best to give a child a fish and feed him for a day or *teach* the child to fish and feed him for a lifetime?"

The Pro chuckles. "You guys are all talking about the same game all right, but you're talking about *parts* of the game instead of the whole game. You remember when we talked about trying to feel the parts of our own personal games so that at some point we could work on pulling everything together? It's the same with the executive game. Each of you must be willing to entertain the possibility that your own priorities and preferred strategies are not all that is important.

"If you are willing to consider other priorities and strategies, then you just need a concept or premise or goal of some sort to help it all make sense. That's what I call an integrating premise."

•

Human beings tend to treat things—including the development of their own games—in a piecemeal, one-at-a-time fashion. In the process they lose sight of the fact that each of us is designed to operate as a *whole*. Our separate tendencies are intended to become joined in larger patterns that, over time, come to define both who we are and what kinds of games we play.

If those of us who manage or teach or parent other people want to play well and enjoy the game to its fullest, we may not be able to afford the luxury of preserving and pursuing our most cherished tendencies as isolated satisfactions, unrelated to the whole. Sometimes there is something else that exists on another less apparent plane of thought, which, once identified, can both give new meaning to our pursuits and arrange erstwhile opposites in a complementary pattern. If we permit ourselves, we can find an integrating premise to make us whole in our executive games.

•

"Pro," Tim says, "I've always been taught that there's a right way and a wrong way to do almost everything. But it sounds like you're getting into some gray areas. What the devil *is* an integrating premise?"

"Well," the Pro says, "let me give you a golf example.

In my business, *lack* of integration is the biggest problem. I see people all the time who are defeating themselves because they've grooved a piecemeal approach to the game.

"Take the basic swing as a case in point. We've already talked about how, on the backswing, you are really only trying to position yourself to deliver the club back to the ball. But a lot of people give it ninety percent of their attention and have nearly *all* their problems on the backswing.

"Tommy Armour, one time, said that nobody ever hit the ball with his backswing, so why give it so much attention? But a lot of people do and a lot of teachers spend a lot of time just talking about how to take the club back.

"Some instructors say just swing your arms. Some say turn your shoulders. We hear about one-piece take-aways and forward presses. And then the same teachers have to warn us against sliding our hips instead of turning them or remind us not to leave our weight on the left side so that we don't get a reverse pivot. It just goes on and on.

"These are piecemeal approaches, and they sometimes cause as many problems as they seek to solve. The solution is to integrate the whole swing. And, believe it or not, I think you can achieve that with your *armpits*."

Tim chortles. "Armpits! Now I'm going to have to worry about golf and body odor at the same time!"

"I'm being a little facetious when I say 'armpits,' " the Pro continues. "But sometimes something that seems totally unrelated to the problem—maybe something off the wall—holds the key to solving it. If we permit ourselves to look outside the boundaries we've imposed on ourselves, lots of times we can find a new aspect of the problem that, properly tended, will solve it for good. That's what focusing on your armpits can do."

Tim is interested. "I can't seem to swing the club back on the proper plane and get a proper body turn away from the target, all at the same time," he says. "How can 'armpits' fix that?"

"A lot of people have the same problem," the Pro says. "They try to compensate. Some of them focus almost exclusively on swinging their arms freely. Others focus on turning their shoulders. They swing *around* themselves, and get big looping pull hooks for their troubles.

"They all lose what teaching pro Jimmy Ballard calls *connection*. Without connection, all the important parts move separately instead of in any proper sequence. And you end up with a swing that, if it works at all, can't be counted on to repeat."

"And focusing on your armpits," says Tim, "helps connect things, right?"

"Right," the Pro says, "and Ben Hogan made pretty much the same point. He used to practice with a handkerchief under his arm and try to keep it there until after he had hit the ball. Keeping the armpits connected integrates the swing. For example, if you focus on keeping your upper arms snug to your chest area when you start your backswing, you *have* to turn your hips and shoulders to take the club back. Just swinging your arms alone breaks the connection."

"What about power?" Frank says. "I can see how staying connected can make you get a good body turn, but don't you lose club-head speed coming back to the ball?"

"Frank, you'll get *more* power. If you can maintain connection, you apply the force of your whole body where you need it—to the ball. *Try* it."

"But what about tempo, Pro?" Larry asks. "People have told me I get impatient and swing too fast."

"Tempo is a very personal thing," says the Pro. "But if you start off with an integrated swing and *keep* it connected through a complete backswing, you *can't* swing too fast.

"And here's the most interesting thing about all this. You remember how this is a game of distance and accuracy? How it seems you have to sacrifice one to get the other? Well, staying connected produces *both* more distance and greater accuracy! That's what true integration can do for us in all our games."

Larry laughs and shakes his head. "This integration stuff is just simple enough that you wonder why so few players ever work on it."

"Ah," says the Pro. "Now there's the real puzzle."

•

An integrating premise can help in getting out of the executive trap. The executive trap, as we have seen, is primarily one of ambivalence. We often are stymied by our feelings about opposing issues like authority and obedience, dominance and submission, independence and dependence. Many of us have opted for fragmented approaches. But there are integrating premises available to us that, much like the Pro's "snug armpits for maintaining connection," can begin to pull the executive game together for us.

Take the issues of dependence and independence, for example. Our executive games often reveal our feelings about the relative merits of being dependent or being self-reliant. We perceive an either/or world, choose up sides, and invest our energies in promoting one posture or the other.

As it turns out, dependence and independence are not even the real issues. Each is but a way station on the developmental road to a fuller realization of our individual and collective potentials. Mental health experts would encourage us to go further and seek *interdependence*, a condition where we are all so self-reliant that each of us is strong enough to depend on one another when we need to. Such mutual trust and reliance is, of course, the essence of *partnership*. And partnership, the ultimate stage in human development, can become an integrating premise for our efforts to pull our executive games together.

•

SELF-ESTEEM: THE GREAT INTEGRATOR

LARRY IS CLEARLY INTRIGUED by the Pro's analogy. "Pro," he says, "are you suggesting that there is some concept that can integrate the executive game the way 'connection' does for golf?"

"Exactly. A teaching pro and an executive have a lot in common. I, too, have to be concerned about how people are performing and feeling, know when to give directions or solve problems, how to set objectives and maintain standards."

"What pulls it all together for you?" Larry asks.

"I think the integrating premise for *my* executive game is *self-esteem*—my own and that of the people I work with. Whatever game we're talking about, the objective is to realize our potential as fully as possible—performing well and feeling good about ourselves as a result. That's self-esteem. But self-esteem is not only the objective, it's also the primary *means* to achieving that objective.

"It's really a pretty simple proposition. People with high self-esteem not only get more satisfaction out of their work, they work more cooperatively with other people and experience less stress. They're less easily upset and just generally more positive about everything.

"So whether you want production or high morale or both, you need people of high self-esteem. But where do you get people like that? Whose job is it to ensure the conditions for people to develop their self-esteem?"

"Executives!" Larry says.

"That's my view, too, Larry," says the Pro. "And that raises an even bigger question. What kind of executive is most likely to feel comfortable focusing primary attention on people's self-esteem instead of on performance and morale and standard operating procedures?"

"A smart one," says Larry.

"It's not that simple," the Pro says. "I think instead that it is the executive who, personally, operates from a foundation of high self-esteem."

•

Unlike golf, the *real* executive game involves relationships among people. Yet it is one of the real enigmas of executive development and education that so little importance is attached to managing the human side of enterprise. We are taught to value and develop executive skills pertaining to technology and economics and strategic planning. And when we get in trouble, most of us look for new technologies, more capital investment, and visionary concepts as the solutions to our problems. We might better consider the effects of our own executive practices on the self-esteem of all those whom we interact with and influence. And, if self-esteem is the great integrator, we might consider just what aspects of our executive games are in need of integration. What "opposites" must we integrate?

LOVE AND WORK

Many years ago someone asked Sigmund Freud what a person must do to be healthy. Without hesitating, Dr. Freud replied, *"Lieben und arbeiten!"* ("Love and work!") Of all the complex and ingenious insights into the human condition fathered by Freud, this simple and fundamental observation may be the most profound.

Freud understood that health and quality of life depend, in large measure, on how effectively each of us adapts to the realities of the world around us. Since there are two environments—social and physical—love and work are our most basic means of accessing and responding to our day-to-day realities. They are our connections.

Through love we establish emotional connections with our social world; affection, caring, and investing of our emotional energy can bind us to the other people in our lives. Through work, on the other hand, we establish physical and intellectual connections with our environment; productivity of mind and body—the solving of problems, inventing of tools, creating of new methods, and making of things—not only help us adapt to the demands of our physical environment, but also allow us to have impact on it and shape it to our own needs. Clearly, health requires *both* love and work.

But we human beings are blessed with just enough intellect to make simple things difficult. Most of us proceed as if everything is a matter of either love *or* work. Many of us behave, in fact, as if there is a competition between the two. As with distance and accuracy in golf, we establish our personal priority and press on without even asking ourselves what game we're trying to play. We just "split off" as unimportant the part that gives us trouble. The plot thickens when we become executives and our views of love and work, and the personal accommodations we have worked out, directly affect the well-being and options of other people.

Mental health and social science literature is pretty clear and consistent on three points where the management of love and work is concerned. First, 15 to 20 percent of those who have effectively integrated love and work in their lives enjoy far and away better personal health and do a better job as executives. Second, the 70 percent of those who pursue a fragmented, piecemeal approach, and the 15 percent or so who have essentially withdrawn from the fray, consistently encounter rather predictable problems in their own lives and in their executive jobs. And, third, the reason the 85 percent majority do a fragmented, one-sided job of connecting with the world is that they are *ambivalent* about love and work per se.

Many executives see love as "weak" and work as "strong." Some see work as onerous and something to avoid, believing that love conquers all. We know that people make decisions based on their perceptions of the probable gains and losses to themselves. Maybe they do the same thing where love and work are concerned. They work from a mental matrix of the costs and benefits of love and work. Such a matrix might look like this:

	Love **A**	**Work** **B**
Benefits (Good)	• prevents loneliness • ensures acceptance • gives emotional support • is empowering • gives a sense of being needed	• has impact • produces what is needed • can be a source of pride • gives a sense of accomplishment • gives a sense of control and needed independence
	C	**D**
Costs (Bad)	• makes one vulnerable • can be taken as a sign of weakness • can make one lose control • can make one dependent • can require self-sacrifice	• can be onerous • can be fatiguing • can be demanding • can take up time • can invite criticism and ridicule

Even from just a cursory analysis, it is apparent that we are all working with some pretty loaded issues. Nothing is all good, without risks, and neither is anything all bad, with no redeeming features. Like life itself, our mechanisms for dealing with our world are a mixed bag. How we use them depends on what aspects of the problem we decide to focus on. It is here that executives differ most.

Executive Styles

There are five basic executive styles. Each reflects the manner in which the executive has resolved a personal ambivalence about love and work.

With people like Frank, Tim, and Fred in mind—consider the following executive styles in relation to the above A-B-C-D matrix.

Taskmasters (B-C)

Work is the primary focus of executives who either view the costs of love to be too great or see love itself as irrelevant to their personal needs—a sign of weakness or an invitation to exploitation. They are interested primarily in results, in tangible evidence of effort and productivity, unencumbered by such distractions as morale or satisfactions. They are distracted by pains of performance and power, but most of their problems will concern *people*.

Comforters (A-C)

Some executives, attracted to the benefits of love and apprehensive about the costs associated with work, put all their energies into building and maintaining a connection with the social part of the world around them. In their management, they focus on giving people emotional support, taking care of them, and protecting or rescuing them from the rigors of work. They are distracted by "people" pains, but their problems will be those of *performance*.

Regulators (C-D)

Some executives value neither love nor work. Perhaps overwhelmed by what social and physical connections have cost them in the past, they decide to risk no more. They disengage to save their energies for themselves and in their management focus on adherence to rules and precedent, so that the more people comply, the less social and physical hassle they have to endure. Theirs is an unemotional, impersonal, and effortless attempt at being in the world but not part of it. They are pained by lack of purpose and power, but *people* and *performance* will suffer most.

The three styles above—based on an inner reality that says we must choose among mutually exclusive possibilities—account for about 60 percent of the executive games played today. They are based in "split" unintegrated priorities.

Manipulators (A-B-C-D)

These are the most common executives. They seek to maximize gain and minimize loss. They are willing to compromise love and work values—and encourage settling for less than possible satisfaction—as a necessary trade-off for avoiding unacceptable costs. They seek to appease and control, dangle the promise of satisfactions, and covertly influence, simultaneously. They take great pride in their abilities to orchestrate people and events. Manipulators see playing the executive game as a personal art form. Believing in nothing beyond themselves, they suffer pains of philosophy; the quality of their relationships and performance will reflect their inconsistency.

Developers (A-B)

Some executives capitalize on the advantages of both love and work. They focus on building and maintaining effective connections with the social and physical realities of the workplace. They work for health, productivity, and growth among those they manage. Developers feel that promoting both love and work is their executive job, and although it's not easy, they embrace the task as a loving chore. They are not without pain; they expect growth to cost something.

Meddling Executives: Games of Mistrust and Interference

Generally speaking, all executive styles, with the exception of the Developers, are meddlesome. And there are two reasons why, as executives, any of us might choose a meddlesome style—both related to our Private Game. First, those of us who meddle have allowed the Meddler to win the game in our own heads. Second, as latter-day Meddlers we don't trust those in our charge any more than the meddlesome authority figures in our lives trusted us. It is hard to trust anyone when we have been taught not to trust ourselves. The pains of mistrust of others' adequacies and intentions *demand* that we try to take over their games and tell them how to play, but our interference not only negates the potential of those we manage or teach or parent, it also damages their self-esteem.

•

"PRO," LARRY SAYS, "if executive success depends on how we manage self-esteem, why do so many of us do such a lousy job? Have we become a nation of autocrats and caretakers?"

"I think," the Pro answers, "there's a lot of talk these days about caretakers, but the real problem is that many executives are—irrespective of style—basically care*seekers*. They try to get other people to do for them what, deep down, they feel they can't do for themselves. Their styles may differ, but they are still trying to get people *to take care of them*. Some use force because they're afraid to trust people. They try to *make* what they want happen, whether that means demanding it of someone or extorting it from them. They do the same thing with their golf swings. They don't really trust the club, so as soon as they get to the top of their backswing, they try to force the club down with their hands and arms as though they can't even trust gravity, either. *They* have to supply all the speed and direction—make it all happen—to get what they want.

"Others spend their energies apparently taking care of others so that they can be sure those people feel obligated to take care of them, at least to keep them around. Careseeking plays out in a lot of different ways. But it keeps not only the executive dependent, it encourages everybody else to be dependent, too.''

"What *should* we be doing?" Frank asks.

"I think we might consider the archer," the Pro replies. "The golfer's backswing is analogous to the archer drawing his arrow back in his bow. The archer's job is to aim and position the arrow to do its job. When the string is taut and the bow fully bent, the archer *trusts* the design of his bow and arrow to take advantage of the natural properties of the situation. He just puts everything in a proper position and turns loose. He doesn't *make* the arrow fly, he *allows* it to fly.

"I think golfers might do the same thing. Use the backswing to establish torque and position the club—and then just turn loose. *Allow* the club to swing. That's what separates the good players from the rest. The same idea applies to the executive game. Meddling executives try to *make* things happen. Good executives *allow* things to happen. Which strategy you use can make all the difference.''

•

There are two kinds of interference with the realization and expression of human potential. As we've seen, we all interfere with ourselves to some degree. But the more we interfere with ourselves, the more likely we are to interfere with others. Some of us not only interfere *directly* with others' potential through the practices we use and procedural constraints we impose, we also interfere *indirectly* by feeding into people's propensity for self-interference. Meddling executives have a real knack for spotting and playing to the Meddler in others' heads.

That is why self-esteem should, as Larry suggested, be an important consideration for executives as they play their games. Moreover, that is why all of us might profit from a studied consideration of the effects of our preferred executive style on the self-esteem of the people we manage.

Careseekers:
Games of Directing and Protecting,
Regulating and Manipulating

It is axiomatic that we will mismanage the self-esteem of others any time our executive style is based more on concern for ourselves than on concern for the well-being and productivity of those in our charge. In addition, a true irony of the executive game is that the less sure of ourselves we are, the more dependent we become on people we're not sure we can trust. We become careseekers, and the more "responsible" we feel, the more irresponsibly we will behave *toward* others. Fearful that they might not produce what we need, we try to make other people's decisions and choices for them and fall into the careseekers' trap.

Let's see how this is revealed in the executive game. If we're Taskmasters like Frank, we will value strong controls. We will personally make most decisions, be firm in our use of power, and stress the importance of orderliness, propriety, compliance with standards, and unquestioning obedience. Not only will we seldom reward, we may even be inclined to punish signs of curiosity, exploration, and originality. If we care at all about others' self-esteem, we seek to make them the kind of "strong and independent" people we wish we were and, as a result, concentrate our efforts on a single aspect of the game: *mastery.*

Out of our own concern that others not make us look bad—coupled with our mistrust of their abilities and intentions—we begin to see people as *objects* for which we are responsible, but upon whom we must reluctantly depend. As a result, we communicate *to* people, but not *with* them. And most of our messages will be in the form of directives rather than information or explanations. We will seldom, if ever, ask for opinions or expressions of feelings. We will not seek the involvement of those in our charge, nor will we really get very involved with them intellectually, emotionally, or socially. We will not necessarily be harsh in all this, as much as we will be perfunctory and aloof.

If our efforts to master those we manage are totally successful, we will create not "strong and independent" extensions of ourselves, but people who are quiet, well behaved, and conforming. They will be compliant and un-questioning, suppressing their curiosity and spontaneity. There will be little quarrelsomeness, negativism, disobedi-ence, aggression, or playfulness—at least that we can see. Neither will there be any originality or eagerness to solve problems.

In our efforts to make others extensions of ourselves, more often than not we end up with people who, lacking in their own self-esteem, look to us—and other Taskmas-ters—for *confirmation*. That inevitably causes resentment, and we may discover, too late, that instead of the independ-ence and sense of industry we hoped to create, counter-dependence and passive-aggressive behavior may be the earmarks of our organization. We may find we have cre-ated competitors so hostile toward us that they cannot con-form because they are intent at beating us at our own game. As Taskmasters we meddle the way we were med-dled with. And we will surround ourselves either with peo-ple who dislike us but comply or with adversarial clones who are set on defeating us. Such people will fail to pro-vide the kind of care we really seek.

Then there are the Comforters, who appear to be gen-uinely nice people—perhaps not entirely honest or reli-able, but nice. If we are Comforters, we have trouble with the demands and stresses of organized living. We are not into control and taking responsibility. We're into love—*being* loved. Trying to be lovable, we prefer to nurture and lend support. We think of *ourselves* as objects and learn to behave accordingly. When we *must* manage or organize, we do so as benign and indulgent Meddlers, more con-cerned outwardly with others' comfort than our own. We exercise little overt control, make few decisions we don't absolutely have to make, and overlook signs of disorder and noncompliance on the part of those who rely on us.

We do not reward independent, outgoing, or exploratory activities. Out of our own displaced fear for the safety of those we meddle with and care for, we will actually discourage such inclinations. We will overprotect. We don't want anything to happen to the people we lean on. We will seek closeness and show our concern for people by anticipating their needs and supporting them, before even giving them a chance to express their desires. We "know" what they *need* and what is *best* for them even if they don't. We may lavish praise for only ordinary accomplishment—in the spirit of confirming them—but seldom will we encourage, much less push, for the kinds of extraordinary accomplishment that would allow them to confirm themselves. As Comforters, by giving in to our own needs to meddle, we create our own ultimate irony; we thwart people's desire for growth and mastery from which they could derive that healthy self-esteem necessary to strengthen them enough to carry us—and they resent us.

The Regulator style also amounts to seeking a form of custodial care. With its emphasis on rules and boundaries, it is an attempt to use the "organization" to take care of ourselves, to achieve security while minimizing the pain and hassle of personal involvement. We seek only enough authority to keep demands on us to a minimum. If we must manage, we will play a passive-aggressive executive game; we will meddle the way we were meddled with long ago —by neglect. We absent ourselves, psychologically and physically, as much as possible. Objects geared to objects.

Careseekers at heart, we put our efforts into taking care of the system—the organization or institution—that takes care of us. In any event, we will attempt to do this by indirect and mechanical means rather than by personal effort, using organizational rules and procedural manuals to deal summarily and impersonally with infractions. We will not tolerate signs of curiosity, exploration, or originality on the part of those around us. We prefer to communicate by written memo, which lessens the probability of personal involvement, the raising of questions or objections, and, thereby, the likelihood of personal confrontation. At no point will we concern ourselves with whether or not we are asking as much as people are able or want to give. Personnel development, after all, isn't a prime issue in our management style.

If we're successful Regulators, we will garner a few quiet, unimaginative, detached automatons who put in their time each day with no complaints and work mightily to preserve all security and comfort. More often than not, however, we will foster rebellion because, once again, we are depriving others of the means to achieve mastery, growth, and self-esteem. Our irony is that, in seeking to escape the hassle, we create people whose chief talent is giving us a hard time rather than tending to our needs.

Manipulators are also heavy into careseeking via control. But they prefer covert and unobtrusive, behind-the-scenes methods whereby they can control people and events without appearing to control them. They use communication toward this end as well. They talk *to* people *about* other people but seldom express a personal opinion. They seek information they can use later, because information is power. And they are supportive of individuals, as needed, in a one-on-one fashion, because it sets up opportunities for their favorite strategy of "divide and conquer." Their performance expectations are primarily for themselves in skillfully maneuvering other people into going along with whatever course of action best serves the Manipulator's own needs. This is not to say Manipulators are unmindful of the importance of self-esteem, but they merely give it lip service (lest, neglected, it backfire on their plan) rather than build it. We are all objects to be used.

We can all wonder about the honesty, integrity, and personal productivity of executive careseekers and meddlers. The questions we might ask about all such executives are: What happens when people are treated like objects? What do they learn? How do they grow? What are the effects of such executive styles on the self-esteem of others —and, when these strategies fail, on the self-esteem of the executive?

•

"WHY CAN'T MEDDLING executives *see* that their approach isn't working?" says Larry. "Are they just blind or do they just *deny* what's going on around them?"

"Both," the Pro says. "They're distracted by their own priorities, by the pains of their Private Game. Remember at the beginning of the week when we paired up for that coaching exercise? When Frank tries to coach, he focuses all his attention on the results, what the ball does, because he thinks the outcome reflects on him."

Tim nods. "And he sure doesn't pick up on how a guy is feeling. I was his partner. And the more lousy he told me my shots were, the worse I felt—like I was an embarrassment to him. I stopped trying to learn anything. I just wanted that exercise to be *over!*"

"Yes," the Pro says, "but when your turn came to coach, Tim, you were so distracted by your Private Game that you couldn't see anything either. You actually *praised* some of the lousiest shots I've ever seen! You were driving Frank nuts. He couldn't see any connection between what he was doing and what you were saying—because there wasn't any connection."

"I was Fred's partner for that exercise," says Larry. "It was just before he walked out, and he didn't give a damn about helping me. He just let me hit and didn't say three words—and asked that I do the same for him. That frustrated me because I could have learned something from Fred if he'd been willing to work with me."

"A concern for learning," the Pro says, "may be what really separates the good players from the rest."

•

Developers: Encouraging Exploration and Discovery, Learning and Growth

The Confucian bible *Lun yü* (The Analects of Confucius) begins, "What a joy to learn, and to put into practice what you have learned." In many respects this thought captures the guiding premise—the working assumptions—of those executives who prefer a Developer style.

Of the four executive styles, only the Developers understand the importance of self-esteem and how to achieve it—in themselves and in others. Developers understand that a sturdy self-esteem flows naturally from joyful learning put into practice. They understand that all executives are *teachers*. *How* they manage the learning process can make all the difference in what people learn and how they feel about themselves. And *what* they teach is just as critical to a successful outcome. They do not view work as something people must be forced to do or as an onerous demand from which people must be protected. They view work as a major means of learning and self-expression—and as a vehicle for acquiring a sense of mastery, self-confirmation, and growth.

Developers, unlike meddling executives, understand that people *value* work for entirely personal reasons. They are not surprised by the results of a recent Gallup poll that revealed:

- Work satisfies a basic need for self-worth; 70 percent of people surveyed said they would continue to work even if they did not have to for economic reasons;
- People who work the longest hours tend to be happier than those who work less rigorously;
- A sense of personal identification with one's work is the crucial link between hard work and satisfaction;
- The amount of stress experienced by people corresponds inversely to the amount of work satisfaction enjoyed;

- Most of all, people want freedom, choice, and responsibility in their work;
- Such satisfactions and desires are the same among people regardless of gender, race, or income and become more pronounced as people grow older.

Developers understand that, as the poet said, labor is love made visible. And when people know how to love and work, they will connect so effectively with reality that their self-esteem will rest on the most solid of foundations.

What do Developers use to foster self-esteem and integrate the games of love and work? What do they do differently from meddling executives?

The answer may be found in the process of *exploration and discovery*. Developers understand that it is only through exploration and discovery that any of us can truly get in touch with, vitalize, and release the hidden potentials that we call the Player within ourselves. Developers address the Player in others.

Exploration and discovery are part of the natural and innate process of *learning and growth*. It is not just coincidence that the emergence of the assertiveness that first brings us into conflict with the people we look to for nurturing is marked by seeking, grabbing, handling, tasting, touching, and chasing kinds of behavior. Many of our problems as adults—and certainly our Meddler's compendia of warning voices from the past—are the direct result of the *mismanagement of this stage of our exploratory urge*—not only when we were children, but at every subsequent developmental stage.

It is during our first attempts to explore and discover that we come to know what people *think* of our attempts at exploratory behavior. Whether we are encouraged or discouraged can have a profound and lasting effect not only on what we learn, but on how we feel about ourselves. It is during this time that we decide the relative merits of behaving in a compliant, aggressive, or detached manner. And it is then that the Private Game between Meddler and Player is set in motion.

Developers are guided by such awareness. They use a wide range of executive strategies, to be sure, but their overall objective is to encourage, not discourage, the process of exploration and discovery, learning and growth. They know that how we feel about ourselves determines how well we play the game.

•

"PRO," LARRY SAYS, "you're an executive. What's your objective? What do you want out of the game?"

"I hear people talking about 'wanting to make a difference,' " the Pro says. "I'd like that. But *all* executives make a difference. I guess I'm more concerned about the *kind* of difference I make.

"I think about guys like Cus D'Amato, who took two troubled street kids and turned them both into heavyweight champions of the world. Floyd Patterson and Mike Tyson were each the youngest boxers of their times ever to win the title. Someone once asked Cus what his secret was. He said, 'I see a spark and I fan it until it becomes a flame. Then I feed the flame until it becomes a raging fire. My kids succeed when they become champions—but I succeed when they don't need me anymore.'

"I guess that's what I would like," the Pro says. "I'd like to send people away from here who no longer need me. People whose belief in themselves is great enough to overcome all the disbelief they're going to encounter. That's the kind of executive I'd really like to be."

THE ROAD TO AWARENESS

Aim, Acknowledge, and Accept

*The difference between amateurs and
pros is amateurs look for the hazards
and pros look for the landing area.*

Lee Trevino

"The more I studied it, the more I loved it," said Bobby
Jones, "and the more I loved it, the more I studied it. . . ."
Jones was talking about the Old Course at St. Andrews. He
did not like the course at all when he first played it; it
exacted its toll. But Jones persevered—until his knowledge
of the course "allowed me to play it with patience and
restraint until she might exact her toll from [those] who
might treat her with less respect and understanding."

Bobby Jones was talking about what good players call
course management—how to assess the hole before you and
select the shot with the least risk but best outcome. Good
course management requires a lot of discipline and a good
deal of self-knowledge. The result is a shot based in sound
judgment. Course management is a bit of a misnomer because to find the landing area consistently really requires
self-management. That's where most of us have trouble—
on the course and on the job.

The Old Course Jones loved is not unlike life itself.
Each of us has had our game tested by bunkers and hazards. But if we persevere, if we learn, each of us still has a
chance to adapt our games to the realities of the course.

We can study our games and the course until we come to understand and love the experience. If we are struggling with the executive game, each of us can still commit to greater awareness of ourselves and the course we are playing.

•

"PRO," LARRY SAYS, "you've stirred up a lot of stuff in my head. Now I *want* to start working on becoming more aware. Where do I start? You still haven't really talked about *how*."

"If you think about it," the Pro says, "we have been talking about *how* to become more aware all week. We've talked about how our personal playing strategies can sometimes work against us, how old swing thoughts can make us operate in the BEWARE mode and can keep us making the same errors over and over. We've even talked about how our own unacknowledged ambivalence can make us play self-defeating games we don't even know we're playing. We've talked a lot about where we are and how we've come to be there."

"You're right," Larry says. "It's just that it doesn't all hang together for me yet."

Frank nods. "I'm not sure, you know, what I *do* with it."

"Yeah," says Tim. "It all sounds like me, but it doesn't *feel* like me yet."

The Pro chuckles. "You've hit the nail on the head, Tim. True awareness is one part thinking and one part feeling. When the two combine you achieve the kind of insight that is more than the sum of its parts. When enough insights combine, you end up with what I call awareness.

"I work with such a mix of people here at the Academy that sometimes guiding them to *any* insight seems impossible. I get some guys who have completely lost touch with their own feelings. They can describe the moves in a good golf swing better than I can but can't play the game because they can't apply what they know intellectually to their own swings. They've never learned what a swing really *feels* like, good or bad.

"Then I get other students who are all *feeling* but don't know how to *think* about what they feel. The result either way is that *nobody talks about feelings.* But to become aware, we have to think *and* feel. That's our only means for understanding reality."

THINKING AND FEELING:
OUR ACCESS TO REALITY

Tim frowns. "Maybe some people just can't communicate as well as others. Maybe it's a verbal problem."

"I think it goes deeper than that," the Pro says. "There's a lot of noise going on. Everybody thinks and everybody feels. But some people are so bothered by their feelings that they bury them. After a while they literally lose touch with their feelings. But that doesn't mean feelings don't still influence such people.

"It's the same with non-thinkers. They're bothered by reason because sometimes facts or logic would keep them from feeling the way they *want* to feel. But without facts or logic they're hard-pressed to understand why they do what they do. They can't explain it to themselves or anyone else.

"No matter how well we may swing the club, we've got to think our way around the course. I hear people talk about how they're really working on overcoming a flaw in their game. Usually, they mean they're *thinking* about it. But you can't really *work* on something until you can feel it, too. We need both kinds of information if we're really going to manage our games enough to play well. Even Jack Nicklaus needs both."

"Why?" says Frank. "He's the best ever."

"Well," the Pro says, "Nicklaus turned fifty and became eligible for the Senior Tour in 1990. He was scheduled to play his first event in April of that year. And, frankly, he was a little apprehensive. Not only had he been having some back problems, but his swing was off and had been for some time.

"Anyway, the tournament was held at Desert Mountain, where Jim Flick is director of golf. Flick worked with Nicklaus on the practice tee before the tournament. And he observed that when Nicklaus was winning all the time, he had always played by feel. Now, Flick pointed out, it seemed that Nicklaus had gotten very analytic and mechanical, as if he was thinking about his swing so much he had lost his feel.

"Nicklaus agreed, so Flick gave him some drills to do —like choking down on his short irons, things like that— to increase his feel for a shot. Nicklaus not only won his first Senior Tour event by four strokes, the next week—at the age of fifty—he finished in the top ten at the Masters. Nicklaus claims he's playing better than he has in fifteen years! Even the best need balance, Frank."

•

There is a tension of sorts—yet another trap of ambivalence—between our needs to be rational and thoughtful, on the one hand, and sometimes equally strong needs to proceed without the constraints that reason and logic might dictate. Sometimes thinking gets in our way or requires too much of us, and we deny the rational so that we can follow our feelings. Although all of us do this at one time or another, some of us—like Tim—make it a way of life. Allowing our feelings to dictate our perceptions and interpretations of reality helps us justify our actions to ourselves.

That's why people like Frank bother those of us like Tim. Not only do they try to keep everything so rational that they challenge our feelings, they seem devoid of the very feelings we depend on in others—feelings of caring, compassion, empathy, and the like.

Likewise, people like Tim drive those of us like Frank

crazy. We fail to understand or sympathize with their inability to express or defend their actions on logical grounds. We may even, according to our own rational criteria and objective observations, question their intelligence. So it is that by choosing to limit our access to reality, we not only impair awareness of our own games, but hinder our relationships as well. Unwilling to communicate effectively with ourselves, we are unable to communicate very well with others.

•

THE PRO CONTINUES. "I'm interested in how people use thinking and feeling to keep from learning the game. How they play games with themselves to keep reality at bay—so they can stay where they are.

"Dave Pelz is a tour pro turned golf scientist and instructor. Not long ago he did an experiment that put to a test the touring pros' claims that they can feel the difference in golf balls, between some wound with a balata cover, some wound with a Surlyn cover, and some solid ones covered with Surlyn. He had these tour pros hit all three kinds in random order with several different clubs and then tell him what kind of ball they had hit each time. He knew going in that players on the tour *prefer* balata.

"Well, they did no better by 'feel' than they would have by chance! Pelz found no evidence that players can actually 'feel' differences based on ball construction or cover material. But what got my attention was that every time the pros made a good swing and caught the ball on the club's sweet spot, they concluded the ball was the one they preferred—a balata. In other words, in their minds the pros equated the *feel* of a good swing with striking the ball of their *choice*.

"This is an example of some very talented people actually using their *feelings to confirm what they already think*. That can be a trap. And my guess is we all do it a lot of the time!"

"Gee," Tim says, "no wonder nobody can understand anybody else. We can't even understand ourselves."

Larry looks troubled. "So what's the solution, Pro? How do we get a balance? How do thinkers talk to feelers and vice versa?"

"I think," the Pro answers, "we have to explore our *purposes*. It does no good to argue about beliefs any more than it does to argue about how somebody feels. But we can talk about what personal purpose is served by thinking about reality or feeling a certain way."

•

COMMUNICATING PURPOSE:
THE KEY TO BALANCE

We explore purpose simply by asking questions, first of ourselves and then, if it seems worthwhile, of the other people we would like to understand. Those of us like Frank and Fred might ask ourselves, "What purpose does trying to keep everything rational and objective really serve for me? What would it cost me to feel?" Those of us like Tim, on the other hand, might ask ourselves, "What purpose do my feelings really serve for me? What might I lose if I put my feelings to a rational and objective test?"

•

"I'VE LEARNED TWO THINGS about true awareness here on the practice tee," says the Pro. "*What may be logically acceptable is not necessarily psychologically acceptable, and without emotional ownership, few of us will put enough energy into anything to get it grooved.* That's why something has to sound right *and* feel right for anything worthwhile to happen."

"So," says Larry, "your job is to figure out a way to make things *sound* right and *feel* right at the same time. How do you do that?"

The Pro leans forward. "By providing a more structured experience," he says. "Creating a guided, step-by-step experience is the only way I've found of communicating with anybody on what awareness is really all about. I can guide the experience, but I have to let the experience do the communicating.

"For instance, if just thinking were enough for true awareness, then we could all read a good book on golf—and then go out and play. Obviously that's not enough for most people.

"By the same token, if feelings were enough, then we could all just randomly pound balls on the practice tee, without any particular objective or swing thought in mind, and be ready to play. But purposeless practice doesn't work, either. Awareness requires something more."

"But how is that a communication problem?" Frank asks.

"Well," the Pro says, "we know that thinkers need to learn to trust their feel for a shot. And feelers need some rational guidelines to refer to when the wheels come off. On a good ball-striking day, they need to take notes: establish precisely where the ball is positioned in their stance, how far their hands are from the body, how closed or opened their stance is. Detailed knowledge of their own mechanics can save them on their off days. I think it's the same with developing awareness. Experience can communicate to non-feelers and structure can communicate to non-thinkers.

"I guess I think of awareness as being like a personal guidance system that keeps us oriented so we always know where we are relative to where we want to go, regardless of distractions and outside influences. And it's assembled out of bits and pieces of intellectual and emotional material. We've been talking so far about the pieces. Now it's time to put everything together.

"I can guide you guys through the steps of the AWARE mode. In the time we have left, I can give you a structured format for having the kinds of experiences you need to achieve awareness."

•

THE AWARE MODE

We have all had the experience of *wanting* to do what's right—while, at the same time, not knowing what that is. We need some thoughts and ideas to guide our efforts. We need some structure. And the more disoriented and lost we feel, the more structure we need. That's what the AWARE mode really is—a structure, a set of guidelines, for building ourselves a dependable and enduring personal guidance system based on a knowledge of ourselves.

Structuring the Game

Structure can be both a blessing and a curse. Most people need to know what to expect and some understanding of the situations they encounter before they feel capable of responding adequately. There's nothing unusual about that. Few of us are comfortable with totally random, formless experience. But some of us are bothered by too much structure, and some of us are uncomfortable when we lack as much structure as we would like.

For example, those of us like Frank want immediate clarity. We often sense a loss of control and feel vulnerable in situations that don't have a clear-cut purpose or appearance of order. We're uncomfortable not knowing what to expect. We react by trying to *impose structure*. We question: Who's in charge here? What's the objective? How much time do we have?

In the process, however, we lose most of the spontaneity as well. We tend to build rigid and sterile places and formal relationships devoid of humor or creativity. Our lives become so rigidly structured that we stop feeling anything, and we become so certain of our view of things that even our wrong opinions appear to us as correct ideas no one else can understand. In our zeal to establish a structure to our liking, we misdiagnose. Consequently, we also mismanage.

Those of us like Tim need structure, too. We become even more anxious than the people who seize control. When faced with uncertain situations, we don't know what to expect or what to do, and we lack the sense of personal control that would allow us to establish structure where there doesn't seem to be any. We become docile followers. Over all, we have a real love-hate relationship with structure. We want it so we can feel less anxious, but we fear it because it may require something of us and sow the conditional seeds of evaluation and judgment. Sometimes we freeze.

Those of us like Fred love structure. It is our refuge, our sanctuary, where we can be both detached and blameless. Structure depersonalizes the process and allows each of us to deny responsibility for what happens. Even if we do not agree, we can justify our actions as simply following the rules.

All games require structure. Boundaries and dividing lines are a part of reality. In general, however, the more concerned any of us is about structure, the more likely we are to become rigid, unimaginative, and anxious in dealing with situations that test our competence. Depending on our own private fears, we play the games of Taskmasters or Comforters or Regulators.

If Taskmasters, we will be impatient. We try to speed things along. We instruct and direct. We devise plans for avoiding our worst-case fantasies, and we prescribe and proscribe—thoroughly ignoring the adaptive genius of the Player the AWARE mode is designed to set free.

If Comforters, we will be afraid. We doubt our ability to handle situations, structured or not. We are fearful of offending someone. We are also inconsistent. Sometimes we look to those we are "caring for" to supply the structure. Other times we jump in prematurely and try to rescue or protect people by deciding what they need and doing what is "best for them."

The Regulators among us will try to make sure everyone conforms so the unexpected cannot occur. We un-questioningly accept and grab hold of whatever structure we can find. But whether Taskmaster, Comforter, or Regulator, we deprive other people of the opportunity to explore and discover and devise a structure of their own. We fail to be very creative personally or to encourage creativity among those around us.

Experience-based awareness will introduce us to new ways of feeling and doing. We will feel differently because we will have discovered and begun to entertain different ways of thinking about ourselves, others, and our common situations. That's what the Pro has in mind for Frank, Tim, Larry, and us all.

•

"AS YOU KNOW," SAYS THE PRO, "the BEWARE mode is a cycle that feeds on itself, a closed system geared to external events. But the AWARE mode is a dynamic, ever-expanding system. We build it from the inside out. Experience is the core, but to start the process in motion, we must take a number of steps."

•

A lot of us design our house and ourselves from the outside in. We are more concerned with appearance and image than we are with function or substance. But, as the Pro has said, we build awareness from the inside out. Our own experiences—our personal histories and stories of where we've been—are at the core. And how we think and feel about these experiences, whether we truly understand their significance—or insignificance—determines our current awareness of where we are. Our task is to use such data in order to build outward, to expand our true awareness so that we can see where we want to go and how to get there.

•

THE FIRST STEP TOWARD AWARENESS

"THE FIRST STEP TOWARD the AWARE mode," the Pro continues, "is learning how to aim, acknowledge, and accept. We need to check our *aim*, how we orient ourselves to our target, or maybe check to see if we even consciously have a target. The touring pros actually help one another with setup and alignment. They know it's easy to miss your aim on the golf course, and if you do, there's no way to turn in a good score.

"In 1989, Curtis Strange was hitting everything thirty feet right of where he intended. He thought he was coming over the top and cutting across the ball with an open club face at impact. That's what it *felt* like. And he was worried because he was about to defend his U.S. Open title. Before making any drastic changes in his swing, he had Carl Welty —a fine teaching pro—videotape him on the practice tee. He discovered he had gotten into a closed stance and was actually *aiming* to the right, causing him to swing too much from the inside on his downswing. He said, 'That's all I need to know,' and went out and won his second consecutive U.S. Open!"

Larry says, "Alignment is as much a mental thing as it is physical, don't you think, Pro?"

"You bet. You can't separate the mental from the physical if you want to play the game well. Frank, you have some superb physical talent, but you play unaware. You're so intent on impressing everybody that you don't bother to aim. Then you refuse to acknowledge the problems that wind, the lie of the ball, or your own impulsiveness can cause you. You try to use your physical skills to overpower the hole. And then when the shot goes awry or falls short, you won't admit that something you did—or didn't do— caused the result.

"Tim, in some ways you're just the same, although in other ways you're the exact opposite. Unlike Frank, you start by *over*aiming. You're so scared, you fiddle with your setup and ball position and recheck your alignment so much, I'm surprised you can take the club back. You can't stand to risk a mistake. And you won't accept your own capabilities. So you pass it off to a 'magic nine-iron' or something—anything that will keep you from being responsible for the outcome.

"If we want awareness, we must begin with taking proper aim, acknowledging all the influences that come into play—especially our own emotional reactions and tendencies when our competence is tested—then accepting responsibility for the shot."

Aiming: Deciding Who We Want to Be

"Aiming," says the Pro, "helps us establish direction. I know we hear a lot of talk about goal setting and objectives, but in my opinion, finding the direction we want to travel is much more important than focusing on goals. Goals can distract us sometimes, actually pull us away from our intended course.

"Curtis Strange knew that his goal was to defend his title successfully—play well, turn in the lowest score. But first he checked his alignment to see if he was going in the direction he wanted to go.

"It's the same in life. Aiming strikes at the heart of ambivalence. We need to be clear about what we *desire* so that we can really evaluate the goals our *fears* make us pursue or cling to. Becoming a millionaire by the time you're thirty, or doing whatever it takes to be number one, getting your kids in the right school—these are goals based in some kind of compensatory fear. But they may not lie along the healthy path you would like your life to take.

"Sometimes we get so enamored of a goal that we forget what we have to do to get there. The tour professionals talk about 'falling in love with the line' when they're trying to sink a crucial putt. They're so intent that they forget to stroke the ball properly. They forget it's still a game of distance and accuracy.

"Knowing the direction we want to travel in gives us a reference point in life. And if our direction is true and we stay close to the course, we'll not only reach all the goals that are truly important to us, we'll discover new ones that lie beyond our imagination. And, as Jack Nicklaus says, aiming and aligning the club face and ourselves is the only aspect of the swing over which we have one hundred percent conscious control."

•

At this stage, no action is required. This is a period for quietly owning up to what we really want and to where we really want to go. Next, we must look for and acknowledge the obstacles in the paths we have chosen—especially the ones we ourselves have erected.

•

ACKNOWLEDGING: GETTING IN TOUCH WITH DISTRACTIONS

"WE DISTRACT OURSELVES," the Pro says, "by failing to establish a course we want to follow. But we really interfere with ourselves when we're trying to get to a place we're ashamed to acknowledge.

"Some of the screwy things we do are due to the screwy goals we're trying to reach. For example, pride and fear and greed have made a lot of golfers do some really weird things on the course. But few will acknowledge that they are so proud or scared or greedy that it interferes with their swing. A *lot* even deny that there's anything wrong with their games.

"So they spend the whole round misclubbing themselves, trying to force shots, and playing out of the rough. And they completely forget about their real objective—to shoot the best score they can. Then, after the round is over, they sit around and blame everybody but themselves—the foursome in front, slow play, poor greens, their equipment. None of them will ever play the kind of game they really want to play until they ask themselves, 'What am *I* doing to cause myself trouble?' "

•

We can continue the process by fully *acknowledging* that there are problems to be solved. Those of us who are in flight, like Tim, may find this step difficult. We have been afraid of our own feelings. We need to acknowledge that. Frank and Larry, even Fred to a degree, are more willing to face the fact that a problem exists. But those of us like Frank and Fred need to acknowledge that our preferred strategy is to find someone else to blame.

•

Accepting: Taking Responsibility for Ourselves

THE PRO CONTINUES. "It doesn't do a whole lot of good to know where you want to go or what you're doing to keep yourself from getting there, if you're not willing to accept the responsibility for your own journey. That doesn't mean you can't get someone to help you. All of us need help on our games from time to time. That's why people get together at the Academy or go to a pro back home."

"But I thought self-reliance was the name of the game," says Frank.

"It is," the Pro says. "And nothing is more self-reliant than doing what *you* need to do to get the problem solved. A decision to seek help is still acceptance that it is up to *you* to do whatever is necessary to get *your* game on track."

•

Some of the people most alert to the existence of problems are least sensitive to the fact that they may in fact *be* the problem. Those of us like Frank and Fred may be painfully aware that we encounter the same kinds of problems wherever we go. Yet we refuse to see that we are the only constant from situation to situation. We will do anything else to keep from personally *accepting* the problem as our own. We neither consider ourselves responsible for solving it nor see ourselves as the cause of it in the first place.

On the other hand, the Tims among us have problems of acceptance in that we are too ready to accept the blame —but not the responsibility for solving the problem. We're inclined to swallow the despair, the blame, the guilt, everything. The AWARE mode prepares us to accept only the problems that are *ours* to solve. We'll find we have work to do.

THE ROAD TO AWARENESS

Willingness, Work, and Wholeness

*I've missed about all the shots I can
spare today; now I'm going to work.*
Walter Hagen

"So, THAT'S IT?" says Frank. "Just line up better, read the situation, think about your swing tendencies, then grip it and rip it?"

"No," says the Pro. "That's just the beginning. You've got to be willing to work at it. The reason we have trouble in the first place is that we've developed habits that work against us. We must learn to do something else in their place—and repeat it until it's natural to us. For as long as we have to force ourselves to remember or rely on somebody else to remind us to do the proper thing, that's a sign it's not a natural part of us yet.

"Insight and awareness don't come easily. Tour players go to the practice tee *after* they've played to try to feel their swings and think about what they're feeling. It's the only way to work out what's wrong and try to groove what's right about your game.

"That's something for you to contemplate, Larry. You think your way around the course pretty well, but I'm not sure you really work at feeling your game. That's why your club selection is not always what you really want. But if you're willing to work, I believe you can have a fine game.

"Frank, the same applies to you. Until you're willing to do the work necessary rather than what's easy for you, you're not going to be as good as you'd like. And Tim, if you can decide the game is important enough to you that you can commit to playing it well, then doing the work required will pay off. But not until it has some purpose for you.

"If the game is really important to any of us, we must be willing to do the work required to realize our own potential—to play it as well as we can."

Frank frowns. "If getting executives to commit to hard work is the key to realizing their potential, we're all in trouble," he says. "Most of the people I know are too busy to get any work done! Going to meetings and giving speeches and checking on everybody else doesn't leave any time for work. I can vouch for that personally."

"Each of us has to decide what a good solid game is worth to us," the Pro says. "We can either work toward a perfect game or duck the issue. It's a matter of choice."

Frank frowns. "I thought you didn't believe in pursuing perfection, Pro."

"Not the way you mean," the Pro says. "I wouldn't encourage anybody to work on developing a game that's free of all faults or shortcomings. But I would encourage everybody to seek perfection as the Greeks did. The Greek meaning of the word *perfect* is 'to be complete,' whole. I would invite all of you to work toward a perfect game in the sense that it is 'whole.'

"Wholeness is the objective. All I'm suggesting is that each of us be willing to do the work necessary for becoming whole so that we can play a *complete* game."

•

THE SECOND STEP TOWARD AWARENESS

Willingness: Committing to a Perfect Game

The second step of the AWARE mode invites us to work to be truly whole, to learn to trust ourselves, and to encourage those natural capacities and impulses that characterize the Player in us.

To accomplish that, we first must be *willing* to open ourselves to the possibility that we can best learn about ourselves by examining where we are, where we've been, and where we want to go. We must begin to entertain the notion that willingness, not willpower, is the true source of personal strength. We must become willing to question ourselves, to ask whether willfulness or withdrawal have served us as well as trust in our own and others' natural capacities might. As it turns out, an *unwillingness* to entertain such questions and experiences is at the core of most defensive posturing and the continuation of our self-defeating practices.

•

Work: Producing a Real Player

"PRO," LARRY SAYS, "today's players work on their games constantly, but Ben Hogan was the first real legendary player to practice much. Why did it take so long for people to figure out they have to work at the game?"

"Hogan was the first to realize," the Pro answers, "that a lot of the problems of the game would yield to the kind of analysis practice makes possible. He really didn't start off with a very good game and even thought about quitting. Then he realized he had something within that would produce a good game, if he could just reach and learn to use it. But he knew it was going to take work.

"In those days the idea of practicing never occurred to players. Those were simpler times. There were fewer people obsessing about how the game *ought* to be played. Hogan was different. He tried to develop his own personal game by pounding balls and thinking about what he was feeling, until it all fell into place.

"Without the benefit of size or much natural talent, he developed what a lot of people consider the perfect swing. You might say Hogan introduced the value of work to the game. Through work, he realized that 'something within himself' and applied it to his game."

•

Work can be both onerous and satisfying. The same is true of the work of awareness. There is one notable exception: this time *we* are the product of our labors. We can produce a *real* Player out of the resources we have inside ourselves.

On the surface, becoming willing to work in our own best interests would seem one of the easier steps toward awareness. In truth, it can be the most difficult. The longer we've been trapped by our ambivalence, the more some of us are inclined to cling to the status quo. Familiar pain seems preferable to the fear of not knowing what to expect, but the longer we wait, the more desperate we become and the harder the work required of us will be.

•

Wholeness: Achieving Harmony Among All Our Games

"PRO," LARRY SAYS, "when you say you want us to play a perfect game—to be complete—you're talking about getting all the parts together, aren't you?"

"The game is made up of so many demands," says the Pro, "so many different tests of competence, that it's easy to feel overwhelmed. We forget that we have the capacity for learning all the skills we need to play a rewarding game.

"It can be confusing. You've got to play a long game and a short game equally well. You've got to get distance and maintain accuracy. You need power and finesse. You need to know how to play in good weather and bad weather, how to come back from trouble, because that's all part of the game. Sometimes reality seems more than we can handle.

"After Ben Hogan had what could have been a fatal crash with a Greyhound bus, he came back to win the U.S. Open at Merion in 1950. And, as if to really make the point, he successfully defended his title in 1951. It was not until Curtis Strange did the same thing thirty-eight years later that anyone was able to win back-to-back U.S. Opens. Hogan's doctors said he would never play again, but he just went back to work on the practice tee. He wanted to be whole again.

"We can all be like Hogan—if not on the golf course, at least in life—if we're willing to work at becoming whole. Playing a complete game can be the most satisfying, exciting, uplifting, and rewarding experience anybody could ever want. Each of us has everything we need—all the parts—to play a complete game. But it's up to each of us to put the parts together and make ourselves whole.

"I don't think it's just by accident that one of the best-selling golf books of all time is called *How to Become a Complete Golfer*. That's what all of us want, down deep in our guts, because that's our true nature. It's just a matter of choice: a commitment to doing what's right for ourselves."

THE ROAD TO AWARENESS

Accounting, Appraisal, Analysis, Admission, and Amnesty

*You can be the greatest iron player in
the world or the greatest putter, but if
you can't get the ball in position to use
your greatness, you can't win.*

Ben Hogan

TIM LOOKS TROUBLED. "Pro," he says, "why do you say I need to decide if the game's important to me? Sure I don't practice much, but that doesn't mean I don't *care*."

"My impression is you hold something back," the Pro says. "I get the feeling you haven't quite let yourself take the game seriously yet. If you want to be aware, Tim—and this goes for Frank and Larry and even for me and Fred— you've got to take inventory, account for all the games you *do* play. At some point you'll have to evaluate them, honestly appraise their utility for you. You'll probably find some of the games you play actually work against you. Then you'll need to analyze why you keep on playing the ones that don't have anything to do with the game at hand.

"I think a little objective soul-searching is good for all of us. And sometimes it's hard to do that alone. Most of us could use some help. You can't see all the moves you make —the compensating and poor timing—nor can you tell sometimes how your game affects everybody else. It helps to get with somebody who can. I'd recommend talking it over with one of your golf buddies, or maybe even your pro back home, someone who can be objective and honest with you. I guarantee you'll understand yourself and your game better.''

"That sounds like a lot of work," Frank says. "Where do we start?"

"With the accounting process," the Pro answers. "You make a list—just like an inventory—of all the games you play *other* than the game you need to play to get what you say you want. Then you evaluate how well those games on your list really serve your overall objective.

"Frank, you like a power game. You want to knock the cover off the ball on every shot. Getting more distance than everybody else gives you pleasure. But how does your pursuit of power and distance affect your score?

"Tim plays a cautious game because he wants to stay out of trouble. Larry experiments all the time. He likes to try different clubs and different shots. As much as he's played, he still doesn't have a real plan for playing the course.

"These are all games that don't have very much to do with your stated objective of scoring as well as you can. I'm just talking about golf, but you can do the same kind of accounting for all your executive games, too, if you really want to play better."

•

THE THIRD STEP TOWARD AWARENESS

The real work of awareness begins with making an accounting of our games and then conducting an honest appraisal of how well they serve us.

Accounting: Taking a Personal Inventory

We begin the accounting by facing up to a little-acknowledged fact: most of us *know* the games we play. For example, by now we not only have a pretty good idea of the games Frank, Tim, Fred, and Larry are playing, but we probably know which of these executives is most like *us.* Voices of pride may tell those of us like Frank that we don't need to do any accounting; voices of fear tell those of us like Tim or Fred that we dare not look too closely. These are the Meddler's utterances of bewareness that help us justify fight and flight.

The Franks among us will be tempted to look only at the public goals we aspire to reaching. We'll be addressing performance skills rather than our *personal competitiveness*, the rewards of influence rather than our *need for status and attention*, and personal achievement rather than our *need to feel superior*. In the process, however, as we focus on our pains of performance, we will continue to deny our real problem and the games we are really playing.

But if those of us like Frank are willing to look inward, we will discover that our real problem is human *relationships*. It is hard for Frank to trust either the competence or intentions of other people. He conveys his fundamental distrust in the way he relates to people, yet unless he is prepared to do *everything* himself, he is dependent on others for achieving his own performance goals.

In taking inventory, Frank might ask himself how he contributes to his own frustration. He might ask how his games of distrust affect other people's performance. He might ask how *he* would perform for someone who neither trusted him nor respected his competence. Frank might also ask himself how his performance on the golf course is affected by his compulsion to beat his fellow players. Is this not a problem of relationships, too?

The Tims among us will focus on the pains of relationships. Although we are committed to the love ethic, we are pained and seldom reassured by the amount of affection we *receive*. More often than not, we blame others for not appreciating all the concern we have for them. Not only will we divert ourselves by a preoccupation with our own good intentions, we will fail to see that our pains of relationship are really by-products of more fundamental problems of *performance*. We might better spend our time clarifying and taking inventory of our feelings about achievement and how well we have done our jobs.

In taking inventory, the Tims among us might ask ourselves what we do to avoid testing our competence—and learning to trust it. Are we a little too ready to pump up the self-esteem of those around us in the fervent hope they will do the same for us? If so, we still have work to do. We might ask ourselves in what ways we and our relationships suffer from our games of nonperformance. How would we feel toward people who not only fail to produce for us, but stifle our own attempts to feel productive?

The Freds among us deny the pain by trying to detach from problems—both those of performance and those of people. We, too, try to blame someone other than ourselves. But we don't want to live unnoticed and pass unremembered. Why else do we constantly call attention to ourselves? Because negative attention is better than no attention at all.

Those of us like Fred might ask ourselves what we should expect from life in return for what we've been willing to invest in it. We might ask what games we play to shield ourselves from the emotional investment that comes with *caring* about something. We might ask what we do to avoid the challenge of taking the initiative and creating meaning in our own lives. We may find that our pain reflects our lack of purpose.

Appraisal: Assessing the True Value of Our Favorite Games

As should be clear by now, we do not randomly choose the Private Games we play. They are set in motion and systematically monitored by the Meddler in each of us, by voices from the past. Most of the problems we encounter in our Public Games are due to our private needs to relive past experiences—perhaps so we can learn to deal with them adequately. We're repeatedly drawn into more current, but always similar, situations to which we always react the same.

Frank, for example, will always find his share of opportunities for confrontation and competition so he might once again force recognition of that personal adequacy he is so concerned about. Tim will gravitate toward other people worse off than he. Fred will continue to find ways to appear above it all so he can avoid the risk and pain associated with being neglected and overlooked once again.

But do such outcomes have value in terms of where we are trying to go? Do our games serve us well, or do they help us defeat ourselves? These are the questions the appraisal process is designed to bring to the surface.

Analysis: What Purpose Do Our Games Really Serve?

If we are committed to ridding ourselves of the distractions and constraints of an irrational Meddler, we must be willing to *analyze* the games we have inventoried and evaluated. When we cling to behaviors that cause us and others problems, it is because those behaviors are somehow important to us. Analysis is an attempt to identify and recognize *why*, by tracing the threads of experience that have intertwined to form the fabric of our lives.

One of the first questions analysis would have us ask ourselves is if the practices that get us in trouble might be traced to our *games of compensation*—ill-conceived attempts to compensate for shortcomings we're sure we have. A second query concerns whether or not *we are angry*—and if so, why? Is it because we're frustrated or because we're scared? Is it the people around us, ourselves, our jobs, or life itself that frustrates or scares us? Or might it be the prospect of disappointing those voices from our past that sets us on our current maladaptive and baffling course? Perhaps we are simply trying to divert attention from a shame we can't acknowledge.

And how do we *feel* about being angry? Those of us

like Frank are comfortable with pointing at the most convenient target and firing. People like Tim, on the other hand, are *afraid* of anger, so they keep it to themselves. The Freds among us neither enjoy nor fear anger as much as resent it. Getting angry signifies *caring* about something.

Analysis might also ask whether we are all ultimately playing the same game. Might we be indulging in a *game of comparison?* Do our own judgments of ourselves—nagging voices from the past—cause us to choose the games we play and how we play them? If those of us like Frank, for example, work to appear superior, is it really higher status —being more "special" than anyone else—that we crave? Do we try to achieve this not by raising our own level of accomplishment, but by disparaging or beating down the accomplishments and skills of the people around us?

The Tims among us may also wonder about our lowered standards for comparison. Are we drawn to those somehow less able than we are as uncommonly good candidates for our relationships? By comparison, do we feel better? Although we might also crave someone who is strong enough to take charge, someone we can depend on to make decisions and get the work done for us, doesn't comparison with these people often make us feel worse?

Analysis may help us understand where we are and why we may be bogged down. We may find that learning to play the game for its *own* sake—not for purposes of comparison—is the major strand of genuine awareness. Then we can consolidate our progress and gird ourselves for the future through the process of *admission*.

•

Admission: Owning Up to Our Private Purposes

LARRY GAZES OUT THE WINDOW. "You know," he says, "it really amazes me sometimes how people will work hard *not* to do better by themselves. The steps we've taken so far have all been solitary work. Boy, is that a setup for self-deception!"

The Pro nods. "That's why the next step is admission," he says. "Not only is the work so hard that most of us could use some help, a lot of people don't really understand it all until they've gone public with it. Sharing what you've learned with somebody else can not only help keep you honest, it can begin to make it *real* for you as well.

"But another thing the admission process does is help you recognize that the self-defeating game you've been playing may have been causing other people trouble, too. It can begin to open up relationships and let in some fresh air."

•

Private acknowledgment simply will not suffice if awareness is the goal. Kept private, the thoughts and feelings triggered by the work we must do will cry out for rationalization and overreaction. Those of us inclined to fight or take flight will soon find a means of displacing or explaining away the things we have learned. We will need clarity at this point. Other people, less personally involved and more objective, can provide that. They can help us focus the issue if we will trust them enough to confide in them.

What we need is a voice of reality—someone willing to challenge our perceptions and conclusions, someone who knows and cares about us enough to help us grow. Such a person may be hard to find or may even turn out to be the very person we would most like to hide from. Whatever the case, we must keep in mind that the short-term discomfort of honest admission can free us in the long term. Admission paves the way to release. It defuses the shame and sets the stage for granting both ourselves and others amnesty. Then we can lay aside the excess baggage from the past and get on with life.

•

"WE WASTE A LOT OF TIME and energy," says the Pro, "tormenting ourselves over old grievances. If we take a close look at our game, we will often find that a major distraction in our present play is the unfinished business from our past. Sadly, a lot of the 'finishing up' amounts to getting even. We can break such painful and energy-sapping ties to the past by allowing everyone—ourselves included—a fresh start.''

Amnesty: Giving Up Our Taste for Revenge

"It's one thing to work on forgiving yourself," says Tim, "but what if you really screwed up and took a lot of people with you? What do you do then?"

The Pro answers. "I think you examine your format. Does your game hold everybody accountable for their mistakes forever, or does it allow for fresh starts? You can decide which format you want to play."

•

Just as many of us still struggle with voices from the past, so too are many of us bogged down under the burden of past deeds. Our values and morality often are geared more to blame and retribution than they are to granting amnesty and renewal. When we apply the former, we condemn both ourselves and others to a life constrained to atoning or getting even; but when we choose the latter, we can free both ourselves and others to profit from mistakes, to try again and perhaps do better.

•

"How does format have anything to do with awareness?" says Frank. "You still get the score you shoot, don't you?"

"Sure," says the Pro, "but the format you play dictates the real significance of your score. A lot of people never get over a bad hole, and they make the rest of the game harder than it has to be.

"Let me give you an example. There are two basic formats in the game of golf, stroke play and match play. In stroke play, everything counts for the whole game. It's a cumulative format, and just one bad hole can wipe you out. In match play, you still give it your best and count every shot, but you play one hole at a time, and each hole is, in a manner of speaking, a new beginning.

"If you're playing stroke play and take a 15 on the third hole, you're out of contention. But if you're playing a match play format, all you've lost is the third hole. There's still hope—maybe even to win. You're free to think about doing better from the present hole on. If you do badly on enough holes, you'll be out of it for good. But I know people who, given the chance, will profit and play their hearts out for the rest of the game. I've seen some guys come back from the brink and go on to greatness."

Larry looks at the Pro. "Match play is a more forgiving format, right? Is forgiveness what you're talking about?"

"Not really," says the Pro. "Some people take forgiveness as *excusing* them for what they've done, as not having to be responsible for their own acts. But people are still accountable for what they do. No one can make them *not* accountable. But we can give up our *personal* need to punish or get even with them—to take revenge.

"There's an old Sicilian proverb that says, 'Revenge is a dish that must be eaten cold.' That means you must be patient, wait and nurse it—don't be in a hurry—so you can enjoy it that much more. But that takes a lot of energy. And it distracts us from enjoying the here-and-now. I think revenge is a dish that is best served only when you've lost your appetite for it.

"We don't have to forgive to be healthy, but we do have to turn loose our need to punish. That's what I mean by amnesty. If we grant amnesty to ourselves and one another so that it's the whole game—not just one or two holes—that really counts, we might be surprised at the freedom of performance we have unleashed."

THE ROAD TO AWARENESS

Review, Reconstruction, and Riddance

*To bring the hopeful out of the
wilderness, I have endeavored to show
that building one's best golf is basically
a matter of laying one little essential
brick of fact on top of another.*

Tommy Armour

"ONE OF THE THINGS some of my students find helpful," the Pro continues, "is to review the history of their games. It helps to get a perspective on what some of your favorite swing thoughts have been. I'll bet each of you has been taught, or picked up somewhere, at least one basic idea that you consciously apply to the way you swing the club to this very day."

Larry begins. "I concentrated for years on keeping my left arm straight. Finally I decided that consciously trying to do that can ruin a person's whole swing. It sure screwed me up!"

"The one that stuck with me was 'Keep your head still,'" Frank says. "You ever try to do that and make a powerful swing? You can *hurt* yourself!"

"Mine was 'Keep your head *down* and just swing your arms,' like a pendulum," says Tim. "A guy I play with told me that. That's where all my fat shots come from—or my slices. Take your pick."

"Everything you guys have said is a valid swing thought," the Pro says. "A lot of teachers see them over and over in good swings and build a model in their minds of what the swing should be like. But there's a lot of room for error in swing models. When you base learning and the golf swing on what you *see*, or *think* you see, happening with good players, you risk building a faulty model of the swing. Not only is what you think you see not really happening, but a lot of other stuff *is* going on that you *don't* see because you don't know to look for it.

"We've all got this urge to make sense of the whole thing. So we zero in on some move or principle and make it the cornerstone of our working model. And the irony is that when we study the swings of good players on slow-motion video, we find none of that stuff is true. The only time the left arm *has* to be straight is at address, during the downswing, and at impact. Studies show the head *does* move, two to six inches laterally, but it stays *behind* the ball. My point is this: If we're going to do any good, we may have to *reconstruct* our thinking and build a new swing model."

"It's the same with management," observes Larry. "For years, people said executives spent their time planning, directing, and controlling. Then a guy named Mintzberg followed them around and kept records on what they did. He discovered they hardly did any of that stuff. They spent most of their time dealing with people—in meetings or on the phone. The old models didn't prepare a lot of executives for how to work with people at all."

"That's what I mean," says the Pro. "If we're willing to reevaluate our favorite models of how to do things, sometimes we discover they hurt us more than they help us. When that happens, we have to be willing to build new ones that are more reliable and productive.

"It's always good to reflect on a round," the Pro says. "Sometimes you can learn more about your real game after a round than you can out on the course."

•

THE FOURTH STEP TOWARD AWARENESS

Review: Reflecting on Critical Experiences

The review process really begins early on. It probably starts during the appraisal stage and gathers momentum during the analysis and admission stages. But it is so critical to awareness that it deserves and requires its own focused attention. We are preparing ourselves for building a new model.

In the review process, our task is simply to lay out *what is*—choices, acts, and outcomes—and try to separate this from what we *believe or feel* to be so. If our review process is successful and productive, we will be struck by the silliness of some of our favorite ideas and conclusions. We may be surprised by a recognition of those persistent influences we've tried to deny for a long time. And we may simply discover the missing data that would help our present circumstances make sense.

Our emotions may be triggered during the process. If so, we should be prepared to accept them for what they are—as part of the fabric we are trying to review and understand. If we can do all this, we may find that here in the present we can gain control over the past by *reconstructing* our perspective of what has happened and what it means.

Reconstruction: Building a New Model

This process begins on a note of heresy. If experience is the best teacher, as we have all been taught, why don't we learn more from it? Although a good deal of conventional wisdom—and many of our Meddler's values—would have us believe experience is the key to knowing and understanding, few of our experiences are so compelling or so focused as to ensure the learning of a particular lesson. Experience is only the stimulus for learning.

Why, for instance, does learning, knowing, and understanding seem to occur *after* rather than *during* the experience? Why do people who appear to have identical experiences often end up learning entirely different, sometimes totally opposite, things?

"We do not learn from experience," says my favorite psychologist, George Kelly, "so much as we learn from our reconstructions of experience." This is the pivotal insight upon which the AWARE mode rests, and it is verifiable through, of all things, personal experience.

If we have an auto accident as we drive through a busy intersection, do we learn something about defensive driving *while* we are having the experience? Very likely it is only after the experience—as we recall all the events and assemble them into a mental model of the experience—that we feel we have learned something. The same is true of those past events that cause us pain and make us struggle in the present. What we have learned depends on the models we've built. Maybe we need to take them apart, brick by emotional brick, and examine them in the light of present events.

As we consider reconstruction, we might ask ourselves who has been in charge of our learning—our model building—so far in our lives. More often than not we will find the difficulty lies with our Meddlers rather than with the quality of our experience. Meddlers help us recall bits and pieces and build mental models based on bewareness. These models are faulty, and our learning is flawed. We make the same self-defeating mistakes and experience the same pains, over and over. That's how the game becomes unmanageable.

There is room for considerable error in the model-building phase of our learning. Meddlesome authority figures, like teaching pros, make errors of perception and interpretation. That is why *reconstruction* of our past experience is so important for understanding and appreciating ourselves.

We may or may not need the help of others in achieving such a reconstruction. But we will surely find that for a more realistic and adaptive model of learning and performance, we will have to eliminate the things that weigh us down and are counterproductive to our well-being. We must say good riddance to lessons learned from faulty models, feelings grounded in irrational assumptions, and practices based on false premises.

•

Riddance: Dropping False Assumptions and Excess Baggage

"IF YOU'RE ABLE TO BUILD a more reality-based model for yourself," the Pro says, "you may find there's no place for some of your favorite swing thoughts. You can grieve for them if you like, but you *must* let them go. In particular, you may find you have no need for a Meddler. Get rid of it."

•

It is when we are deciding what to keep and what to let go that the ultimate nature of our Private Game is determined. But if we are to master the Private Game, we must free ourselves of the burdens that voices from the past have told us we must bear. We must learn to trust our natural capacities and skills and not the Meddler's bewareness games that thrive on false connections with the past.

We must examine our maladaptive and irresponsible practices and question whether and to what extent they might be the result simply of faulty learning. We will find strengths upon which we can build, but other ideas and feelings—probably more embedded and deeply held—will stand the tests of neither logic, reality, nor productive self-interest. More often than not we find it is these that bind us to the past and keep our natural capacities mired in bewareness.

Cleansing ourselves of long-held and valued connections can be a difficult task. Our Meddlers will erect fear as a barrier. Success, however, rests on a simple and straightforward premise: *The past is important to our present and future well-being—and, therefore, worth recalling—only when it is a basis for learning a responsible lesson.* All else is excess baggage. If we are unwilling to rid ourselves of such messages, judgments, apprehensions, and fears, we will block our path to true awareness. But good riddance can free us to both see and entertain new possibilities. We call that *growth!*

THE ROAD TOWARD AWARENESS

Experimentation and Evaluation

It's not your perfect shots, but your good misses that help you score consistently well in golf.
Carl Lorhren

"YOU KNOW," LARRY SAYS, "it bothers me that there are so many different schools of thought on the golf swing. How are we supposed to know which approach is right or which teachers we can trust?"

"That's not as tough as it might seem," the Pro says. "Most qualified teachers pretty much stress the same basic things. They may differ on how you initiate the swing or how to distribute your weight, but by and large, good instructors teach the same fundamentals."

"It *is* like management theory," Tim says, chuckling. "But how do we know whom to believe?"

"The key to believing is personal experimentation," the Pro replies. "Be willing to try different things once you're satisfied they have merit. This may sound like a contradiction and an oversimplification, but you'd be surprised how many people rush wholeheartedly to embrace the latest fad or gimmick without trying it out first, and others won't try anything new—even when there's overwhelming evidence it'll help them.

"But if you're going to grow, you've got to be willing to experiment by using a systematic program of trying something that could improve your game. Now I'm *not* saying *change* what you're doing. I'm simply saying be willing to experiment for your own information.

"Good players experiment all the time. You guys all know that Jack Nicklaus won his sixth Masters not long ago. He attributes the win to a *new* putter and a *new* approach to the short game. Chi Chi Rodriguez was teaching Jack's son, Jackie, how to approach the short game. Jackie, in turn, taught it to his father. And Jack took it to the Masters. Now *that's* experimentation. And it makes my main point. You don't have to be bad off to want to get better. Good as he is, Nicklaus still wants to grow.

"That's what I recommend to you. If what you're trying *really works* for you and is *repeatable*, groove it. That's how you begin to take your awareness from the practice tee and put it to work on the course. And remember, sometimes we have to explore the 'wrong' way of doing something before we're ready to discover the 'right' way. That's what experimentation is all about."

•

THE FIFTH STEP TOWARD AWARENESS

Experimentation:
Trying the "Wrong" Way to Discover the "Right" Way

For our purposes of awareness, the Pro's words capture both the promise and difficulty inherent in the step of *experimentation*. To experiment—to willingly and purposely explore something we may have been taught is "wrong" in order to test the possibility of discovering a better way— is a Player's game of awareness. Our Meddler, of course, would have us beware. It will remind us of the risks involved in letting go and encourage us to continue as we have in the past. Very likely it has been the Meddler all along who has labeled our options "right" and "wrong" and, thereby, dissuaded us from trying new ways of thinking, feeling, and behaving.

Experimentation implies a willingness to learn and adapt. Rather than trying to fight or flee from the problems that test our competence—strategies that feel "right" to us —we can face and attempt to solve them. Experimentation guided by a better understanding of our games and their effects on ourselves and others is the safest available approach to problem solving. In the final analysis, however, we're simply looking for a better way, for a more adaptive and productive response for ourselves. Therefore, when we experiment we must give equal attention to evaluating the outcomes.

Evaluation: Testing for Utility and Reliability

Our criteria of evaluation are simple: utility and reliability. If our behaviors yield the effects we desire and serve our needs for competence and healthy self-esteem, we may conclude those practices are useful and will further our growth and development. If they yield essentially the same results time after time, we may judge them reliable. In fact, utility and reliability are the only two requirements that our experiments must satisfy for us to learn, renew, and grow. We are now playing the game with awareness.

Experimentation and evaluation are neutral experiences. In and of themselves, they are neither good nor bad. And, as the experimenters, none of us is either "right" or "wrong"; we do not succeed or fail in our experiments. We simply learn. There's an old story about Thomas Edison as he tried to find a workable filament for his electric light bulb. "How did it feel," he was asked, "to fail a thousand times before you got the right material?" Edison replied, "I didn't fail a thousand times. I learned about a thousand things that didn't work." Let it be the same with you as you experiment with new ways.

•

"IN THE FINAL ANALYSIS," the Pro says, "the whole process is a matter of determining what *works* for us. It's not really about 'right' or 'wrong' or what any of us *should* do. It's about what genuinely serves our needs for self-worth. All of us need to feel good about our games. That's the only true objective. What works for Frank may be different from what works for Tim or Larry or Fred, or for me. What works is a decision that each of us has to make for ourselves. And it is a decision that we *can* make once we have achieved awareness.''

•

A REVIEW OF THE STEPS TOWARD AWARENESS

If we choose to embark on the road to awareness, we will take some of the steps so easily, we may think we've bypassed them. Others will be so difficult that we'll feel the need to go back and start over. And we'll find some steps overlap, so that we seem to be doing two or more things at once. All of this is to be expected. However the process plays out, there are two things we must try to do for ourselves: be patient and be tolerant. No one is an expert at becoming aware.

In summary, the AWARE mode requires that
- **A** we take *aim* and identify where we are trying to go. We *acknowledge* the existence of those circumstances —both inner and outer—that cause us problems and *accept* responsibility for engaging and solving them.
- **W** we become *willing* to do the *work* required for problem solving. Our objective and our reward is *wholeness* of mind, body, and spirit.
- **A** we make an *accounting* of the games we play that either contribute to the problem or allow it to continue unsolved. We make an *appraisal* of the effectiveness of these games in moving us in the direction we wish to travel and *analyze* why we have chosen to play those that do not serve us and distort our aim. And we *admit* to ourselves and at least one other person the scope and purpose of the games we have been playing. And when we find that we have played a less

than flawless game, we grant ourselves and our fellow players *amnesty*.

- **R** we *review* the facts and threads of experience that have brought us to our present circumstances. We begin a *reconstruction* of past experience that is more consistent with reality and rational analysis. Then we are ready for *riddance,* for ridding ourselves of those misperceptions and false premises on which many of our most counterproductive games have been based.

- **E** armed with a new model of personal performance, we *experiment* with different ways of responding to demands. We risk doing the "wrong" things in order to discover what is "right" for us. We *evaluate* the reliability and utility of our efforts and our rationale for moving us in the direction we wish to go.

Then we can become true users of life.

NEW SWING THOUGHTS

Preparing for the Game Back Home

*In golf, as in life, it's the follow-through
that makes the difference.*
Anonymous

THE PRO LOOKS AT HIS WATCH. "Well, guys, it's just about time to close 'er down. I'm sorry about the weather, and I want to thank each of you for your patience. You could have just taken a rain check and come back later."

"I'm sort of glad it rained," says Larry. "I feel like I learned more just talking with you than I would have out on the course. You've helped me see some new connections, Pro."

"I'll second that," Tim adds. "I haven't liked everything I've heard, but at least I've got a handle on the work I need to do."

"I feel I got my money's worth," says Frank, "even if I didn't get in as much golf as I hoped. I'd like something more in the time we have left, though. I need some playing exercises or something to work on back home. What can I work on?"

"Frankly," says the Pro, "I'm reluctant to get very prescriptive with any of you. My goal is to encourage awareness. But let me think about it a minute."

"I've got an idea," Larry says. "You said experimentation is the key. So why don't you suggest some *experiments*

—rather than the prescriptions you don't like—that each of us can conduct back home? Can't you give each of us a program to experiment with that will produce an awareness of some new swing thoughts we can use in *all* our games?''

Letting Direction Determine Goals

''Sure,'' says the Pro. ''But first I need to reemphasize a couple of earlier points for the experiments to make sense.

''I'll start with my personal favorite thought. Watch Jack Nicklaus line up a shot. He goes through the same routine every time. He stands behind the ball and sites the line from his ball to his target. Then he walks around to take his setup and addresses the ball. He waggles the club, checks his alignment, and lets it fly.

''He's determining the direction he wants to go in,'' says the Pro. ''But he's not aiming at the long-range target. He picks a spot about three feet in front of his ball that is *on the line of his desired direction.* Then he aligns himself and aims his club face at this intermediate target. The use of an intermediate target is his key. It allows him always to establish his direction *first* and then to set intermediate goals that are always on that line.

''My thought for you guys is: *Proper direction is the most important thing you will ever have to decide. Keep all your intermediate targets—your daily goals—on that line and be faithful to the direction you've chosen.* If you'll just do that, I will guarantee you a good game.''

Responsibility, Rectitude, and Reality

''But how do you know,'' Larry says, ''when you've really decided on a *proper* direction? How can a person really be sure what's good or bad, healthy or unhealthy?''

''I have some thoughts on that subject, too,'' the Pro says. ''They're not original, but they sure influenced the way I play. I call the program I try to follow the 'Three R's of Good Judgment.'

"The best way to capitalize on whatever talents we have is to play *responsibly*. That's the first R. We must do what we can to feel good about our own games, but we can't do things that keep other people from doing what they can to have a good round, too. Responsible players respect both themselves and the rights of other people on the course.

"Further, our games must reflect a personal sense of *rectitude. We all need to believe in standards of right and wrong, a personal code.* If we want to play well, we must play according to some set of rules. Not just those specified in the rules book, but our personal codes as well. Good players play the ball as it lies. We don't claim a lower score than we actually achieved—or a higher one just to inflate our handicap. This R lets us evaluate ourselves.

"Responsibility and rectitude are important to me on their own merits. But, combined, they keep me in touch with *reality,* the third R. Another thing good players do is play realistically. Some people describe this quality as 'playing within yourself,' but I think it's staying based in *reality.*

"Good players nearly always choose the high percentage shot. They measure their capabilities against the difficulty of the shot. They look at what it will cost them if they fail and whether or not what they might gain is worth what it might cost. Most important, they have a long-range as well as a short-range view of things. They know if they keep plugging along their chosen path, things will even out.

"Even the good players aren't flawless. What sets them apart is that they are *always* working on their games. And you guys can do that, too. For example, as executives you might check daily on the direction you've chosen by asking yourselves:

- Do my actions serve my own needs for self-worth without depriving others of their similar needs? If so, *you are responsible.*
- Are my actions consistent with my own sense of right and wrong? If so, *you are ethical.*
- Do my expectations jibe with my capabilities and the demands of the situation, and are my short-term actions in line with my long-term goals? Is the gain worth the cost? If so, *you are realistic.*

"Committing yourself to a responsible, ethical, and realistic direction will allow you to go a long way."

The three executives sit quietly. Then Frank says, "I need a more personal plan. You know, a game plan specifically for *me* to work on back home *now.*"

The Pro smiles. "I've got some ideas for each of you. But you'll have to decide if they make sense to you and what you're willing to do with them when you get home."

When Strength Is Weakness

The Pro continues. "Frank, when you have bets riding on the game, I want you to play with only four clubs. You can use your four-iron, six-iron, pitching wedge, and putter. That's all. For a month."

Frank is aghast. "You've got to be kidding! The guys I play with are a bunch of cannibals. They would make their own grandmothers walk and carry their bags if they thought it could help them win. If I do that—no driver, no long irons—you've taken away my *power.* I'll be a laughingstock."

The Pro nods his understanding. "I'll tell you something I've observed this week, Frank," he says. "Your power doesn't do you any good. You spend all your energy dealing with the problems that your reliance on power creates. If you want to play up to your potential—and I'm convinced you do—you're going to have to consider laying the power aside. And don't seduce yourself by compensating. I want you to throttle back. Don't try to hit the six-iron harder; drop back to an easy four. Learn the real essence of the game.

"You see, Frank, *what you consider your greatest strength may be the greatest weakness in your game.* What I'm really taking away is your *crutch.* I want you to work toward playing a *whole* game."

Frank is quiet for a moment. Then he says, "I don't have to bet all the time, right?"

"I *want* you to bet," the Pro says. "I don't think you'll take it seriously or stick with it if you don't. I want you to feel what it's like when the possibility of losing and looking foolish is part of the game. And after every round, I want you to call me and tell me your score."

"Only for a month, though," Frank says. "And I'm telling everybody why I'm doing it."

"That's good by me," the Pro says, "but after you see what happens, you may not want to give away the key to your success."

When Fear Is Opportunity

The Pro directs his attention to Tim. "Now, Tim, what are you looking for?"

"Well, I was hoping you'd recommend some new clubs for me. New clubs, you know, to sort of compensate for my swing?"

"How many sets of clubs do you have now?"

Tim's answer is barely audible. "Four," he says.

"I don't deny that equipment can be important," the Pro says. "But sometimes it's just something else to depend on. If you can get your game straightened out, Tim, you can play with anything."

"What do you want me to do, Pro, play with only four clubs, like Frank?"

"No, I want you to play with every club in your bag. Especially your *driver!* No more safe four-wood shots off the tee. And get reckless; take no more than twenty seconds a shot. And I want you to swing from your heels on every shot but those around the greens.

"You see, Tim, *the thing you fear the most may be the very opportunities you need to play really well and enjoy the game to its fullest.*

"I want you to learn what it's like to play without being afraid you might look foolish. There are some definite risks involved. Maybe not just the ones you've thought of. But the people I've known who decided to get really good at something invariably started off from the premise that the potential rewards outweighed the potential risks. I guess that's what you've got to consider where your own game is concerned."

PARTNERSHIP: LEARNING TO BE DEPENDENT AND SELF-RELIANT AT THE SAME TIME

"Now," says the Pro, "the fun begins. I'm signing both you guys up for the Academy's Scotch Twosome Tournament. It's a two-person team format where you alternate shots, sort of like they do at the Ryder Cup. You both hit tee shots, but Tim goes to Frank's ball and plays it, then Frank goes to Tim's ball and hits it, and so on until you get to the green. Then you alternate putts until one of you holes out."

"We have a tournament like that at our club every year for husband-wife teams," Tim says forlornly. "We call it the Divorce Open."

The Pro grins. "You're right. It can sure test a relationship and cause lots of arguments. But I want both you and Frank to see what it's like to have to depend on each other and to be accountable to each other at the same time. It's a great format for learning not only how somebody else plays the game, but something about yourself as a team player. And you may discover the true value of partnership and that it's okay for each of you to be dependent and self-reliant at the same time, as long as you move in the same direction.

"There will be times, Tim, that Frank will be in trouble and have to lean on you. And you'll come through. The same with Frank. I want both of you to learn that when you need help, the other is strong enough to depend on. That's the beauty of partnership. It takes self-reliant people. But when *both* of you are strong, there's no telling what you can accomplish together."

STAYING CONNECTED: THE LIFELINE

After a long silence, Larry shifts on his chair. "You know," he says, "I can't help but wonder, Pro, what you would be saying to Fred if he had stayed with us."

"I'd extend him the same invitation I'd like to extend to you, Larry."

"You'd recommend the same thing to Fred that you'd recommend to *me? You're serious?*"

"You two guys are a lot alike in some ways. You both have an unusually good understanding of what it takes to play a decent game, and you both stop short of your potential. Fred leaves his best game on the practice tee. He isolates himself. But so do you, Larry, without knowing it. I get the feeling that it's strictly a private affair for you. It's *your* game and *your* satisfaction. And I can understand that, but I worry that your talent might isolate you a little bit if you don't watch it. Most people *struggle* with the game. I don't want you to forget how it feels to struggle.

"Sometimes you say things that people aren't ready to hear. Not out of malevolence or anything like that. It's just that sometimes, because the game is easier for you, you forget how hard it can be for other people. This game is seductive. The better you get at it, the easier it seems to be —and the harder it becomes to understand why other players are having the problems they do."

"Are you talking about sensitivity, Pro," asks Larry, "like they do in management seminars?"

"Not really," the Pro says. "I think *humility* is a big part of what I'm talking about. Maybe *compassion*. Maybe *tolerance*. But mostly *empathy*. We work on getting in touch with our feelings, but sometimes our own feelings can get in the way. It's not enough just to understand how we feel about our own games; sometimes we need to be aware that other people have legitimate feelings, too. We need to respect the way they feel, whether we agree or not. It's a sign of our maturity.

"There are a lot of people in my business who don't really *care* how their students feel about their games. I can't do that. I think if I ever stopped caring about your swing, Larry, I'd lose sight of the Player in you. I wouldn't care about your Player. And that would be the first step in losing sight of the Player in myself—of caring about myself as well. I want to stay involved in the struggle because it keeps me connected."

"So what's the solution?" says Larry.

"Okay," says the Pro, "two thoughts for you, Larry. First, *all of us are self-centered, but none of us is truly self-sufficient.* And second, that means to me that *all the talent in the world is wasted if it's not connected to something vital.* Sometimes we forget to stay involved in the game because we get self-centered and things come too easily. That's when the spirit starts to die. The more content Fred is just to practice, and the better you get at playing for your own enjoyment, the more disconnected each of you is going to be—unless you take the initiative and reach out to other players.

"You've both got a lot to offer somebody who's struggling. I don't want you to lose sight of the Player in other people because you'll lose sight of the Player in yourself. So for a start, I'm inviting both of you to assist me in our Big Brothers and Sisters Junior Golf Program. I'm calling Fred tonight. I'll tell you one thing: you and Fred will get connected. Kids don't let you leave your game on the practice tee *or* on the course! You'd better be prepared to bring it with you."

The four men hear the horn of a taxi driving up in front of the clubhouse.

"Okay, guys," the Pro says. "I guess we'd better close it down. There's your taxi. Thanks for coming. This one has been special for me. I've learned a lot. I hope you'll stay in touch and let me know how you're doing."

Tim says, "Just like that? Is that all? Don't you have any last-minute words for us, Pro?"

"Yes, I do," the Pro says quietly. "I thought of it when I saw the taxi pull up. On the road from Prestwick Airport to St. Andrews—you know, in Scotland, where the game began—there's a sign that says 'A Little Care Gets You There.' That applies to you guys. Just *care*. Make a real commitment to the game, and I think you'll get where you're trying to go."

THE ONLY-NESS OF IT ALL

Productivity Begins with Me

*Success in this game depends less on
strength of body than on strength of
mind and character—on qualities such
as determination, dedication, and plain
old hard work—the same qualities that
bring success in the workplace.*
Arnold Palmer

As THE TAXI MAKES ITS WAY toward the airport, Larry says,
"You know, guys, I feel like Hale Irwin."

Tim grins. "You mean you learned enough this week
to win three U.S. Opens?"

"Not by a long shot," Larry says. "But somebody asked
Hale Irwin one time what made golf so challenging. And
he said, 'It's the only-ness of it all. It's knowing that I'm
the only one who can play my game.' That's the way I feel
right now."

"Yeah, I know what you mean," says Frank. "Some
caddie can advise and warn all he wants to, but I'm the
one who has to swing the club."

"That's my point," says Larry. "The caddie is a resource. He's like an expert, an adviser. But he's alone, too.
He's got his job to do and I've got mine. It's only when we
put both jobs together that we get the really good score.
That's where being a good executive comes in. In my
game, I'm the one who's got to start the partnership. That's
where the real only-ness lies. And it's the same back home.
I think this whole week has been about learning to accept
and make the most of the only-ness of it all—on the
course, at the office, even at home."

•

Only-ness evokes all our ancient fears—of separation and abandonment, of trading the comforts of dependence for responsibility and self-reliance, of growing up. And these fears compete with our desire for productivity. But those of us who are yet to know the Player within can have no sense of our own capacity for producing what we need to play the game well. Moreover, if we don't have a sense of *our own* productivity, it is most unlikely we will have any sense of *others'* productive potential. And if we don't have a sense of their potential, it's even more unlikely that any of us will use our executive authority to supply what people need to be productive.

We are faced with the executive paradox that most characterizes today's authority relationships and flawed leadership practices: the productivity of those we lead is limited by the degree to which we, as executives, perceive them as competent and productive people. And since our perceptions and expectations of others are rooted in our own sense of adequacy and self-esteem, productivity begins not with the people we are accountable for, but with each of us in an executive position of authority. That's the only-ness of being an executive that we must learn to accept and come to terms with effectively. Otherwise we will stay trapped. To get out, each of us must face up: Productivity begins with *me!*

THE COMPETENCE TRAP
WILL WE ACCEPT THE CHALLENGE—OR DENY
THE PROBLEM?

Accepting the only-ness of executive responsibility—learning to embrace self-reliance rather than fighting or fleeing its demands—is the way out of the trap. Too many executives have failed to come to terms with the only-ness of the game. Too many of us have become inclined to a

self-serving displacement of blame or a plea of helplessness.

   Why? What is our problem with only-ness? Does it lie
with our Public Games? As executives, do we simply make
poor decisions, exercise too much or too little control, provide poor direction, and fail to coordinate people and proj-
ects effectively? Is it that we do not know what we need to
do? I think not. Our Public Games are but outer symptoms
of what's going on in our Private Games, between personal
potential and self-interference, between Player and Meddler. We can accept only-ness and achieve executive
awareness only when we allow the Player to win. Mismanaged in the past to such an extent that today we doubt our
own productive potential, will we stay in the competence
trap and dig it even deeper for everybody—or will we commit ourselves to releasing and nourishing all the potential,
our own and others', and escape the trap once and for all?

●

AS THE TAXI CONTINUES, our three executives reflect on their
week's experience.

   "You know," says Frank, "this may be the most productive experience I've ever had."

   "What?" Larry exclaims. "You didn't agree with anything the Pro said. How was it productive?"

   "Well," says Frank, "I've decided the whole game boils
down to managing the sand trap."

   "The sand trap?" Tim says.

   "I figure," Frank says, "that I lose at least five strokes
in an average round because of sand traps. Take off those
five strokes and I'm a pretty good golfer. And it dawned on
me that I don't usually get in a trap unless I'm trying to
force something, trying a shot that's beyond my capability
or getting cute with my approach shot. So the first thing
I've got to do is be more realistic about myself and my
game and try to avoid the traps by playing within my capabilities.

"But the main thing is to get out of a trap in as few shots as possible. I completely lose my poise in a trap, take three shots most of the time, and if I do get out the first time, I blade the ball and knock it clear over the green into another trap. Not after this week.

"I finally heard the Pro when he said, 'All you have to do is swing naturally and the club will do the rest.' I tried to do what he said and I learned to *trust* my sand wedge. I was disregarding the capability that is literally built in the club and trying to *help* it do its job. I learned you've got to trust the tools of the game."

"That sounds almost philosophic, Frank," Larry says quietly.

"But, more important, I think I do the same thing with people," Frank says. "I ignore their built-in capacities and try to force things, make them do their jobs the way I want. I've spent most of my life trying to get out of the executive traps I've put myself in. Maybe I can solve that, too, by trusting the potential at my disposal."

•

Let's examine the trap we put ourselves in by assuming, for the moment, that we are *accurate* in our perceptions that people are, in fact, not adequate to their tasks. Now the executives and managers among us will either have to give up on task accomplishment altogether or figure out ways of meeting lowered standards of production and quality geared to inferior workers. Some of us have reacted in both ways, but most of us have attempted to "prevent something bad by forcing something good."

We want to "redesign" and "help" the tools of the game. We talk about "motivating" people and creating motivation where there isn't any; providing proper "incentives" for them, enticing people to do better what we don't really believe they can do in the first place; and "leading" them, providing vision and a model of exemplary practices for people whom we believe are too dull to see beyond today and want only to be told what to do and when to do it. So we put ourselves in a real double bind. The competence trap founded in our own doubts about the competence of others presents us with problems none of us is competent to solve. As a result, we will be found wanting as executives. We may have chance moments of success, but we will fail over the long haul.

PRODUCTIVITY: A MATTER OF DEFINITION

An alternative is to trust the natural performer in ourselves and others. If, as executives, we have a genuine sense of our own competence and productivity, it will be easy for us to appreciate the potential of those we manage. But to achieve such awareness, many of us must first redefine ourselves. Remember, if we can't manage our own games we can't play in the tournament. Once again, the trap may be of our own making.

Traps of Self-Definition

Tim defines himself as a guy who must turn his game over to a "magic" nine-iron. He's an executive without self-confidence. Frank is busy defining himself as someone who can *will* his putts into the hole—except on poorly maintained greens—and strives for perfection because to do less is to lose respect. He's an executive who merely *appears* to be self-confident. Both have the capacity for productive play. But both rely on magical thinking. Their belief in a "personal magic" obscures their true competence; they both lack a conscious awareness of that human capacity in *themselves* to get things done.

If Frank and Tim can succeed in becoming more aware, they will come to appreciate their own potential and capabilities for productive action. They will define their own capabilities differently, and their approach to executive leadership will likely change. So will their organizations. Productive executives create productive organizations.

Developing Self-Definition

Not all of us are as fortunate as Frank and Tim. We don't have a pro to guide us. We may have to pursue awareness and redefinition on our own. How we define ourselves is especially critical if we are executives, because self-definition is a Private Game that strongly influences our Public Game. We push for our own personal Scratch Ideals and evaluate situations and people according to our views of ourselves. We leave our marks on the organizations we serve, and our qualities and traits affect our transactions with those we manage. But if we are to lead, we are obliged to understand how we have defined ourselves *before* we impose our definitions on others.

Some of Us Wait for the Gifts to Arrive

For example, we might wonder why some of us, like Tim, choose the role of Comforter. Is it because, defining ourselves as unproductive, we have split the world into good and bad, productive and unproductive, and concluded further that "the source of all good," as psychologists have called it, lies beyond our own productive capabilities? If so, we come to feel the only way to get what we want or need is to *receive* it from some outside source. We look for someone else to give us directions or make decisions rather than making even the smallest personal effort. So dependent on Meddlers in the past that we never came to know the self-reliant Player in ourselves, we now look for Meddlers in the present upon whom we can depend for what we need.

We play all our games the same. We procrastinate, observe rather than get involved, and wait passively for someone to tell us what to do. We comply to avoid appearing ungrateful or demanding. We do produce something from time to time, but we take little pleasure from our accomplishments. We do only those things that are easy for us rather than the things others need or want. Mainly we wait to be prodded, to receive the energy necessary from an outside source. In short, we have traded responsibility and self-reliance for reassurance and dependency. With such an unproductive orientation to life, those of us like Tim might ask ourselves, "What kind of executive am I? Do the people I manage have a sense of their own productivity?"

Some of Us Pillage and Plunder

Then there are those of us like Frank. We can't admit it, but we also define ourselves as unproductive. We still believe the things we want—respect, recognition, status—depend on others, events sought outside ourselves, and must be won by outstanding performance or taken by force or cunning. We work, but our lack of confidence in our own adequacy is revealed in our compulsive need to convince others of our productivity. We forget that truly productive people are content to let their products speak for them. We must *take* to enjoy. If things are given—if we don't have to win or earn or take them—we mistrust the giver and wonder if we are being set up for exploitation.

Fearful of being exploited and made to look bad, we become convinced that we cannot concern ourselves with hurting people's feelings, because the weak and dependent don't understand us anyway. Those who are strong and dependable, able to follow orders and earn their keep, will understand how things work. They will appreciate our efforts and show their loyalty by producing what we need. Too bad there are so few.

Given such an unproductive orientation, the salient questions for us are, again, "What kind of executive am I? What kind of self-definition do I allow others, productive or unproductive? How does it *feel* to work for me?"

Some of Us Are Content to Count Beans and Arrange Shelves

The Tims and Franks among us are quite caught up in how we play the Public Game. Those of us like Fred, on the other hand, have little faith we will get any reward from the outside. This renders the Public Game meaningless and the Private Game irrelevant. We find our satisfactions in predictability and the security of hoarding and saving what we already have. We seek to build a protective wall around ourselves so that we can keep all we possess —what, at some time, has been given to us or left for us to claim.

We are unwilling to engage in productive thinking of our own. Workplaces are hiding places in which we can spend our time in pedantic orderliness, arranging our things, thoughts, time, and feelings in sterile and rigid patterns. There is reason to believe among us Freds that we are where we are as a last resort, a final refuge. We can seek out such a place in our teens or after forty years on the job. It is a self-definition based in neglect, dashed expectations, and unanswered prayers.

Somewhere along the way, the Meddlers in our lives neglected us and we were forced to hope that maybe personal effort or unique gifts alone would save us. But unconfirmed and alienated, we were not prepared for the unfairness of chance and bad bounces. Already victims of poor management, we decided the pains of the game were more than we could handle. So we gave up on Meddler and Player and the game itself. Not surprisingly, we are angry a good deal of the time. We resent those who pose tests of our competence, those who have achieved what we wanted to achieve, and we are contemptuous of ourselves for reacting to such tests as we do.

Our problem is we tried to *think* our way through the game at the expense of our feelings. Now, bitter and preoccupied with the unfairness of life, we engage in formulaic pursuits in an effort to survive. Executives like Fred might ask what sense of collective productivity and its rewards they promote. Where is the sense of purpose, the means to joy?

Some of Us Make Deals with Others' Products

Frank, Tim, and Fred are "primitive" types, almost arrested in their original reactive states. Many executives, equally lacking in any sense of personal productivity, have learned to be less obvious and, perhaps, more socially acceptable. No more productive than the Franks and Tims and Freds at their core, they have honed their social skills so that they can "sell themselves" and make deals on behalf of the productive people they know.

Executives like these not only make deals concerning goods and services, they also trade with lives. They have learned to view both people and products—including themselves—as commodities, all for sale to the highest bidder. Life, they have concluded, is a process of exchanging goods. Why not become a master of exchange? Instead of working at becoming personally productive, why not manage the exchange process to get what they cannot produce for themselves?

The questions for executives who define themselves as deal makers might be: What happens when there are so many deal makers that nothing is being produced? What will we trade then?

UNPRODUCTIVE ORGANIZATIONS: AN EXECUTIVE CONSPIRACY OF NONPERFORMANCE

If those of us like Tim and Frank and Fred are not satisfied with our answers to the executive questions posed so far—and, frankly, I hope we are not—we might change the answers by redefining our productive orientations. Before we can do any of this, however, we will have to examine the organizations—the workplaces and primary relationships—we have assembled. We may find that we have designed them to keep us just as we are—to keep our denial and dependence intact. We may find that, as executives, we have put ourselves and everyone else at risk.

Let's examine, for a moment, how executives try—perhaps unwittingly—to perpetuate their own preferred playing strategies by selecting the kinds of people with whom they are willing to play or work. Let's look at the kinds of relationships they prefer. And let's see how unproductive executives build unproductive organizations.

Although most of us have pretty clear ideas about the kinds of people we prefer to be around, we may not have given a lot of thought to *why*. Many executives look for people who seem compatible with the way things are done. Some of us look for people who share our orientation and values. Others look for people who complement our own characteristics and inclinations. All are logical and productive choices for those of us with self-confidence and a sense of our own competence. But for those of us without it, there is the real danger that we may surround ourselves with people whose characteristics serve more to magnify our inadequacies than to reflect our strengths. We may choose people to *compensate* for the games we play.

For example, whom might Frank choose to work for him: Larry, Fred, or Tim? Those of us like Frank have shown a definite preference for Fred-like associates. We like someone who will simply follow our orders, go by the procedures manual, make few demands, and stay out of trouble. They quietly allow us to stay as we are because they want to stay as they are, too. But sometimes Franks are attracted to Tim-like associates because they are so eager to please and so exploitable. Sooner or later, however, we become disenchanted with their nonperformance. Those of us like Frank create dependent, conventional, and uncreative places to work.

Tim's first choice is Frank. He needs someone strong, decisive, and ambitious upon whom he can lean and look to for what he needs. It does not bother him that Frank might take his authority and run with it; Tim doesn't want it anyway. But at some point—after he has had enough abuse and known enough indifference—Tim may decide to retreat to the safety of a relationship with Fred. At least he will have someone to protect and care for, a person with whom he can share passivity. Passivity is the hallmark of all Tim's organizations.

And Fred? He is equally attracted to and bothered by Frank and Tim. On the one hand, he will take comfort in Frank's commitment to production. On the other hand, Frank is a little aggressive for Fred's tastes. Fred likes the undemanding cooperativeness of Tim, but he recognizes there will be problems of nonperformance. So Fred prefers not to select anyone at all.

It is noteworthy that although productivity is our goal, many of us overlook or bypass Larry when we form our relationships. We are faced with another paradox: the Larrys among us are, more often than not, seen as trouble-makers. They challenge us to be competent and produc-tive. Frank looks at Larry and sees a competitor. He is also bothered by Larry's almost Tim-like caring. Who would want to lose to a guy like that? As for Tim, he can see how Larry's sense of his own productivity might well serve his goals and meet his needs of dependence. But there is also a nagging apprehension that Larry won't be content to leave Tim as he is, so he feels pressured by Larry and by the example he sets. For Fred, Larry is the embodiment of evil. He will not abide by rules without challenging their logic or utility. He questions constantly whether things might be done better if they were done differently. He is never content to leave well enough alone. He may be *nuts!*

And Larry, whom would he select? Larry wants only to realize his own potential for productivity and simply seeks a partner who wants the same thing. He is willing to work with Frank or Tim or Fred as long as they are willing to work with him. Larry tries to avoid the competence trap altogether. Should he find himself in one, however, he has a pretty good idea how to get out. Productivity and creative problem solving are hallmarks of Larry's organizations.

With the exception of Larry's position, the picture that emerges is one of counterproductive alliances formed around a premise that none of us is truly productive. We form relationships with other people whom we feel will not challenge our own inadequacies. The executive game is played with people, and—unlike a club or ball—people think and feel. Imagine clubs or balls with Private Games of their own. Then the relationship between player and equipment becomes as important as the separate attributes of each. The equation has too many unknowns that must become known before the problem of performance can be solved. That's how the executive game works. And that's why becoming more aware is so important.

A PRODUCTIVE ALTERNATIVE

Tim or Frank or Fred do not play the game the way they do because they are incapable of producing, but because they operate from unproductive outlooks and have adopted executive orientations to compensate for what they lack. If we become aware of how our basic orientation was formed, however, it can *change.* The possibility of development and progress and growth, and the reality of personal choice, is really what the game is all about. Regardless of a mismanaged past, we can choose to play today's game more productively.

All of us have already had experience with the process of change. None of us is the same person who started grammar school, or worked at a first job, or married, or had the first baby. Each of us changes constantly. And regardless of what some Meddler may have led us to believe, each of us can be more productive. We can redefine ourselves in terms of the person we want to be.

•

"Larry, I've got to ask you something," Frank says. "Your game was already in pretty good shape when you came to the Academy. Do you feel you got your money's worth, or was it all something you already knew?"

"Oh, it was worth it," Larry says. "The Pro showed me some finesse shots around the green that I'm going to make some money with. But the real thing I got was a *concept*, sort of a guiding premise. I *know* there's a part of me that can play any game I ever have to play if I try to understand where I am, how I got here, and where I want to go. I feel like I've put a lot of pieces together into just one strong piece.

"When I look back at myself, I see a whole crowd of different people. When I was a kid, I was like Tim. I really wanted to be one of the gang. I worked *hard* at not offending them. I learned to tell jokes; I'd share my allowance; I'd help them with their homework. But I resented the hell out of them.

"As I got older, I kind of went into a shell like Fred. By the time I went away to college I only had one or two friends that I really cared about. But then I made a conscious decision that I was going to be different. I didn't know how, but I damned sure wasn't going to suck up to anybody or be pushed around anymore.

"Next, for some reason, I got involved in campus politics and found out that I was a real wheeler-dealer. My self-confidence soared—never enough to run for office, but I was pretty sure I could get anybody else elected. Boy, was I full of myself. Everything and everybody was just a commodity to be sold. I went from dumb-ass to wise-ass."

"Then what?" Frank asks.

"Then," Larry says, grinning, "I became a horse's ass like you, Frank. I went in the army and started giving orders, and taking names. I thought that's what leadership was all about—until I got out and started working around people who didn't have to be *afraid* of me."

•

Larry's experience illustrates three important elements of human development that are common to us all. First, throughout a natural process of simple maturation and changing circumstances, Larry was able to redefine himself, to adapt. Second, he showed that important changes can be wrought by conscious choice. Each of us has known many endings and many beginnings, but few of us have chosen to capitalize on the transitions. Some of us, unaware, fail to recognize the opportunities for growth presented to us. But we have exercised choice. A choice not to go further is a choice nevertheless.

The third feature of Larry's experiences is that little by little he became aware of the different aspects of himself among which he could choose. None of us is a *pure* type, limited to one way of behaving, feeling, thinking, and responding to tests of competence. Each of us is a mix of Meddler and Player. It is up to us to decide which will win the game in our head. We can decide, out of all the influences within us, whom we want to become. If we decide wisely, and go to work on ourselves, our aptitudes, practices, knowledge, capabilities, and potentials will complement one another. We will achieve a harmony between our Private Games and our Public Games. And we will become whole.

We might all examine our *total* approach to the games we play. We might ask ourselves, as Larry apparently has, what utility a particular mix has for us. If the answer triggers a desire for change, we might take comfort in the fact that we have changed before and can change again.

•

"I won't bore you guys with my résumé," Larry continues. "Let's just say I've learned to be a pretty fair executive—and play a pretty fair game of golf. But I've known for some time that some of the methods I've tried just didn't work quite the way they were supposed to. I was getting stuck, but sooner or later I would surprise myself or other people would surprise me with new capabilities that would pop up irrespective of what we thought we were doing. I began—intuitively, I guess—to address myself to the unexpected. It was like 'Here's the problem. Surprise me! Surprise yourselves!' But I didn't understand what was happening.

"Now I think I understand. I was discovering the Player in me and in the people I manage. The Player is responsible for all the surprises. He's a lot more capable than we give him credit for. I think, with some work, I can orient myself to freeing up the Player in all my games. I can minimize all the interferences that keep that potential from showing up. That's what I learned this week."

"What makes you think you can do that?" Frank asks.

"You do, Frank," Larry replies. "And Tim does and I do. I can see real Players all around me. I mean, that two-iron you hit, Frank, and the nine-iron you hit, Tim, couldn't have been hit any better. Both balls went in the lake, but that was poor judgment, not poor execution or lack of ability.

"I'm talking about *potential*. One of the things the Pro helped me realize is that there aren't very many flukes on the golf course. The potential we see from time to time is the Player in us trying to get out. But if we explain away the tangible evidence of our own potential, we'll keep on getting in our own way. It's the same with the people we work with."

"You're saying everybody's got potential just waiting to be released?" Frank asks.

"Exactly," Larry says.

Frank laughs. "What about at work? I know guys who've made a career of laziness, people who couldn't make a decision if their lives depended on it. Where's the potential? Where are all the Players?"

"As the Pro said, it's a matter of definition," Larry replies. "What we *see* happening isn't really what's going on. I don't know any more than you've told me about how you operate, Frank. But I do know self-interference isn't the only thing that detracts from expressing potential. Outside interference will, too. We have to deal with self-interference *plus* whatever interference the people in authority, all the Meddlers, put on us. It's a wonder we ever get anything accomplished. I think you're a Meddler, Frank!"

Tim speaks up. "I'm afraid I agree with Frank," he says. "I don't see much evidence of the Player in people. I've got people who are scared to death of making a mistake, no matter how much I praise or encourage them. Don't get me wrong. I don't mind people leaning on me. What I don't like is being the guy in charge and having to push to get things done. I'll be honest with you, I don't think anybody, myself included, would really work if they didn't have to. I just try to make it as bearable as I can for everybody. I guess I believe the real Player wants to be somewhere else."

Larry looks at Tim intently. "If that's the truth, then you're playing the wrong game—or playing the right game the wrong way. We get a lot more than money out of work. My work connects me to the world around me. And it feels good when I do something well. Like the feeling you had, Tim, when you got that birdie Wednesday on the hardest-rated hole on the course. There's a Player in every one of us who wants to feel like that all the time."

•

Like a lot of us, Frank and Tim seem to have trouble with transitions. They're not yet sure they want to transfer what they learned about themselves on the golf course to their roles as executives. Yet without awareness and a faith in the natural performer in both ourselves or others, we will not allow excellence because we do not understand our own executive role of interference in the performance equation. Frank and Tim perhaps are afraid to turn loose, to let go of what they have that, ironically, also holds them and everyone else back.

•

"I'VE GOT SOME WORK TO DO," says Larry. "I need what the Pro calls an 'integrating premise,' to pull things together in my own mind and give me a sense of direction. If there is a part of each of us that *wants* to be productive, then that's the part I want to play to. I want to learn how to *play to the Player*.

"That will take some work on my part because—especially as an executive—I've got to learn more about Players, how they operate and feel and what they respond to. But can you imagine what things would be like if we could release that kind of talent and energy!"

•

Implicit in Larry's comments are positive visions of human potential, faith in his own and in other people's capabilities, and a recognition and acceptance of the role they play in true productivity. If we can learn to listen to the Player in ourselves, we will discover the Player in others. We will begin to understand human relationships better and thus be able to manage them better. We will learn that interdependence, not independence or dependence, is the developmental goal of productive people. We will discover that a desire for personal growth and expansion, not submission to the will of others or submitting others to our will, is the real stimulant to productive activity. And we will learn that labor and care, respect and knowledge, and concern for continuing growth are the foundations of the authority and influence of those who function as truly *productive executives*.

THE PRODUCTIVE EXECUTIVE: LEARNING TO
PLAY TO THE PLAYER

If those of us in authority really *believe* there is a Player in everyone, we will want to orient ourselves to its release. But how might we proceed? It is one of the ironies of the executive game that much more attention has been given to troubleshooting and problem solving—handling the symptoms of illness—than to promoting health. That is why the first problem of leadership many of us have encountered is one simply of not knowing what to do.

But there are data about what productive executives do; they show that as we learn to play to the Players, we will achieve more, personally and organizationally, than most of our unproductive meddlesome colleagues.

Productivity and Personal Achievement

At 8:14 A.M. one morning a few years back, Jane Pauley of NBC's "Today" show had this to say to her television audience about achievement:

"And here's a timely piece of news for Monday morning. Nice guys finish first. You won't find any of that in any of your taking-care-of-*numero-uno* books where success is how big the office, how many buttons on your phone, how long the lunch hour, how wide the stripes on the tie. Nice guys finish first. It's that simple."

Pauley told of a firm in Texas that had gone to the trouble to find out what *does* succeed. It studied over sixteen thousand executives, from some five hundred different organizations, and, as Pauley continued:

"Here's what they found. High achievers were as concerned for their subordinates' job satisfaction as for their own. They were open, candid, and welcomed subordinates into the decision-making process.

"Merely moderate achievers were the status hounds collecting symbols of success for their hungry egos, huddling with higher-ups and shutting out subordinates. Low achievers didn't trust the underlings, didn't talk to them, and feared always for their jobs. Now, if there's any advice to be had here, it's put away your how-to books and find yourself a real nice boss. High achievers breed other high achievers."

Since the research project described by Pauley was one I conducted, I have some opinions about the findings. Although the study became known as the "Nice Guy" research, I am convinced that "niceness" was not the really distinguishing feature of high-achieving executives so much as it was that they *played to the Player* in building their authority relationships. They were true Developers.

I am equally convinced the average and low achievers were executives who, lacking a sense of their own productive capacities, were Careseekers who meddled with people. Average achievers were Taskmasters, while low-achieving executives preferred a mix of Regulating and Comforting practices. Finally, I am convinced that the people on the receiving end of executive practices reflected the nature of those practices in their work and in their expectations. The data clearly showed that achieving executives produced achieving subordinates, while executives of limited achievement held their subordinates to limited achievement. Most important, however, the data proved that productivity began with the individual person in charge—with executives like you and me.

High-achieving executives had a different approach that we might all benefit from studying.

A Belief in the Player

One thing we can learn from high-achieving executives is that a belief in the competence, resilience, and good intentions of those we manage is critical. Then we will be inclined to employ policies and practices that *minimize interference with the potential* of those who must perform. If we believe in others' productive potential, we will encourage them to define themselves as productive people. We will be Developers.

Appreciating the Player's Need for Mastery, Self-Expression, and Enjoyment

Guided by our belief in the Player who does the work, we will be more aware of *why* people work. We will be mindful of the importance of monetary returns and job stability, but we will not deceive ourselves that these suffice either to define or satisfy those who work. We will understand that doing good work is a major means of self-expression and a major source of self-esteem. As a result, we will seek motivational policies and practices, job designs, assignments, and incentives that are geared to making work a meaningful and personally satisfying experience for those we manage.

Involving the Player in the Game Plan

No one knows as much as Players themselves about what they can do, what they need to do it well, and what they will find most satisfying and rewarding. Those of us who want to play to the Players will extend an invitation to productive people to explore the problems and strategies of work with us so that together we might discover the right, most workable and productive solution. We will encourage the release of people's expertise and an openness to experimentation. And we will be rewarded with their commitment and creativity, the cornerstones of truly productive effort.

Playing a Natural Game

One of the most intriguing factors found to distinguish high achievers from average- and low-achieving executives was their sensitivity to differences in authority. They didn't appear to have any. They conducted and presented themselves to their bosses and colleagues the same way they did with their subordinates. In all encounters they were open, authentic, and spontaneous, unconstrained by power differences. They dealt simply with respect and understanding. They were genuine in playing the Public Game.

The more genuinely open we are in expressing our opinions and feelings and in attending to those expressed to us, the easier and more productive our relationships will be. We will seek partnerships, not relationships based on obedience or dependency. We will listen and respond authentically when people talk; and we will encourage them to do the same. We will find they are willing and able to respond in kind.

We must accept the responsibility for our own practices and encourage those we manage to do the same. When we make mistakes, we should feel neither guilt nor any reluctance to admit our error. Indeed, the only guilt we might appropriately feel is that which comes to us when we do not do what we know needs to be done.

The game is simple; but this does not mean it is easy. If we aspire to executive achievement, we may have to review our assumptions and where they came from, rid ourselves of those that do not serve the Player well, and reconstruct our approach so it encourages competence and health among those we manage. Additionally, if we're to release the Player in ourselves and others, we may have to learn to experiment and evaluate the utility and reliability of what we do. As we become more personally aware and learn to build relationships based on the potential that surrounds us, we will find that productivity truly does begin with each of us.

And, from time to time, we may want to pause and reflect on the process. We may want to ask ourselves again why we have chosen to play the game as we do.

•

THE BOARDING CALL for Larry's flight can be heard above the hubbub of the lounge in which the three executives are waiting for their planes. Larry begins to gather his things. "Well, guys," he says, "thanks for sharing an important experience with me. And remember, I'm serious. I really think we ought to get together in a month or so. I'll even spring for the tab at the 19th hole!"

"Wait, Larry," Tim says. "I need to know one more thing. Why has all this meant so much to you? I mean, Frank and I both learned a lot this week, but it seems to go deeper with you, even to the way you want to manage. Why?"

"I don't really know, Tim. But I guess as an executive I'd like to be a positive force of some sort. I'd like to see people grow and flourish and know that I had a hand in it.

"But speaking from the other—more personal—side, as a consumer, my life would sure be simpler if there were more Players doing the work and fewer Meddlers. I mean, if we could tap all that potential, we wouldn't have to worry about productivity or quality. I could trust my car and my toaster. I could trust the school system and the government. I could even get information when I need it —from people who are supposed to provide it. Part of my concern is just enlightened self-interest. In some respects, you could call it just pure old-fashioned selfishness.

"But, mostly, I guess it's like somebody said. You can curse the darkness or you can light a candle. I guess I prefer lighting candles. It may not help any overall, but it'll sure be brighter where *I* am. At least *I* can see to do my own work.

"Not a bad note to leave on, right, golf fans?"

Afterword

A LETTER TO THE PRO

Some weeks after the Academy experience, the Pro received a letter from Tim McBride.

Dear Pro:

Here's a *friendly* and *appreciative* voice from your past. (What else would you expect from me?) Larry, Frank, and I have gotten together three times since the academy and are learning to enjoy one another quite a bit. We invariably think of you and what you taught . . . no, what you helped us discover.

You will be pleased to know all of our games, not just golf, have improved dramatically. All three of us have worked on our Private Games, and if any of us is to be believed after a few scotches, we are each playing our Public Games far better than would have seemed possible.

I am learning to take a stand on things and speak my mind. Frank has started asking people what they think about things and is still amazed by what they have to offer. Larry has started a Tuesday night seminar series for his hourly workers—he's really a teacher at heart.

The best part is that Frank and I are teaming up for a best-ball tournament at Larry's club. With my handicap, we figure we've got an edge. One weird thing—are you ready for this?—Larry invited Fred to be *his* partner. Frank thinks he's nuts! But Larry said it has something to do with "staying connected." Said you would understand.

One thing bothers us, though. We all agree people are beginning to look at us a little funny, as if they're not quite sure what to make of us. We *know* we are more effective and productive, but, especially at work, it's as if people are not quite ready for us.

So, the three of us—not entirely in jest—came up with a deep, philosophical question for you to ponder: We've all been taught that in the land of the blind, the one-eyed man is king. If that is true, why is it that in the land of the "crazies," the sane person doesn't have a chance?

Fore!
Tim

A few days later Tim received a reply. The Pro wrote, in part:

I know what you mean about becoming a better player and suddenly finding that people don't quite know what to make of you. Being aware and confident can really set you apart. But don't let it. Each of you has the option, if you choose, of guiding others—particularly the people you really care about—to discover what you have come to know.

We are all struggling. Maybe in different ways, with different things, but it's a hard game we're trying to play. The terrain may be beautiful, but it can also be treacherous. Sometimes the score we get won't reflect how well we've really played. It helps to know there are some people along the way who have made sense of it all, who understand, care, and maybe, just maybe, can serve as a signpost to help us find the path we want to take. That could be you!

> May your aim be true
> And your swing smooth,
> all the way from tee to green.
>
> Pro

He very well knows what he has to do.
As for the rest of us? We can but
watch and wait.

Henry Longhurst, *Golf Commentator*